Emotional Stress *and* Your Health

BRIAN INGLIS

Emotional Stress *and* Your Health

Foreword by

HANS SELYE, M.D.

CRITERION BOOKS
NEW YORK

Library of Congress Catalog Card Number 58-9628

Manufactured in the United States of America

To my colleagues
on the "Spectator"

FOREWORD

EMOTIONAL stress is one of the most important factors affecting the health of man. It can be harmful or it can be invigorating —depending upon the way we take it.

Stress is the rate at which wear and tear is induced in the body by the process of living; but there can be no life without some wear and tear, so our object must be not to avoid stress, but rather to learn how to live with it. Indeed, as the great English physician John Hunter put it some 160 years ago: "There is a circumstance attending accidental injury which does not belong to disease—namely, that injury done has in all cases a tendency to produce the disposition and the means of cure." There is some healing force in nature, *vis medicatrix naturae*, which tends to cure from within, and this force is activated by stress. The various shock treatments (e.g., insulin shock, metrazol shock, electro-shock) have amply proven this fact.

During the last two decades we have by scientific analysis learned a great deal about stress, but the concept itself is very old. Even Hippocrates, some 24 centuries ago, distinguished between the *pathos* (suffering) and the *pónos* (toil) of disease. The idea of *pónos* comes quite close to what modern medicine now recognizes as stress. For so many centuries the concept of stress lay dormant, because it remained a more or less abstract philosophic idea that did not lend itself to accurate scientific experimentation.

We physicians have attempted to dissect the stress reaction of the body into its constituent elements by examining the chemical and structural changes that take place in living beings exposed to stress. In this manner we have learned a good many things which help doctors to recognize and cure certain diseases, but our technical data are of little use to the layman. Yet stress—and particularly stress due to emotional factors—pervades man's life in health and disease to such an extent that any educated person is naturally curious to learn as much about it as circumstances permit. To satisfy this need, it is perhaps best that a general outline of the subject should be written by someone who is not a physician himself and, hence, not too close to technical details that might blur his vision for the over-all picture as it applies to daily life. It is fortunate, therefore, that Brian Inglis has undertaken to do this in EMOTIONAL STRESS AND YOUR HEALTH. As Editor of *Spectator*, Mr. Inglis has had ample experience in the clear expression of complex thoughts, and—as he explains in the first chapter of this book —he became intensely interested in problems of this sort during a chance encounter with a doctor in Italy. Mr. Inglis subsequently visited my laboratory in Montreal, and in the course of our conversation it became clear that although he is not a physician himself, he has a keen, instinctive feeling which helps him to sort out the important from the unimportant in medicine.

It may be questioned, of course, whether the general public should be apprised of progress in medical research not fully concluded. Undoubtedly, much more work is needed before we can completely elucidate the concept of stress and of the so-called "disease-producing life-situations." Yet, I believe that, as the work develops, it is quite appropriate to issue progress reports in terms generally understandable to the non-medical reader. I have no technical knowledge of celestial physics, and cannot, as yet, buy a return ticket to the moon; yet it interests me to read—in terms understandable to me—what physicists and astronomers have found out about space travel. Actually, at this time, the general reader is much more likely to profit personally from knowledge about emotional stress than from data on space travel. Many of the general lessons learned in the laboratory by chemical or histological studies not directly accessible to the uninitiated can be translated into rules of conduct in everyday life. Once this translation has been accomplished—a task in which Mr. Inglis succeeded remarkably well—it may be felt that the results are self-evident. It is just "good common sense" to behave accordingly in life. But we need an objective, scientific basis to decide what is good common sense, and what is common superstition, about the way to behave under stress. It is common knowledge that "too many cooks spoil the broth," but also that "many hands make light work." It is common knowledge that you must "look before you leap," but of course we also know that "he who hesitates is lost." It is common knowledge that "everything comes to him who waits," but then "nothing attempted, nothing gained." In many complex life situations, Mr. Inglis' careful analysis will help to distinguish the "common sense" behavior that works from the one that doesn't.

The famous English surgeon Sir Heneage Ogilvie—in his introduction to my own book THE STRESS OF LIFE—quoted Juvenal, who said, "Let us pray for a sound heart in a sound body; for a bold spirit that does not fear death but looks on extended life as on a gift from nature." I think that Mr. Inglis' book can help many to attain this aim.

HANS SELYE,
University of Montreal.

CONTENTS

Emotional Stress *and* Your Health

ENCOUNTER IN ITALY

SOME years ago while on holiday in Italy I was introduced at a party to an English doctor. Curious to know how he had come to be practising there, I asked him about his career; and he told me that he had come to Italy on his way home, after his retirement from a job in the East, and liked the country so much that he had decided to settle down. He had been specializing in tropical medicine out East; but he had retired young because, he felt, there was really nothing left for a specialist in tropical medicine to do. Inoculations and vaccines, antibiotics and penicillin, had eliminated many diseases, and reduced the treatment of others to simple routine, which a nurse could attend to better than a doctor.

Besides, he felt that he wanted to learn more about the relationship between emotional stress and disease. That there must be some relationship (over and above the obvious one—that prolonged strain of any kind, such as fatigue, makes it easier to succumb to an illness, and more difficult to throw off its effects) had struck him in dealing with, of all things, cholera. He had come to the conclusion, he told us, that cholera was "psychological".

The rest of us treated this statement as a joke—as he admitted that it was. He insisted, though, that cholera tended, in his experience, to single out as its victims the breadwinner and the housewife, rather than the very old and the very young—the dotards and the babies. The cholera germ is not discriminating; it attacks anybody and everybody; yet not everybody gets cholera. Why? Common sense would suggest that the people most likely to succumb are those whose resistance is low. But "resistance" is not simply a matter of physical vitality; cholera often strikes down the healthy with the weak. Could a person's emotional vitality, the doctor began to wonder, have something to do with it? In cholera freedom from worry, he thought, is important, because worry alters the rate of the secretion of acid in the stomach; and the capacity of the body to resist an invasion of cholera germs, he believed, is dependent in some way on its acid secretion rate. In a cholera epidemic the dotards do not worry, as they are going to die soon anyway; and the babies do not realize there is anything to worry about; it is the husbands and wives, made nervous by the epidemic around them, whose acid secretion rate is most likely to be affected—and who may therefore become cholera's victims. If this theory could be scientifically demonstrated, he argued, cholera would be shown to be attributable, to some extent, to emotional stress.

I do not think any of us took the theory very seriously; I am not even sure how seriously the doctor did himself. But he had certainly taken seriously the train of thought into which it led him. If cholera, he asked himself, why not other types of illness? The relationship between worry and stomach acid was only one example of physical repercussions following emotional stress: everyday life provides many more—the blush of shame or embarrassment; the flush of anger; the pounding heart before a big occasion; the otherwise courageous soldier fainting on an inoculation line, or vomiting at the sight of blood. Does not common sense, again, confirm that chronic worry may in time produce chronic physical symptoms? And that emotional stresses of other kinds may also lead to illness?

Intrigued with the possibilities of the theory, he began to make it his normal practice to ask patients, when they arrived to present him with their symptoms, "have you anything on your mind? Any troubles? Any worries?" And soon he found they usually had. This did not mean that his patients' illnesses were "psychological" in the derogatory colloquial sense of the word. When they came with, say, indigestion, he would often find something to account for it. But he no longer assumed, as he had assumed in the early days of his medical career, that the "something", whatever it might be, was the sole cause of the indigestion. Why, he asked himself, should patients whose digestions had been functioning well suddenly begin to have trouble with them? The answer, he began to find, was that the onset of the trouble often followed episodes from which the patient had suffered emotional stress.

He could not imagine why he had paid so little attention to the possibilities before, knowing as he did how easily our stomachs are affected by stress, of various kinds—how emotional tension leads to a loss of appetite; how alarm loosens the bowels, and so on. In any stressful situation it can reasonably be expected that the digestive mechanism will no longer function normally; and if the stress is excessive, or prolonged, the mechanism may break down. It should follow, then—the doctor concluded—that in cases of stomach trouble it is not enough simply to repair the mechanism and restore normal functioning; the patient should be encouraged to find out whether emotional difficulties precipitated the breakdown, in order to be able to deal with them should they recur—or, better still, to prevent their recurrence.

None of us who was present that evening had heard this theory advanced so systematically before. We knew that there are certain illnesses which sometimes accompany emotional crises: headaches, or nervous rashes, which tend to afflict some people. And thinking back afterwards, I could recall innumerable instances in the family circle, and among friends and colleagues, where illness had followed severe emotional stress. But I had not realized how close, how frequent, the connexion was—largely, I can only assume, because I had been brought up, like most people, to consider illness as a physical condition.

At home, at school and afterwards, it had been assumed that an illness was an act of God (except if we had brought it on ourselves by failing to keep sufficiently fit through exercise, or by over-indulgence in éclairs). Even mental illness was usually attributed either to the fact that the patient had been dropped on the head when a baby, or that he suffered from some hereditary taint. And though "nerves" might sometimes be excused on the grounds that some people worked too hard or overstrained themselves in other ways, it was considered weak-minded to suffer from them; the feeling was that such people ought to take a grip on themselves, and stop being silly about nothing.

It was not until I went to work on a newspaper that I began to see—though still not fully to realize—that the form which my colleagues' illnesses took did not fit in with these preconceived ideas. Contrary to a general impression, reporters are not usually hard-boiled (the best of them are often oddly child-like in character. Possibly it is their ability to see events through the eyes of a child that makes for success in their profession; like good child actors, they have some way of appealing directly to the emotions of their audience, and dispensing with the need for literary embellishments or mannerisms). Many of them, I quickly found, were oddly susceptible to what I had regarded as the diseases of childhood: coughs and colds and chills and tummy-upsets and headaches. Their illnesses were often called by more important sounding names, "gastritis" or "sinus"; but they were not discernibly different from those I remembered by less glamorous names from childhood.

I had cause to notice their prevalence because, as junior reporter, I commonly had to take on the jobs which had been allotted to seniors, when they rang up to say they could not come into the office because they were ill. Some of them got ill rather often. Each reporter tended to have his particular weakness; one would specialize in "throat"; another would get colds so bad as to be indistinguishable from 'flu; a third would be a martyr to headaches. And each of them had a characteristic attitude to his illness. Mr. L. would accept it as natural and inevitable, almost as desirable; he would detect it coming on, and warn the chief reporter, anticipating the symptoms with gloomy satisfaction. Miss C. would fight it, staying in the office, coughing, sneezing, and blowing her nose, until the chief reporter ordered her to go home, and not to be distributing her germs around the office! Germs were still assumed to be responsible; but with a subtle difference. The illnesses were personalized; their individual nature was cherished. A wandering germ or virus, if such were reported in the city, would be blamed; but the actual manifestation of the illness took on an individual character, as if it were a collector's piece.

I do not mean that these reporters were a particularly unhealthy lot. In every office there are some people who get ill often, some who get ill occasionally, some who never seem to get ill. I might not have noticed the illnesses of my colleagues, if it had not been for having to do their work when they were away. This was by no means always a chore; on the contrary it often meant interesting assignments that a new reporter could not normally expect to get. But occasionally it meant boring or unpleasant work; and on such occasions it was natural to wonder whether the reporters might not simply be malingering.

But they were not malingering; not as a rule. They had undeniable symptoms, in most cases; or at least they looked bad enough to carry conviction. And yet the feeling grew that in some inexplicable way they *wanted* to be ill. They did not, of course, want the actual symptoms, the headache or the streaming cold; but they needed to be able to show they had the symptoms—to have an excuse to retire, for a time, from the struggle, because it was nerve-racking, or tedious, or frustrating. It was as if they needed their occasional illnesses in the same sense as a man needs sleep—as a period of withdrawal and recuperation. And their illnesses were caught almost with the determination that a man catches a bus which takes him in the direction he wishes to travel—though in their case, they were not aware of it.

In this respect, it may have been significant that in practice little distinction was made between them and the one or two other members of the staff who carried out a similar withdrawal, but with the help of drink. The procedure differed according to the individual, but the general outlines were similar. Some celebration would come up, a birthday, or a party following a match, or a visit of old friends; and T. would get hopeless, roaring drunk.

The next morning, half-chastened, half-proud of himself as recollection seeped back of the events of the night before, he would go over to the pub for a "cure"; there to be joined by friends, they with their tales of the magnificence of his drunkenness, he with his description of the magnitude of his hangover, until he was fairly drunk again. This might continue for days. T. would do his routine work as best he could, his colleagues "covering" him when he was incapable; but most of the time he would be in one pub or another, a maudlin rather than an active drunk, longing for somebody to bore. Then, something would happen to bring him to his senses; a threat of reaction in the office; a fall on the way home; or, as often as not, an empty pocket. T. would reappear in the office, very bleary, rather self-conscious, and announce that he was for the wagon; on which he would remain for a few weeks, or days, until the next excuse for a celebration broke his resolve.

As far as our employers were concerned—in theory, as far as we all were concerned—there should have been a definite distinction between a man in bed with the 'flu and a man at large on the booze. But in practice little differentiation was made. Nobody thought of T. as a malingerer; it was known that he did whatever work he was in a state to do; and what he could not do was done for him almost as ungrudgingly as it would have been if he had been at home in his bed. In fact the only grouse we had against T. was that he persisted in coming drunk into the office, where he was a distraction, and into the pub, where he was a bore. Otherwise, we behaved to all intents as if he were a sick man; as he was.

All this I saw while I worked in the reporters' room; but I did not fully grasp its significance, mainly because of the difficulty of resolving the apparent contradiction between "wanting" and "not wanting" an illness. Had anybody suggested that old M. *wanted* his headaches, I would have dismissed the idea as fantastic; why would any man want to give himself pain! An explanation was not to come until much later; but at least the experience of the reporters' room prepared the ground for an understanding of what the doctor I met in Italy was driving at; I did not reject his thesis out of hand, with derision, as I might have done earlier.

The effect of my encounter with him was to make me plague doctors at home with questions about how many illnesses might have their origins in emotional stress. But I had little evidence to go on, outside my own limited experience and the, on the face of it, ridiculous story about cholera; and the doctors I discussed the subject with were sceptical. It was not so much that they denied the theoretical possibility of a link between emotional stress and illness, as that they virtually ignored it in their practice—they would never even have considered the idea of asking their own patients about their worries. And as I had no acceptable evidence with which to back the theory I got little further until, some years later, I came across the story of "Tom".

Owing to a childhood accident, "Tom" could not swallow food in the normal way; he had to feed himself through a tube inserted through his abdominal wall. Two doctors working in a New York hospital realized that this provided them with an unusual opportunity to study directly the effects, if any, of emotional stress on the stomach. One day Tom, who worked in the hospital, mislaid some important papers. The sight of a doctor angrily looking for them frightened him—he was afraid he might lose his job; and his stomach promptly and startlingly reflected the fact, in a variety of changes—one of them being (this naturally struck me as a notable vindication of the worry/cholera idea) that the rate of acid secretion in his stomach altered sharply.

It astonished me, reading of this experiment, that I had never heard the story before. The popular press was, then as now, running many medical stories of far less interest. Conceivably I might have missed it by being away at the time it was reported, but so remarkable an experiment ought surely to have been rebounding into the news from time to time, as fresh discoveries followed from research. I was soon to find that nobody I knew had heard of it, not even members of the profession; and then I determined to do what I should have done long before: to read everything I could find on the subject for myself. It was not easy going; I had no medical training, and the bulk of the material—Flanders Dunbar's *Mind and Body* being one of the very few exceptions—was written by specialists for specialists. But it was not necessary to read far to discover how much research had been done into the relationship of stress and disease; and how very revealing its findings had been.

While I was studying the subject, admittedly in a desultory way, one aspect of it began to come into the news: mental illness. In America Mike Gorman and others were beginning to bring home to the public how serious the problem of mental illness had become; and in Britain, the Ministry of Health launched a travelling exhibition to bring the facts around the country. I attended the opening ceremony, and depressing facts they were; in Britain, we were told, patients suffering from mental illness and mental deficiency occupy well over a third of all the hospital beds available in the country (in America the proportion is still higher). As journalists, we were begged to try to get people to realize this; and I wrote a couple of articles in the *Spectator* incorporating what I had picked up from my reading on stress. They brought in a few friendly, and a few irritated letters from correspondents in Britain; and from New York, the surprising invitation from a publisher to expand the articles into a book.

This is it.

★

I have written it from a lay viewpoint, using words in their colloquial, not their clinical sense. But a difficulty remains: a revolution in medicine inevitably creates turmoil in terminology. It takes time before descriptions and definitions settle down to become acceptable to the medical profession; and in the meantime they may pick up loose or misleading meanings in their everyday use. This has happened in the case of some of the terms invented or adopted by Freud and his successors in psychiatry. Where I have felt that pedantry is preferable to misunderstanding, I have discussed terminology either in the text or in the index—which I have used, where appropriate, as a glossary.

Most of the research which I have described is to be found in the standard works on the subject, from Weiss and English's textbook onwards. Where the research in this field is reasonably familiar (into the relationship, for example, between emotional stress and asthma, or skin diseases) I have not named the authorities; where it is less familiar, I have. The works which I have found most profitable for anybody interested in the subject to read are listed in the bibliography. I have also taken the opportunity, in a separate listing at the end of the book, to acknowledge my thanks to all those who have helped me before and during the writing of this book, with ideas, comments, and criticism.

I

RESEARCH

I

A MAN CALLED TOM

I HAD not gone very far in my explorations before I was heartened to find—in the introduction to a formidable collection of research papers published in 1950 under the title *Life Stress and Bodily Disease*—a reference to the possibility of a change in the profession's attitude to the causes of disease, and what might bring it about:

> "Of course, there is never one cause for any phenomenon in nature or in science. It is always a constellation of causes that brings about a change. . . . The constantly negative results of the physico-chemical search for the cause of asthma, hyperthyroidism, ulcerative colitis, peptic ulcer and hypertension had made some physicians more open to look for other, less tangible factors. But these circumstances did no more than incite curiosity and pave the way. The real stimulus, the spark that ignited the chain reaction of investigational energy, came from the encounter with a seemingly unimpressive small man, called Tom."

But although Tom's case had made such an impression, the research done in two other kinds of illness impressed me, at first, even more forcibly; because the connexion between emotional and physical states was even more obvious, and because I could remember cases which seemed explicable only by the theory that stress was responsible: in particular, asthma.

In a village not far from where I grew up a girl lived who suffered periodically from asthmatic attacks. They could be cured temporarily, her parents found, by sending her abroad; but they returned whenever she did. She was never sent away to boarding school, because she was considered too delicate; but when she grew old enough to earn her own living she moved into the nearest town. Thereafter the asthma virtually ceased; though she suffered mildly from time to time, the attacks were never again serious enough to worry her.

The assumption was—and for all I know still is—that there was something in the air of the village that was bad for her asthma which was not present in the air of the town. She knew, and her friends knew, that the attacks often coincided with episodes which caused her distress (the worst of them was when her mother died); yet nobody thought to attribute her attacks to her emotional make-up, rather than to the village air; and nobody would have taken seriously the suggestion that her asthma might be the result of the rather stifling relationship she had with her family, who were very united and very possessive.

Yet the knowledge that asthmatic attacks can be brought on by the onset of emotional stress is at least as old as Hippocrates. As late as the beginning of the present century they were commonly attributed to nerves. Around the turn of the century, however, came the discoveries in connexion with allergy; and very soon the profession began to think that the cause not only of asthma (which involves the lower respiratory tract), but also of hay fever (which involves the upper respiratory tract) would be found to arise out of the fact that the human body sometimes has an unnecessarily high sensitivity to some substance, leading to an unnecessarily strong reaction to it, which takes the form of wheezing, or a running nose. A person who suffers from asthma or hay fever or bronchitis is in much the same position, on this thesis, as somebody who sneezes too easily. A sneeze is the body's reaction to the presence of, or suspected presence of, something which may prove to be an irritant. But if the mechanism which sets off a sneeze is triggered off without good reason, life is made a misery of sneezes. In the same way (it was suggested) asthma or hay fever may be the body's reaction to the threat of invasion by a potential irritant, such as pollen; and it was hoped that ultimately some such culprit—pollen being only one of many—would be found to explain the reaction in every case. Then, it was hoped, an appropriate antidote might be found for each, so that even if the onset of asthma could not be prevented, its effects could promptly be mitigated.

Some striking advances were made along these lines. It was found possible to employ tests which showed what each asthma or hay fever sufferer was allergic to: pollen, or horsehair, or cats' fur. Many patients were then able to avoid attacks, so long as they took care to avoid the culprit, knowing what it was—by banishing the horsehair sofa, or selling the cat. Pollen could not always be avoided but it was sometimes possible to prescribe an appropriate antidote and mitigate the unpleasant effects. Before long, however, it began to be realized that the discoveries about allergy, valuable as they had been, were not telling the whole story. People who had laboratory allergies—that is, who reacted positively to the laboratory tests—did not always suffer from attacks in their normal lives; and people who reacted negatively in the laboratory were sometime sufferers outside it. In one experiment, 254 medical students were used as a sample, all being studied by means of interviews, questionnaires, physical examinations, and allergy skin tests. Rather more than half of the students gave a positive reaction to tests, showing that they had laboratory allergies. But of these, only 75 *per cent* had ever actually suffered from any allergic reaction, that they were aware of. And of the students who gave a negative reaction to the tests, 11 per cent had suffered from allergic illness.

Why? The most likely explanation was that although foreign bodies can cause asthma, and often do, their effect on the individual varies according to his condition. His physical fitness could be one variant: a really healthy man might survive the presence of substances to which he is allergic in the same way as a fit boxer can survive a blow to the solar plexus which would have finished him if he had not stuck to his training schedule. But this theory, though attractive, did not accord with the facts; often otherwise physically fit, healthy men and women suffer badly from asthma.

By this time, too, experiments were beginning to show that the old-fashioned and, it had come to be thought, outmoded notion of an emotional basis for asthma was not so far off the mark after all. An early discovery along these lines was that some patients who blamed pollen from certain flowers for their hay fever could also get the symptoms from artificial imitations of the flowers, though there was no pollen. This could have a simple explanation: if, as Pavlov's celebrated experiments had confirmed, bodily reactions can be governed to a great extent by conditioned reflexes—so that our mouths may water not only at the sight of food, but also at the gong which announces that the food is going to be served—a similar mechanism may operate in the case of hay fever. But numerous experiments have revealed the existence of another link between emotional stress and asthma symptoms. Researchers at Cornell University found it was possible to take patients into a room where, though they were not aware of it, there was a concentration of the pollen to which they were sensitive. They did not at first experience much of a reaction; but if the doctor then began to bring up for discussion subjects which were emotionally disturbing to them, the hay fever symptoms would develop—to disappear again when the discussion returned to neutral channels.

Another researcher, investigating bronchitis, found that when the patient's thoughts were on his insecurity and frustration, his bronchial tubes contracted—he suffered from a bronchial spasm; when the thoughts returned to ordinary subjects, his tubes relaxed. A few years later some New York doctors investigated the reaction more scientifically, by measuring the quantities of sputum a patient brought up under different emotional conditions. They found that whenever those conditions caused him distress, the amount of sputum increased. The experiment was continued for eight months, during which time it was found that events causing great emotional tension could increase the flow of sputum by as much as eightfold, the flow returning to normal as the tension receded.

It need come as no surprise to find that the normal functioning of the breathing apparatus should sometimes be upset by emotional crises. All of us have experienced the way that a sudden fright makes us catch our breath; a surprise takes our breath away; boredom provokes yawns; and desire makes our breath come short. That serious or prolonged emotional stress may result in sporadic or chronic trouble with our breathing is consequently likely enough.

The difficulty lies not in conceding the possibility, but in acknowledging that it could happen to ourselves. As soon as I thought about it, though, I recalled a couple of instances where my own breathing system had been disrupted, though not seriously, by what were obviously the results of emotional tension. One had been after the first time I had been unhappy in love. I then began to experience what I had—for some reason—previously only read about: a lover's sigh. The term "sighing" had meant for me only that contrived intake and expulsion of breath which people perform to indicate exasperation. Acquaintance with the real thing showed me for the first time that we do not heave sighs: sighs heave us. Mine came from deep down, usually when something had happened to remind me of the broken link. They were almost alarming in their intensity, as if they were trying to warn me that the deprivation was greater than I was aware that I felt (for I was trying to pretend to myself that it really did not matter, that I was well rid of the girl). The other example was the tendency of my throat to constrict just before or during broadcasts, leading to an apparently urgent need for a clearing cough—but the cough does not satisfy the need. This is obviously a nervous reaction, and a very common one.

The lover's sigh, the broadcaster's need to clear his throat: both, in effect, are illnesses. They do not have sufficiently painful or disabling symptoms to rate as such; but is it not reasonable to suppose that asthma, bronchitis and hay fever are often simply more serious examples of the same process? If so, it is still necessary to account for the fact that for so many people attacks are associated not with emotional stress, but with pollen, or cats' fur. A clue to the answer has been found in the discovery, in cases of asthma, of a link between the initial attack in childhood and some emotional conflict. In their study of allergic patients, Miller and Baruch found that the early patterns of asthma-attack-following-emotional-stress was repeated through life: "over and over again, it is evident that the adult allergic individual continues to live out his childhood role, repeating in adult but not in mature manner, the scene of the allergic child in the family". The attack may be caused either by the emergence of some emotional situation similar to the childhood conflict, or by something which may be quite irrelevant, but which acts as a reminder of the conflict—in the same way that a gong may induce salivation. How the individual reacts, Miller and Baruch explain,

> "depends not only upon the nature of the happening and upon his sensitivity and tolerance, but also upon what the happening means to him, upon what he makes of it in his mind, upon what he fantasies, even unconsciously, in connection with it. So events which seem insignificant, as well as those actually calamitous, may equally trigger grave emotional reactions that find expression in emotional illness".

A child who imagines, utterly erroneously, that his mother has ceased to love him, or has left him, may be brought to a pitch of suffocating emotional alarm in which sights, sounds or smells he is experiencing attach themselves, as it were, to his emotion; so that the same sight, sound or smell may thereafter continue to reproduce the alarm symptoms of suffocation in later life.

It was thought, at one time, that the alarm might be real; that asthma attacks might in fact be performing, though in an unnecessarily violent and distressing manner, a similar function to sneezing, and one quite as necessary. They might be repelling the invading pollen, which could otherwise damage the body's tissues. It has since been found that this is not the case. As an experiment, allergic subjects were desensitized, so that they did not react to pollen in their usual asthmatic way. They were then subjected to pollen; it did them no harm. Obviously the allergic reaction was unnecessary: it had arisen not out of necessity but from some fault in the body's self-regulating mechanism; the body had acted like a general who is deceived by a feint attack from an enemy into sending an unnecessarily large concentration of troops to repel it.

A further significant fact has been uncovered by research into asthma. At an investigation in London University twenty-five asthma patients were examined by means of psychiatric interviews, during which readings were taken of oxygen content of their blood. "The topics introduced at this interview were deliberately chosen by the investigator to cover a number of life situations, and stresses arising in interpersonal relationship, all of which had been previously noted clinically to be upsetting, and to be related in time to the onset of asthmatic attacks." The investigators' conclusion was not that the emotional stress directly caused the asthmatic attack, but that the stress in some way disturbed the normal self-regulatory mechanism, reducing the amount of oxygen in the blood; and that the asthma represented the body's gasping attempt to restore the balance, by bringing the oxygen in the blood system back to normal.

But if asthma, like sneezing, represents an attempt on the part of the body to recover from something, to restore the body's balance—if it is not an action, but a reaction—then obviously particular care is needed in treating it. A drug which stopped us sneezing might save us from a certain amount of inconvenience; but it might also lead to irritants establishing themselves in the system, and possibly causing severe damage. In the same way, if an attack of asthma is designed to help the patient to counteract the physical effects of an emotional crisis, it may sometimes be desirable to leave the asthma alone, at least until the emotional processes behind it are understood. For in this case, asthma may be performing the same function of giving relief from emotional stress that some people get from crying.

Some researchers have become convinced that there is, in fact, a close link between asthma and crying—or, rather, between asthma and *not* crying. Early in the 1920s E. Weiss put forward the theory that an attack of asthma represents a repressed cry for the mother; and researchers have since reported that attacks of asthma cease when and if the patient can relieve his feelings by crying. The wheezing, too, which is characteristic of ineffectual attempts to stop crying resembles the wheezing of the asthmatic. Asthma may sometimes originate in the conflicts which arise out of a child's inability, for some reason, adequately to express emotions aroused by conflicts in which his mother is the dominant figure: "the repressed dependence upon the mother", according to Franz Alexander

> "is a constant feature . . . everything which threatens to separate the patient from the protective mother or her substitute is apt to precipitate an asthmatic attack. In children, the birth of a sibling who threatens to absorb the mother's attention is found with conspicuous frequency at the beginning of the asthmatic condition".

⋆

Some of the research which has been done into the relationship of stress with asthmatic symptoms has been rendered suspect by the researchers' preconceived ideas; and some of it has been criticized because it was carried out under unscientific conditions. But the results achieved are sufficient to suggest that asthma research can now profitably be concentrated on an examination of the relationship between emotional and physical causes (rather than in trying to establish the primacy of one or other); and the reluctance of the profession to accept the importance of emotional stress in practice is surprising. It is still more surprising in the case of skin diseases, where the link between emotional stress and the onset of physical symptoms is so often close—something which has always been realized and, until this century, accepted as a matter of course. "The limits between the physiological and pathological," the dermatologist Erasmus Wilson said in

1870, "are barely discernible. The blush of transient erythema or urticaria, and the too frequent repetition and the permanence of the blush become a confirmed erythema." It requires no technical knowledge of dermatology to know what Wilson was driving at: most of us have encountered people, usually women, who are afflicted by what is to outward appearances blushing, but which does not appear in immediate relation to events—after, say, some gaucherie—as the ordinary blush does. Can "too frequent repetition"—arising out of the existence of some deep-rooted feeling of guilt—lead in time to a permanent physical change? And can the same mechanism apply to the many other ways in which emotion can affect the skin—through excessive sweating, or itching, both common responses to emotional stress?

The answer is, yes: to say that skin troubles are often stress-induced is to do no more than confirm common observation. Nevertheless it was with a shock that dermatologists, and the profession in general, read the remarkable case described in the *British Medical Journal* in 1952 of a boy aged sixteen who had been suffering from "congenital ichthyosis"—a black, horny layer covering almost his entire body, as if his skin had been turned into a mass of warts. The condition is usually considered resistant to all forms of treatment and, as such treatment as the boy had been having had already proved useless, he was eventually sent to East Grinstead, the hospital where the remarkable feats of plastic surgery were carried out during the war, to see whether the grafting of skin from his chest (which was normal) to his hands (which were "thickly covered with a rigid horny casing which cracked, fissured, and became infected, rendering him unable to work with them") would help. The experiment failed: within a month the grafted skin had become indistinguishably horny from the rest.

A few months later, however, the suggestion was made to the boy under hypnosis that the left arm would clear (the left arm alone was chosen, to avoid any chance that general recovery might be from some other, coincidental reason). After about five days the "rhino" layer on the arm softened, and fell off, revealing skin underneath of almost normal texture and colour. Freed from its black and armour-like casing, the skin became pink and soft in a few days; and at the end of ten days the arm was completely clear, from shoulder to wrist.

The treatment was then continued over the rest of the body; and though the results were less complete, they were substantial enough to make a human being out of the patient, where before he had been virtually an outcast. The improvement in the patient's mental state, the report ran,

> "has been as dramatic as his organic improvement. Previously his schooling and social contact had been reduced to a minimum, his sensitivity towards his smell and appearance causing him to become lonely and solitary, with a hopeless attitude towards future friendship and employment. Now (a year later) he has become a happy, normal boy, and is already being employed".

If even the scaliest of skins may be brought back to normal health by suggestion, under hypnosis, states of the skin clearly may reflect, or be linked with, states of mind; and a wealth of evidence is available to show how often they are. One instance is the report of an investigation in the early 1950s into industrial dermatitis, called for when it was found that half the insured workers attending skin clinics in Britain were attributing their malady to something they caught at their work. An obvious weakness in this explanation was that so many other workers on the same jobs were not getting skin diseases, so it was decided to hold an investigation. After interviewing, examining and following up eighty consecutive cases, the researcher came to the conclusion that social and emotional disturbances are often an integral part of, and perhaps a cause of, the disease; that industrial dermatitis is commonly an occupational neurosis, its incidence being a reflection less of bad working conditions than of the unhappiness, dissatisfaction and general emotional ill-health of the worker.

From the result of many experiments of a similar nature, Wittkower and Russell argued in their book on the subject that skin disorders may have either an emotional or a material basis, or arise from a combination of the two; and that specific types of skin disease may be related to particular emotional disorders. Acne is one instance: adolescent pimples have long been associated with sex troubles, and an old saw suggests that the only real cure for them is marriage. Irrespective of their general characteristics, Wittkower found, a feature common to the majority of acne patients is an inhibition of their sexuality, based on an unconscious sexual guilt. Although he could not demonstrate this finding statistically, he was left with the firm impression that it may arise out of a cleavage between emotional and physical development after puberty, when emotional development is sometimes arrested or retarded. He did not claim that acne was in all cases attributable to this, but he felt that the emotional stresses of puberty ought to be considered as strictly relevant to the common onset of acne at this time of life, and to its persistence later.

Some researchers went further, and argued that the area where skin disease breaks out may reflect the type of emotional disturbance; for instance, that eruptions on the nape of the neck are usually associated with family troubles; and on the thighs, with sexual disorders. In case this should sound ridiculously far-fetched, it is worth remembering that the only reasonable explanation of why blushing is so often confined to the face and neck is that face and neck are normally visible: it is as if they are deliberately selected by our consciences to ensure that we are punished for whatever guilty thought or deed has caused us to feel shame.

Other researchers were meanwhile seeking to relate particular skin diseases to particular personalities. Three Pittsburgh doctors who made a study of patients with one variety of eczema were impressed by the fact that the patients seemed to be of a similar personality type—which was odd, considering that they were selected only because they had the same skin disease.

> "It was found that they had primitive personality structures, and various immature character traits were demonstrable. They showed crippling inhibition of their aggressive and erotic drives, and depression was very prominent in their emotional make-up. Repeatedly there had been an unhealthy child-parent relationship in their lives; with parental rejection often strikingly evident. Invariably, exacerbations of their eczema in adult life could be correlated with stressful situations."

Even if such assumptions could not easily be scientifically verified, they provided further evidence of the emotional background of skin disease, which dermatologists should have found it hard to ignore. But ignore it they did, to a great extent; and where they have accepted it, the tendency has been to insist that the emotional condition serves merely to intensify, not to cause, skin disease. As one such critic, quoted by Wittkower, has argued:

> "Itching is another important physiologic reaction which can be initiated and decisively influenced by the psyche. I need not stress that itching leads to scratching, and the secondary skin changes which appear after scratching are manifold . . . it is perhaps not sufficiently well known that latent skin diseases such as psoriasis and lichen planus, and a group of other skin diseases, will sometimes appear to localize in areas which are scratched or otherwise traumatized."

The writer's object was to produce an adverse and sceptical criticism; but if what he says is true, skin conditions obviously cannot be considered without reference to the emotional factors which precipitate them. Scratching may cause the condition: but if so, it is surely important to find what causes the patient to feel the need to scratch; in theory, if this can be found the skin disease need not appear at all.

It is not, of course, quite so simple in practice. What causes itching? Why does itching occur? Why does it occur at certain times; and not at others? And why in certain parts of the body, not in others? Are the times, or the places, directly or indirectly connected with some emotional disturbance? The answers, could they be found, would be of far greater benefit to sufferers from skin diseases than all the injections, drugs, ointments and powders in current dermatological fashion; and a London doctor, Desmond O'Neill, who has made a prolonged study of this subject, has produced evidence which strongly supports the belief that there is a "tension-itch-scratch" mechanism which operates in such cases:

> "The onset of the skin disorder, in twenty-three of the thirty patients, occurred at a time of especial stress for the patient. Relapses and exacerbations, in all thirty, were related to situations arousing prolonged tension which the patient could neither dissipate nor avoid . . . a common pattern of events in our patients was this: at night, warmth and contact with bed-clothes stimulated the skin; emotional tension, which had been held in check by various defences during the day, mounted; the skin itched; and the patient scratched. Scratching irritated the skin, increased itching, and caused further scratching. The act of scratching then came to fulfil one of two functions; it might provide a satisfaction which the patient could not achieve by other means, or it might serve as a form of punishment."

Itching and scratching, O'Neill concludes, particularly round the genital area, are closely related to the denial of normal sexual outlets; and closely related, too, to the stressful situations which arise in such circumstances. Where patients were co-operative, and sufficient time could be devoted to discussion and solution of their problems, it was found possible in most cases to relieve the tensions, and thereby to remove or reduce the itch-scratch urge which arose out of them. Sometimes a single decision, where making it meant much to the patient, was enough to remove the symptom; one man finally made up his mind to emigrate, and from that time on he was no longer troubled by itching.

O'Neill's investigation is only one of several in this field, confirming the closeness of the relationship between occasions or conditions of tension, and outbreaks of skin disease. In view of the evidence, the continued attempt to treat skin diseases without reference to the patient as an individual is as ill-advised as the celebrated practice of curing measles by cutting off the spots, which is what dermatological treatment still often amounts to. Visited by patients with skin trouble, a general practitioner normally prescribes specifics—lotions or powders; if these fail, the patients are sent to a dermatologist; and only when the specialist's own armoury of remedies is exhausted does the question, can the trouble be due to emotional stress? arise.

Usually not even then; as a great many skin diseases are transient anyway, their temporary disappearance is often attributed to the ointment or lotion, both by the doctor and by the patient. Many sufferers go through their lives unaware that their symptoms may be emotionally induced; that it is the emotional background, not the scaly or spotty foreground, which really requires treatment. Even where it is accepted that a rash is "nervous" in origin, either because all attempts to account for it in other ways have failed or because it invariably accompanies some occasion of stress, the tendency is not to seek to understand and remove or modify the effects of the stress, but to apply some soothing lotion to lessen the irritation, and to wait till the rash disappears of its own accord.

*

The reluctance in everyday medical practice to accept that it is the patient who requires the treatment, and not his symptoms, is also strong in the case of stomach trouble. Yet the feeling that certain stomach disorders, and particularly stomach ulcers, are the product of emotional stress is of long standing. A century ago William Brinton, in the course of the first book to be written on the subject, argued that "mental anxiety so frequently coincides with ulcer that we are fully entitled to regard it as a more or less immediate cause"; and though his advice was ignored, the notion that there is a link between anxiety and ulcers was never quite abandoned. It is now quite widely accepted; the idea of stomach ulcers being the occupational disease of tycoons, because of their responsibilities, has penetrated down to the music-hall joke level. Nevertheless the stomach ulcer is still regarded as the province of the physician, and if he fails, the surgeon—though as long ago as 1948 a distinguished surgeon asserted (I can remember reporting him, for my newspaper) that in many cases his stomach ulcer patients ought really to have consulted a psychiatrist.

Not long after reporting this heresy, I heard that a friend of mine, G., who had been working abroad had come home suffering from a stomach ulcer, whose existence had been revealed by X-ray photographs. After dieting had failed to make any improvement, an operation had been recommended; but rather than put himself in the hands of strange doctors, he decided to come home to consult a surgeon who was an old friend of the family. When he arrived home it was suggested that he should first try the effect of rest and a still more severely restricted diet; for three weeks, he complained when I saw him, he had been persuaded to live on malted milk; and every time he drank the stuff it was as if it had touched off a red-hot golf ball in his stomach. Eventually he made up his mind to visit the surgeon to tell him to go ahead and operate.

To his surprise, the surgeon brushed aside the X-ray photographs, and paid little attention to the recital of symptoms, contenting himself with asking G. whether he had ever tried a valuable medicine, marketed under various proprietary names, but commonly known as whisky. G. said he had been forbidden any form of alcohol since the ulcer was first diagnosed. 'That,' the surgeon replied, 'must be what's the matter with you,' and he poured G. out a large glass. G. drank it, without ill effects. When he had finished, the surgeon said, 'Now go home, and start leading the kind of life you used to enjoy leading when you were here before—before you thought you had an ulcer.'

It happened I was at G.'s home the evening he returned from

the consultation. I suggested that we might start on the prescription at lunch-time the next day. I do not know what he ate for breakfast; but for lunch, after several aperitifs, he sat down to a dozen *escargots*, an underdone fillet steak with onions and chips, some camembert, a bottle of red wine, and liqueurs and a cigar to follow. And he was none the worse.

The interesting part of the episode to me was that the X-rays had apparently showed an ulcer at the time they were taken, about a month before. It was possible that the ulcer had cleared up, but that the symptoms and the pain had continued in his imagination. Or, it was possible that the ulcer had not cleared up, but that the surgeon, through some form of faith healing, had managed effectively to prevent him from feeling any further pain. But either way, I felt bound to assume, mind must in some way have conquered matter.

Then, some years later, I read the story of "Tom". "Tom" obstructed his gullet at the age of nine through inadvertently drinking scalding hot clam chowder; and from that time on he could not swallow. He would put food into his mouth, enjoy its taste, chew it up, and then transfer it into his stomach through a pipe, with a funnel. He obtained employment in the laboratories of a New York hospital; and there, many years later, the idea occurred to two doctors, Harold Wolff and Stewart Wolf, that here was a ready-made living laboratory in which they could study the effects of emotional stress on the interior of the human stomach. The best-known episode is the one in which Tom thought that he might lose his job; and they observed that his stomach immediately paled, in much the same way as a man's face can pale with shock. The colour of the stomach lining blanched, by their method of computation, from 90 per cent redness to 20 per cent redness; the stomach's mucous membrane altered, thickened and congested, eventually becoming so fragile that friction, or even light pressure upon it, caused it to bleed. On being reassured about the job, Tom quickly recovered his normal composure; so did his stomach.

This was not, I was later to find, the first time that the

effect of emotional disturbance on the gastric system had been observed in this way. Over a century before a doctor, William Beaumont, had treated a French Canadian trapper who had been accidentally shot in the stomach at close range; and when the wound healed, a small opening remained in the trapper's side through which Beaumont was able to observe the digestive processes at work. He conducted well over two hundred experiments, and his observations led to the scrapping of older theories about digestion. Beaumont was a physiologist, and chiefly interested in the effects on the stomach of different types of food and liquid; but he observed reactions which, he assumed, must be emotionally induced. On 12 March, 1830, for example, he noted that the food passing through the trapper's stomach was considerably tinged with yellow bile; and this he attributed to the effects of a violent fit of anger. Anger and feverish excitement, Beaumont assumed, diminish the secretion of gastic juice.

Although the effect of violent emotion on the digestion has been actually observed in this way, a reluctance remains to draw the obvious conclusions in diagnosing various types of stomach trouble. To begin with, it should be impossible any longer to hold the belief, still surprisingly widely held in the profession, that emotional stress cannot actually cause real, organic illness. The reactions of Tom's stomach lining to the fear of losing his job clearly demonstrate that if there could be said to be a single cause of an ulcer it might well be emotional stress. My friend G., for example, had a digestion which could normally tolerate his erratic eating and drinking. It is impossible to be certain, but the likelihood is that the breakdown of the mechanism came as a consequence of certain domestic worries which, I know, had accumulated for him at the time. If his stomach lining reacted the same way as Tom's did, he would have lost the protection normally afforded by his stomach's mucous membrane; food and drink, instead of gliding safely down, would chafe the stomach lining, causing his ulcer.

The observations on Tom, too, help to explain away the seemingly miraculous nature of some recoveries. G. again is probably an example. His return home removed him, partially at least, from his domestic stresses; but he had hanging over him the worry of the ulcer itself and the impending operation. That worry once removed, his stomach's lubricating system was free to return to normal almost as quickly as Tom's did; enabling G. to resume the eating and drinking habits of his past, so long inhibited by worry.

But perhaps the most important result of the experiment with Tom is the light it has thrown on the way illness happens. The tendency in the past has been, and still is, to think of the cause of illness as something exclusively physical (or, more rarely, exclusively psychological); and also to think that it must be one or the other—that there is a single cause. But this need not be how a stress disorder operates. In Tom's case, the shock he got would not necessarily have made him ill. He would have got ill only if, like G., the emotional stress was accompanied by his eating or drinking in a way that put too much of a strain on the weakened stomach lining.

The same is true of any mechanism; pieces of dirt or grit in the system may cause no trouble if the lubricating system is in good order; conversely the lubricating system may work adequately even if the rate of flow of the lubricant is poor, provided there is little grit around; but if the flow or lubricant is poor and there is grit present, damage follows. In the case of stomach ulcers, damage may be averted or lessened by keeping the patient on a diet (removing the grit) or by an operation (reboring the cylinders); but the problem can only be finally solved if it can be found what is preventing his lubrication system from functioning properly. It is of little use to concentrate, as doctors tend to do, on analysing the grit, and forbidding consumption of any fuel which may contain it; the human digestion is so powerful an instrument when it is working properly that this should not be necessary, provided that the secret of proper lubrication can be regained—provided the reasons for the emotional stress can be found, so that it can be avoided in future.

What was true of "Tom", of course, is not necessarily true

of Dick or Harry. Different people react to the same type of emotional stress in different ways. Different people get different types of ulcer. But the existence of a link between emotional stress and stomach trouble is demonstrable; and one reason, according to Harold Wolff, is that situations in which people feel strong emotions of alarm or desperation "are associated with the almost complete cessation of gastric activity".

"This is compatible," Wolff continues, "with the view that an assault that has shocked and perhaps overwhelmed the organism evokes a pattern in which the digestive function is irrelevant, and therefore is abolished." In other words, when primitive man had to escape from threatening situations, all his reserves of energy were marshalled to assist him in fight or flight or both, his bowels and bladder evacuating themselves, and his digestion ceasing to function, as a reflex response; and to this day, civilized man finds echoes of the same response—in situations of extreme stress he may lose control of his bladder and of his sphincter, and his digestive processes may cease. What is far more common, though, is for the pattern to assert itself not suddenly but through the prolonged operation of chronic emotional tension—of worry; this, too, may in time disrupt the digestion, and create the situation in which ulcers, or other disorders, can develop.

The development of a stomach ulcer induced by emotional stress, Flanders Dunbar suggested in her *Mind and Body*, is normally in four stages. First, an unduly large number of impulses, caused by emotional disturbances, are transmitted to the intestinal tract. Second, these impulses affect the production of acid, sending up hunger pangs, though food is not required. Third, tension develops in the muscles which govern the traffic of food, leading to indigestion and vomiting; and fourth, the mucous membrane of the stomach having been weakened, the lining of the digestive tract is irritated by food passing through: the acid and the muscle tension combine to aggravate the blemish, and it becomes a painful and infected sore—an ulcer.

Against this theory, it has been argued that many stomach

ulcers are only the natural result of ill-advised eating habits—incomplete mastication, over-fast consumption, swallowing of air, immoderation, or unwise selection of food. But any of these bad habits may themselves be the reflection of emotional states. In stomach trouble, as indeed in all illness, emotional stress can operate at different levels. It may produce symptoms directly, like a quicker heart-beat; or at one remove—as in "Tom's" case, where it precipitated certain changes in the stomach which would have meant, had he then tried to eat a normal meal, that he might have suffered pain; or at a further remove, when it creates a state of mind that causes somebody in time to fall into faulty eating habits, or bad posture—thereby increasing the possibility of illness in much the same way as preoccupation with worries increases the possibility of getting run over, because we are not careful to look around properly before crossing the road.

As with asthma, too, there is a possibility that emotional stress may have arisen in childhood—the product, perhaps, of a child's early training. If the conditioning of a child's habits is attended by some emotional crisis, the pattern may be repeated in the adult. A pattern continually being reported by psychiatrists is the link between the wish to be loved and the wish to be fed. For the sake of simplicity (though these things are usually very far from simple) this can be explained as a carrying over into adulthood of the primitive association of love and food which an infant finds at his mother's breast. Complex and devious though the ways are in which individuals react to deprivation of love, in adults it is found time and again that the wish to be loved—to be dependent on somebody—can, if it is frustrated, be converted into the wish to be fed. The "fat white woman whom nobody loves" may be fat *because* nobody loves her—because she is substituting food for the love she cannot obtain, or give; and she cannot stop eating, because when she does her stomach sends up violent hunger signals, till the craving becomes too much for her.

Whether emotional conflicts arise from this or other causes, their existence is now the chief problem confronting the doctor and the research worker who have to deal with stomach ulcers. And not only with ulcers: with all the commoner ills of the digestive system. Yet much remains to be done. Until recently the great bulk of the work covered the purely physical aspects of stomach disorders. And articles on the subject still appear in the medical journals, dealing with different types of stomach troubles, but ignoring the possibility that much of the physical treatment by drugs and operations is at best a palliative, designed to remove the hurtful symptoms temporarily; at worst a dangerous misinterpretation of the real nature of the illness.

Instead, the authors concentrate on endless and often ridiculous division and subdivision of symptoms—demolishing old theories and putting up new ones, soon in their turn to be abolished. Every now and again it is discovered that some elaborate system of identification, on which for years past firm diagnoses have been made, and treatment—often surgery—prescribed, is in fact worthless: only recently research revealed that patients can have chronic gastritis without having a single gastric symptom; "the type of gastritis," the report ran, "most prone to be associated with dyspeptic symptoms turns out not to be 'gastritis' at all". In spite of such damaging admissions, no suggestion followed that the time has come for research to turn to examination of the relationship between gastric symptoms and emotional states.

Not that doctors deny that emotional stress may precipitate stomach trouble; a "nervous stomach" is far too common for that. But they usually insist that it is not the primary cause; and the great majority of them continue to treat patients coming in with stomach trouble as if it were exclusively a physical phenomenon. Naturally in some cases the trouble has indeed been caused by some exceptional physical condition, such as food poisoning. Where stomach trouble persists, however, and where no such explanation can be found, common sense suggests that attention should be turned to the patient's environment, personality, and emotional background, to see if it is here that the trouble really lies. But how seldom is this done! Much more commonly, the sufferer returns again and again to his doctor, or to different doctors, to be sent by them for tests and X-rays and examinations, and to be given whatever physical remedy the doctor believes in, or has just read about—with no attempt to consider the patient, only the symptoms.

A classic example has been described by Michael Balint, of the Tavistock Clinic in London. Mrs. D., aged 42, came to a doctor with constipation. At first he considered that she showed improvement, but then she got into an anxiety state. Suspecting nervous disorder, he decided to get her records from her previous doctor. Among other reports, these included:

> January 1948: "while attending an out-patient department for her bowel complaint she had a cold axillary abscess which was successfully treated."
>
> October 1948: "difficulty with her defaecation; nothing abnormal found; treated with confection of senna."
>
> February 1950: "She must, I think, be suffering from spastic colon, I could find no abnormality clinically or on proctoscopy. Arranging barium enema, X-ray and blood count."
>
> March 1950: "Symptoms must be largely functional."
>
> April 1951: "Found to have second degree piles . . . give a sheet of instructions on bowel function, and some Normacol."
>
> July 1951: "Signs of supraspinatus tendinitis . . . put on treatment in the physiotherapy department."
>
> October 1951: "Incomplete intestinal obstruction . . . Laparotomy was performed . . . she made an uneventful recovery."
>
> June 1952: "Abdominal and rectal examination failed to reveal any abnormality . . . she was reassured about her condition and liquid paraffin was prescribed."
>
> August 1955: ". . . I am wondering whether there is some stricture formation at the site where the adhesions were divided. I have arranged a barium meal. . . . She also complains

of feeling depressed and requested a consultation with a psychiatrist. I am arranging for this."

In all, Balint comments, "hospital surgeons performed four operations on Mrs. D.—all successfully—and so they closed her case, proudly improving their statistics. But what about the general practitioners? They had to go on attending Mrs. D., still suffering from exactly the same complaints as before or between the operations". The world has many Mrs. D.s; and many more people—relatives, colleagues, doctors, nurses—whose time and patience the Mrs. D.s are wasting, to no purpose.

2

THE ANALYST'S DOG

At this point a question arises. If, as the evidence so firmly suggests, emotional stress can be reflected in the physical symptoms of illness, how is it that some doctors still examine patients, diagnose their illness, and prescribe treatment without even bothering to inquire about their emotional condition? And how do doctors account for those illnesses which resist diagnosis by all the orthodox physical tests?

In practice, the answer is, doctors rarely have much difficulty in finding, or at least assuming, a physical cause. Germs and viruses are usually present, and they can be blamed as "the cause"; even though, for all the doctor knows to the contrary, they may themselves be the symptoms of the patient's illness—the signs that his defences have broken down; just as gangs of looters in a city are a symptom, not the cause, of a breakdown in the machinery for enforcing law and order. To tell a patient that his troubles are due to a microbe is to tell him very little; but the chances are that he does not realize this—that he will go away and boast to his friends about how he must have picked up this wandering pest in a bus, or in a cafeteria.

Much the same applies in the case of patients who are diagnosed as suffering from one of the many forms of inflammation distinguished by names ending in -itis. Again, the doctor is only recognizing the symptoms by his diagnosis, not accounting for them; but the patient is usually satisfied; at least his trouble has been recognized, so that the appropriate treatment can be prescribed.

But the profession has also provided itself with an escape hatch, which it can use when diagnosis fails—"functional" symptoms (as we have just seen in Balint's story of Mrs. D.). The accepted medical definition is that a functional disorder does not involve any change or disease in the body's structure (by contrast with an organic disorder, which does); symptoms of illness are present—the patient has pains, or a fever, or incontinence of bowel movements—but they cannot be traced to any specific source. Most doctors privately admit that functional symptoms are common, but few care to admit as much in public, because "functional" has come to be thought of in the profession as the equivalent of "not diagnosed"—an admission of failure. Rather than make the admission, most doctors prefer to find something, anything, which can be blamed; an attitude of mind which is mainly responsible for the process Bernard Shaw ridicules in *The Doctor's Dilemma*, where his specialists each has his private fad. Sometimes it takes forms even more unpleasant than Shaw visualized; like the mania a few years ago for removing all the patient's teeth, on the grounds that they were the source of the infection that was poisoning his system. In any case, doctors do not care to tell the patient to his face that his illness has not been diagnosed; "functional", as a result, has never come into colloquial usage.

There is really no firm distinction between organic and functional; the terms merely reflect the profession's desire to be able to recognize and explain all illness in precise physical terminology. And if it is accepted that physical symptoms are not necessarily the product of physical causes, this whole system of diagnosis will have to be revised, to allow for the fact that organic and functional are inextricably intertwined—as in the way hay fever sufferers' symptoms may develop either from pollen or when they see a picture of the flower whose pollen normally brings on their attacks. But doctors still cling to physical diagnoses; so the tendency has been, for obvious reasons, for the label "functional" to be applied to symptoms which cannot be accounted for. Many of these arise in times of emotional stress—usually as a result of protracted worry, or frustration: but sometimes from a sudden shock.

The classic example of a functional illness of this nature is Saul's attack of blindness on the road to Damascus. History abounds with similar cases of people who at moments of great emotional crisis have been struck blind, or deaf, or dumb; and most of us, if we examine our own lives, can find some such instance on a less striking—indeed, often at an embarrassingly trivial—level.

I had one such, at my first school. I had committed some breach of the school rules, and it was considered serious enough to be reported to the headmistress. She came up to give me what she would have called a good talking-to; but, though she was less than a yard away, I did not hear a single word she said. In some way, my mind contrived to lock out the reports which normally are transmitted through the sense of hearing. For all I know I have had functional blockages on occasions since which have passed themselves off as "organic"—often, there is no way of distinguishing.

The extent to which this type of functional disorder exists, but remains hidden because it is not distinguished from organic disease, can hardly even be guessed. I heard of a striking and unpleasant example just after the last war. In his capacity as house-surgeon at a hospital, a friend of mine was put in charge of the routine work at the V.D. clinic. Full of a new broom's zeal, he became dissatisfied with the perfunctory way in which diagnosis was carried out there, in particular with the assumption that everybody who came in suffering from the symptoms of syphilis should get the routine treatment for syphilis, without detailed examination to make sure he really had it. My friend insisted on a full battery of all the known tests for all patients—less because he suspected that the diagnosis might be incorrect, than because he thought that with more information about symptoms he might be able to work out greater refinements of treatment. To his astonishment, and to the chagrin of hospital and patients (for the treatment at that time was long, painful, and expensive), the tests revealed that several of the patients did not have syphilis at all. Outwardly their imitation of the symptoms had been close; but they had no tell-tale spirochetes.

Had these patients been the victims of their sense of guilt? Is there some mechanism by which people feel so strongly that they deserve to be punished for sexual laxity or promiscuity, that their bodies reproduce the punitive symptoms? Whatever the reason, such mimicking of V.D. symptoms is still quite common. An advertising agent of my acquaintance, to whom I happened to relate the story of the clinic, admitted that he developed chancres every time he slept with a woman who was not his wife. As it turned out, the doctor he went to the first time it happened guessed their "functional" origin, and explained it. But—presumably because the feelings of guilt lay too deep to be reassured—he never failed to reproduce the symptoms when he slept with other women (which he did frequently) even when he was certain that there was no fear of catching venereal disease from them.

Clear evidence of the astonishing power of mind over body in the production of symptoms has been provided by experiments with people under hypnosis. Quite a common parlour trick of hypnotists is to suggest to a subject in a trance that he is about to be burnt by a red-hot needle; if a cold needle is then placed on his skin he will still cry out in pain, as if burned; and, what is more remarkable, the skin may later reproduce the characteristic blister, as if it really had been burned. Evidently suggestion, under hypnosis, can reach down to that area of the mind which sends out orders to the body to carry out anti-burn procedures; and the body obeys. Conversely, if a patient in a hypnotic trance is actually touched with a red-hot needle, but assured that the needle is in fact cold, he may appear to feel nothing, and have no characteristic blister afterwards.

This power of mind over body operates through suggestion—though "suggestion" is too mild a word. Some people are extremely suggestible; they have only to be told that their symptoms will disappear, and their symptoms do disappear. Others are capable of inducing their own symptoms: one of the felons in the book *My Six Convicts* could reproduce the signs of the zodiac at will, on his body; and numerous saints have reproduced the stigmata. All of us, probably, have some capacity to mimic illness; though not all of us use it, and when we do use it, it may be masked by the skill of the mimicry. One common form is paralysis of a limb: it is sometimes possible to show, under hypnosis, that the limb is not paralysed; all that has been lost is the patient's control of the mechanism by which he normally moves that limb—control which, under hypnotic suggestion, he may regain. Or, the deception—which is unconscious—may be detected because the mimicry is too grotesque (as in the case of certain forms of madness). And where a doctor can detect it—where he is able to demonstrate that the illness really is "functional" in this sense of the term—he is no longer embarrassed at the thought that he may be making an inadequate diagnosis; in fact he will congratulate himself at his astuteness.

★

This type of functional illness is normally referred to in clinical usage as hysterical. Colloquially, "hysteria" has come to mean a particular complex of symptoms exhibited by people (and animals) who appear to have been suffering from over-charged emotions, when they discharge them suddenly and involuntarily, in fits of grief, or rage, or exaltation, or a medley of passions. Usually, the term no longer carries the implication that the individual is using the hysterics to gain his own ends—as it did, for instance, in Dickens's novels, where wives were fond of going into hysterics in order to get their way with their husbands. The result was that the term began to be used in a derogatory sense; the assumption grew that hysterics were an act, put on for the performer's benefit—an assumption which annoyed those members of the profession who, though they did not attempt to understand its mechanism, were aware that hysteria ought not to be confused with malingering (one doctor went on record in the 1870s objecting—in much the same way as doctors now object to the abuse of the term "psychological"—to the use of the word to indicate that a patient "is silly, shamming, or could get well if she pleased". About this time, hysterics began to go out of fashion (because they no longer brought the desired results?) and the term has drifted into a different colloquial meaning.

The mechanism of hysterical disorders is still not understood, but its operation has been well described by Dr. A. E. Clark-Kennedy. When an ordinary man finds himself committed to some unpleasant obligation which he knows he cannot morally escape, he normally manages to adapt himself to it, even if he hates to do so; he does not run away, or malinger. Certain individuals, however, possess a way out. They are highly suggestible; they can pick up the idea of disease whenever it is to their advantage. Faced with awkward situations or unpleasant obligations, they manage to adopt the symptoms of disease subconsciously. "Subconsciously", Clark-Kennedy insists,

> "is the point. To adopt symptoms deliberately is to malinger, and hysteria is not that. What to the patient appears to be genuine pain renders it impossible for him to go to work and essential to stay at home and be waited on. Weakness or dizziness may necessitate staying in bed. So-called heart attack may enable a woman to get her own way and keep her daughter at home. Persistent headache after a minor head injury may even result in the disgruntled man getting the compensations to which he feels entitled. Sudden loss of memory (hysterical fugue) and wandering off are always one way out of any very awkward situation. Again and again during the first world war a man in the trenches managed to stage fits or paralysis and so get invalided back home."

Subconsciously is the point—but in our everyday lives even those of us who are disposed to regard psychological disorders with sympathy find it hard to concede that a man may contrive to imitate an illness without being aware of it, to escape responsibility—especially if the escape throws the onus on us. We may even prefer the straightforward rogue—the malingerer. Most of us confuse the two. That a man can be capable of planning and carrying out what appear to be the most elaborate schemes in his own interest, but not be aware that he is doing so, is something that few of us can easily accept—or put up with, even if in theory we feel we ought to accept it.

Hysterical symptoms range from the simple capacity to have a headache whenever some particular household chore requires to be done, to the most incredible and elaborate mimicry of serious diseases, even of injuries. The existence of these extreme versions is, however, comparatively rare in civilized countries, and although it is still fairly common among more primitive peoples, it does not appear often enough in consulting rooms to embarrass doctors by reminding them of their confessed inability to explain it.

The first serious attempt to account for the phenomenon of hysteria was made by Breuer and later developed by Freud, whose explorations of the unconscious mind made it possible to understand how and why people acquired hysterical symptoms. They arise, Freud believed, in response to emotional conflicts, when the emotions cannot find an outlet through which they can be expressed—and thereby relieved—in the ordinary way. The symptoms may themselves be emotional, but they can also be physical. There is nothing odd in this: for all of us have experienced how, in the grip of great mirth, we can lose control of our bodies, so that a clown may have us literally rolling in the aisles; and tragedy moves us to tears. Gripped by other powerful emotions, we may develop other uncontrollable physical symptoms. Sometimes we can mimic the symptoms of those around us. Freud cited as an example the recurrence, known to hospital workers, of "psychic infection" where patients "catch" symptoms of illnesses which are not infectious from somebody in the same ward. Identification in this case, Freud considered, is not so much imitation as assimilation; it is as if the patient in some way contrives to absorb the illness whose symptoms he is copying.

The strongest evidence of how widespread hysteria is comes from the vast number of "miraculous" occurrences on record. The great bulk of cures attributed to the relics of saints or to holy places are of hysterical or, in the wider sense, functional symptoms—a fact which the medical advisers to the Catholic Church are well aware; they take elaborate precautions to ensure that no cure is accepted as miraculous unless there is evidence which satisfies them that the illness was really organic, and as a result only a very small proportion of cures claimed at, say, Lourdes are considered for elevation to the status of attested miracles. And even in the case of those cures which have been accepted by the Church as miraculous the evidence is not, as the investigations by D. J. West have recently shown, of a kind which satisfies the increasingly rigorous demands for scientific proof in such cases. Still, the weight of evidence that there have been innumerable cures which to all outward appearances are miraculous is overwhelming.

Scepticism about this is surely unreasonable. In view of the remarkable capacity of the body not merely to simulate illness, but actually to reproduce the physical symptoms of illness, it is not at all surprising that the converse should also hold: that if the mind so orders, real as well as mimic symptoms should disappear, as if by magic, overnight. Again, relatively little is known about how the process works; obviously, what we think of as "faith" has a hand in it, but then, relatively little is known about faith. There is clearly some link with suggestibility; but all that can safely be said is that the human mind, in the widest sense of the word, has powers as yet uncontrolled—and barely tapped by man for his own benefit.

I have kept a couple of curious illustrations of these powers until now, because they illustrate what might be called the twilight zone between functional and hysterical symptoms. Over twenty years ago G. D. Bivin and M. P. Klinger, two Indiana doctors, collected details of 444 cases of the condition from which the first Queen Mary traditionally suffered: false pregnancy, or "pseudocyesis". Every woman will have come across stories and possibly actual instances of this malady, in which all the symptoms of pregnancy—morning sickness, gradual swelling of the abdomen and breasts, and suspension of monthly periods—are imitated. What was remarkable about the Bivin/Klinger findings, though, was that in no less than 42 per cent of the cases in which the duration of the false pregnancy was recorded, the condition lasted the full nine months; labour pains occurred in 138 cases. The capacity to carry on hysterical self-deception of this kind for so long is clearly a reflection of the intense feelings related to childbirth; feelings either of longing for a child, or of fear of conception—sometimes, perhaps, a mixture of the two.

There is another even stranger story of a false pregnancy. The last volume of Ernest Jones's biography of Freud includes an extract from a letter from one of Freud's friends about his chow.

> ". . . a psychosomatic case, indeed! She supposedly had too narrow a pelvis for ever having puppies without danger to her life. For this reason, she had to be watched carefully whenever she was in heat. Once, on a Sunday, sitting in the garden with the dog, I fell asleep, and when I awakened the dog had disappeared. Franctically searching for her, I found her finally in the neighbour's garden with a beautiful male poodle. The chow looked very sheepish, but no real evidence of a love act could be established. Nothing could be done at the moment more than to wait and see. Several weeks went by without any change in her behaviour. At the end of the second month, however, the teats began to swell and colostrum appeared. She began to get fat rapidly. When on the street, she scratched and dug holes in the ground, altogether unmistakable signs of pregnancy. I resigned myself to the inevitable, but nothing happened. On the contrary, in the fourth month, instead of increasing, these signs started to decrease. I rushed with the dog to the vet. Diagnosis: pseudocyesis. Have you ever heard

of a dog with a false pregnancy? I am almost inclined to say, 'That can only happen to the dog of an analyst.'"

The truth of this tale is not now verifiable, but it no more than confirms the assumption that the mind—of dogs, as of humans—has remarkable powers to influence the body; in dogs, as in humans, the mind can signal "baby on the way", and the body will take the appropriate action, even when no baby is on the way.

★

There is another type of disorder which falls into the category of functional, though it is normally kept differentiated by doctors: neurosis. Neurosis is if possible an even vaguer term than functional; and its common colloquial derivative, neurotic, has been stretched to mean almost anything. But for ordinary clinical purposes, a neurosis is normally a functional illness which manifests itself in nervous rather than in physical symptoms—in worry, anxiety, tension, and so on. Anybody can be worried for a real reason—the fear of losing a job, or of failing to get promotion; the point at which the worry becomes a neurosis is the point at which there is no reason, or insufficient reason, for worrying. All of us have experienced times when we have been irked by some gnawing sense of anxiety which we cannot explain, or by reactions which are disproportionate to the reason for them (some days we are hardly affected by a certain noise; other days it drives us to distraction); so all of us have first-hand experience of what neurosis means.

Freud attributed neuroses to the existence of repressed emotional conflicts. People develop neurotic symptoms, he thought, when they cannot satisfy some innermost desire because they do not know what the desire is, as they have pushed it away into an inaccessible region of the mind; the neurotic symptoms are a substitute for the missing satisfaction. This was originally ridiculed as far-fetched, particularly as Freud made it clear that the missing satisfaction was basically sexual; but a glance at the people of our acquaintance whom we class as neurotic reveals that it is usually true in an everyday sense—the form their neurosis takes often contrives to give them a pale imitation of the satisfaction that conscience or circumstance denies them. Thus, one of the commonest examples of a neurotic is the man who is always "put upon"; he gets what pleasure he can from gathering together innumerable real and imagined examples of how malice and misfortune conspire to prevent him from achieving his just deserts.

Neuroses, Freud further claimed, arise out of emotional conflicts which have taken place in early childhood, when intense desires are repressed because the child cannot bear to face the guilt feelings they arouse in him. The neurotic symptoms cannot ordinarily be removed until the source of the original conflict has been traced, and the emotions arising out of it, released. But there is an alternative explanation; that neuroses are simply bad habits. John B. Watson, the Behaviourist, succeeded in inducing a neurotic fear of rabbits in a three-year-old boy, who had previously been fond of them, by loudly banging an iron bar with a hammer whenever the boy tried to stroke one; in time, the boy could not even bear to have a rabbit in the same room. Then, gradually, by giving the boy chocolate whenever he saw a rabbit, Watson was able in time to remove the phobia, and to recondition the boy's reaction to rabbits to where it had been before the experiment started.

After recounting this story, H. J. Eysenck, the most provocative champion of the school of thought which has developed along the Behaviourist-Pavlovian lines, argues:

> "Behaviour is essentially learned, although, of course, it has a strong inherited basis. Neurotic behaviour is equally learned; although now maladapted to the individual's needs and desires, at some previous period it fulfilled an important function (i.e. it enabled the boy to avoid the fear-producing loud noise). . . . From this we might generalize and say that perhaps all neurotic symptoms are simply habits which have

ceased to be adaptive, and that the cure of neurotic disorders lies essentially in the elimination, through deconditioning or extinction, of undesirable habits."

This thesis, it has been argued, is supported by the fact that neurosis is not exclusively a human disease; it can be observed, and experimentally induced, in animals. One researcher, H. S. Liddell, put a flock of sheep in a barn-yard laboratory where the only distracting feature was a metronome, normally working at fifty strokes to the minute. Whenever the animals were fed the rate was increased to 120 strokes a minute; and the sheep soon learned to open their feed-box as soon as they heard the faster beat. Liddell then increased the normal rate of the metronome to 100 strokes a minute; the sheep were unable to distinguish between this rate and the feeding rate of 120, and they could never tell when it was feeding time. They fell rapidly into what in a human being would be described as a pitiable state of nerves. Actually their hearts beat faster and irregularly; other bodily functions became upset. Before long the sheep could not even discriminate between the 50 and the 120 rate of the metronome. By this time little barn-yard disturbances, previously unnoticed, bothered them a great deal. They could not relax at night, even when they were lying down. Liddell put them out to grass with other sheep and gradually they recovered. It took a year or more, and even then the recovery was contingent upon continued peace. If they were brought back to the laboratory, the beat of the metronome set them trembling. They suffered palpitations, and old worries obviously crowded back upon them. Some of the sheep did not have to hear the metronome; the laboratory with its year-old associations was enough to arouse the symptoms of collapse.

The fact that animals as well as humans can suffer from induced neurosis is not, though, proof that humans suffer only from learned habits which have ceased to be adapted to their surroundings or way of life. It is quite possible that the Pavlovian explanations may be correct for one patient, the Freudian for another; they are not, in this context, contradictory—though the tendency has sometimes been, on both sides, to maintain that they are (a point I will be coming back to later).

Either way, two things are clear. One is that the time when neuroses are most likely to be contracted is in early childhood, when the mind is more susceptible to conditioning (as the Jesuits long ago discovered)—or, more capable (if the Freudian theory is correct) of repressing feelings which arouse a sense of guilt. The period of training is consequently of incalculable importance to the child's future because—as Flanders Dunbar points out in her book, relating and commenting on Liddell's experiment—babies are not necessarily tougher than sheep; they, too, can be "over-trained". The other is that neurosis is an emotional, not a physical problem. Neuroses can arise as a by-product of physical conditions; Lord Byron's erratic love life has often been attributed to his early shame over his misshapen foot. But in general—and here again, there is no contradiction between the Freudian and Pavlovian schools—they reflect conflicts in the mind; no physical defect is necessary, and the mind's difficulties can be resolved by reconditioning or by psychotherapy—though sometimes with assistance from physical treatments which have been evolved.

It is interesting in neurosis, too, to find that there are a number of physical symptoms which most doctors now concede are emotional in origin; stammering, nervous tics, and twitches, not to mention the thousand and one habits which all of us have in some degree—nail-biting, strumming our fingers, twiddling our thumbs, whistling through our teeth; some trivial, some irritating; some periodic, some chronic; all reflecting, it is now assumed, some inner tension arising out of repression (or maladaptation); all of them reminders of how imperfect is our control of ourselves. What is much less widely accepted is that if such symptoms are neurotic in origin, the physical symptoms of ordinary illness may also, and by a similar mechanism, be the product of neurosis. It is scarcely possible to do more than outline the possibilities of this subject, so little is known about it. Briefly, the suggestion is that if emotional stress can produce physical symptoms (as we know it can) then it is natural to suppose that neurosis, which has so powerful an emotional content, can also exercise a powerful effect on the symptoms.

To take a hypothetical example: let us assume that the form our neurosis takes is a desire to escape from the treadmill of home/bus/office/bus/home for a few days (this, of course, is to to skip out the intermediate stages—the mind does not work as straightforwardly as that, but it is capable of taking undisciplined unconscious urges and translating them into such practicable terms). The best way to get out of going to the office is to have some illness; and if possible, an illness which is not going to be called neurotic, because that would gain no sympathy, and might even lead to the suspicion we are shamming. Therefore we use the mechanism which Freud called assimilation: we imitate any illness so well that to all outward appearance, we have it—though we are not conscious of any deception. Say that we get appendicitis: if we are operated on the surgeon will find nothing wrong, but nobody is going to know that, and we can eat our grapes contentedly. Indeed, it is by no means unlikely that we will fall ill with symptoms—an asthmatic attack, or a rash—which will be indistinguishable, as far as our doctors are concerned, from what they would consider a real, organic illness.

In the circumstances, it is obviously absurd even to try to calculate how widespread neurosis is, and how serious its effects. All of us haye small phobias, minor mannerisms; we are all neurotic. Even if, for convenience, the category is limited to those whose symptoms are so distressing that they feel compelled to visit a doctor, no figures can give a true picture. The number of patients who present themselves to their doctors with any idea that their symptoms are neurotic is a tiny fraction of the whole; and normally, it is not in the doctor's interest to diagnose neurosis even if he suspects it; which he rarely does, as the physical symptoms usually appear to be classifiable under various heads—skin disease, asthma, and the rest. Opinion within the profession of what constitutes neurosis varies enormously: and estimates which have appeared in medical journals during the last few years have ranged from 2 per cent of all patients, to 50 per cent.

The extent of the problem is, however, hinted at by an analysis of certificates of incapacity given by doctors to workers in 1953-4, which the British Ministry of Pensions examined in the course of an investigation into absenteeism in industry; it revealed that neurosis came fourth on the list, behind only the rheumatic diseases, T.B., and bronchitis—this, in spite of the natural tendency for doctors to put "neurosis" down only when the patient has some obvious nervous disorder, and when he has no other specific form of illness. Workers normally prefer, too, if they can, to quote some physical illness as an excuse for absence, so that they cannot be accused of malingering—in fact they often ignore nervous, and wait for physical, symptoms before going to a doctor. Even allowing for the possibility that some cases get put down as neurotic because the doctor has failed to make a correct diagnosis, the incidence is certainly far heavier than any statistics could show.

*

There is another difficulty: how to separate neurosis from mental illness. Until quite recently the distinction was clear for all to see; a man who was neurotic was left outside, while a man who was insane was shut up in an asylum. The distinction was primarily legal—whether or not a man was capable of looking after his affairs; and whether or not he was a public nuisance, or danger. But the distinction has now broken down. Mental illness has been sub-divided into a number of categories; and there is a growing tendency for patients to come voluntarily to asylums—renamed mental hospitals—for treatment. At the same time, neurosis, alcoholism and other unstable personality traits are being treated in mental hospitals, so that the old division between sane and insane, neurotic and psychotic, has become blurred. Whether there is any real distinction, even clinically, is still being debated; for practical purposes the old jest is probably as easy a definition as any—that the neurotic builds castles in the air; the psychotic lives in them (to which somebody has since unkindly added that either way, the psychiatrist collects the rent).

For many of us, though, the old emotional distinction persists. Like most people who grew up while the old habit of imprisoning the insane behind high walls still continued, I formed the impression that insanity was a form of violent, or at least potentially violent, mental disturbance. The ninth hole of the course where I used to play golf looked out towards a large lunatic asylum; and occasionally one of the inmates, a little, mild old man, used to come and watch us. He stood always in the same place, saying nothing, except some murmured friendliness when he pointed out where a ball lay; but I could never quite rid myself of the feeling that he might one day assault and—madmen having supposedly the strength of ten—strangle some player.

This feeling about the insane is still very far from extinct; but notable efforts have been made in the past few years to break it down. The number of people who are compulsorily sent to mental hospitals is rapidly declining; when people are persuaded to undertake treatment voluntarily, the stigma of entering a mental hospital begins to disappear. As more and more patients arrive for treatment who by no stretch of the imagination could be considered lunatic, but whose mental or emotional symptoms need examination and treatment, the assumption must be that the division between neurotic and psychotic will cease to have so much emotive meaning for the public.

At the present time, anything up to a half of the available hospital beds in Western countries are occupied at any one time by mental patients; and as all these patients are sufferers from emotional stress (sometimes the cause, sometimes the effect—usually both—of their illness) the need for greater understanding of the nature of these stresses is obvious.

Obvious, too, is the need for greater effort and expenditure on treatment and research. Psychiatrists are continually complaining that the proportion of public funds spent on mental illness is dangerously small. In the middle Fifties, for example, the amount allocated for research per T.B. patient in the U.S. was over $25; per schizophrenic patient, less than $5. In the same period, New York State was spending more money on maintaining its criminals ($4.40 a head) than its mentally ill patients ($3.70 a head). Although conditions in mental hospitals improved after the scarifying publicity some of them got in the press and in films like *The Snake Pit* after the Second World War, much remains to be done to civilize and humanize them, and to provide them with adequate staffs. As it is, psychiatrists are often kept so busy on administrative work that they have little time to carry out psychotherapy—so that what is given is really little more than occupational therapy, designed to keep patients busy.

An argument often heard recently is that this may not matter—that psychotherapy, though a useful adjunct to treatment, is not all that important because many psychoses are attributable solely to physical changes in the brain. A great deal of research has recently been done on this aspect of mental illness; and a growing body of psychiatric opinion has it that mental disintegration, hallucinations, and delusions are the product of physical changes in the brain's structure, or chemical composition, which the patient's emotional condition reflects, but does not cause. If this is so, the first step in psychiatric treatment ought properly to be to prevent or cure such changes by means of the appropriate physical techniques—electric shock treatment, drugs, or operations; while psychotherapy—treatment of the mind by psychology, in contrast to treatment of the brain by physical methods—can be left to fight a rearguard action, helping to rehabilitate the cured patient; in much the same way as physiotherapy is needed to rehabilitate patients after a prolonged physical illness, though the cure may have been first effected by an operation.

But although the onset of delusions may be traced to the degeneration of a part of the brain, the question still has to be asked: what caused the degeneration? Some forms of insanity are occasionally accounted for by the discovery that the patient is suffering from a tumour on the brain—but what causes the tumour? It is at least possible that if, by some stroke of fortune, research workers had the chance to observe the relationship of physical changes in the brain to emotional stress, in the same way that the relationship was observed in "Tom's" stomach, they might find that sudden or prolonged emotional stress was the first stage in the process leading to physical degeneration.

Significantly, research into schizophrenia appears to be confirming this view. Discussing the subject in his *Drugs and the Mind*, Robert de Ropp says:

> "Stress of one kind or another is usually involved in the development of schizophrenia. Several research workers have sought for the cause of this condition among the mechanisms which have to do with the body's response to stress. Under stressful conditions a chain of nervous and chemical reactions is initiated . . . there is, in the schizophrenic, some defect in the chemical machinery that enables the body to cope with stress."

The stresses involved may be of different kinds, but very frequently it appears that in schizophrenia, and in other forms of mental disorder, a powerful but unresolved emotional conflict may be the precipitant which pushes the individual over the brink into illness.

A personal experience helped, for me, to illuminate this obscure problem. I was invited in my journalistic capacity by a friend of mine, an anaesthetist, to witness a demonstration of the use of the drug "curare", as a muscle relaxant in electric shock treatment of the brain. Recalling its association with schoolboy stories of South American adventure—curare is the poison with which the Indians tip their blowpipe darts—I had expressed an interest in it. This was at a time when the shock treatment had become rather fashionable, particularly as the use of curare helped to prevent the effects of muscular spasm on the patient when the shock was administered. In fact the only signs that the current was passing through the terminals attached on either side of the patient's forehead was a slight tremor in her toes, and a clamping together of her jaws on a "bit" which had been placed in her mouth to prevent her from biting her tongue.

Immediately the shock was administered, and her jaws clamped, I was reminded of an incident that had happened a few weeks before, when I had seen a friend, B., having an epileptic-type fit—the first I had ever seen. The expressions on the two faces were so startlingly similar that the explanation leapt into my mind at once: that this electric shock treatment must be a way of inducing a fit artificially. But with what purpose? The anaesthetist had already explained to me that nobody knew why shock treatment helped some people with mental illness; the treatment was given simply because it had been found to work, not because anybody had reasoned out in advance how it would work. Could this mean—I thought to myself, while the treatment proceeded, with other patients—that a real fit might also have the same result; that it might be a mechanism by which an epileptic threw off approaching mental illness? Certainly, I realized, this would help to account for my friend B.'s case.

B. had always, since I first knew him, evaded responsibility by running away. In small matters and in big, whenever he was faced with a situation which promised embarrassment, he escaped from it simply by putting it out of his mind. If, for example, he found himself unable to keep an appointment, he never thought to ring up and excuse himself; he simply failed to appear. After what had promised to be an exceptional university career he had left college without taking a degree, and had since then been unable to settle down to any particular line; but he was still young enough to live with and off his family, and he continued to be irresponsible, until he fell in love with a girl who knew his ways, and was determined to change them.

The girl insisted that it was all a matter of discipline; that he was grown up, and ought to put away childish things; and that really, he could not expect her to marry him, if he did not learn to behave himself. B. was sufficiently in love to want to carry out these instructions; and he knew the girl well enough to realize that she would not marry him if he did not. So he did his best to conform to her requirements. The trouble was that he had conditioned himself to irresponsibility. Certain episodes in his past, too, which he had been content to ignore, or managed to blot out of his mind, came up at him when he tried to become responsible (responsibility being often, of necessity, retrospective); and he could not face them.

It was on one such occasion immediately after he had, as it were, tripped over his past, that he had had his fit. Could it be—I wondered—that he had in some way managed to summon up the fit to relieve him of the necessity to accept responsibility at that moment? His wife-to-be was with him: if he had run away, he might have forfeited her love; had his mind turned instead to a physical expedient to help him out? If this was the explanation, it was a striking demonstration of the ability of the mind to select an appropriate illness, in time of need.

I decided to put this idea to the psychiatrist who had given the demonstration. After thanking him, and saying that I was interested in the whole subject, I described the case of B.'s fit, saying,

> "... the point that struck me at the time was that the fit, so far as being the frightening thing his family all thought it was—specialists were brought in to test everything from his eyes to his urine—was a release mechanism; and if it hadn't existed he might have gone mad. That led me on to wonder whether the same is not true of epileptics—that their fits are a way of avoiding lunacy, or mental disequilibrium of some kind, in the same way that vomiting may be a way to prevent poisoning. The twitching toes, the clenched teeth of your patient yesterday were identical with my friend's symptoms. I don't know enough to carry the speculation further, but I thought you might be interested to hear a lay reaction. ..."

The reply came a few days later:

"My dear Inglis,

Many thanks for your letter. I am glad you enjoyed the demonstration, though if I'd realized you were really interested I would have tried to show you what a real fit looks like, uncontrolled by the administration of S—— (the relaxant). It is far more impressive!

About your friend's fit: it seems to me that if he had no previous history of behaviour of this sort it was probably a hysterical fit which can often closely resemble an epileptic one, and is, as you say, a release mechanism to get away with an intolerable situation. The true epileptic however has no control of when the fit may occur . . . it appears to be due to a discharge of electrical impulses in the brain which suddenly come to a crescendo and need not necessarily have any emotional tone connected with its occurence. Not all epileptics develop insanity—in fact, only a very small proportion of them.

What one tries to accomplish with ECT is of a different order, and the actual fact that a fit occurs with it is incidental; but it gives the measurement of the force of the electrical stimulation. What one is trying to do is to upset the part of the brain which carries the association fibres, and thereby upset their memories so as to make them form different memory patterns, and stop them thinking in their present kind of vicious circle. When they have reformed their memory patterns, one hopes they will be reformed in a more healthy way.

This is all very badly stated but you will probably get the gist of it. . . ."

On the contrary, it was very clearly stated. A couple of points struck me as significant. First, doctors I had asked had not even known that the induced fit theory existed. There was no particular reason why they should—no doctor can be a specialist in every field—but they had argued as if they knew. So had the brain specialist who had been brought in to see my friend B. after his fit. He had ordered a battery of tests on B.'s brain, blood, nerve responses, and urine; and from their findings announced confidently, greatly to B.'s family's relief, that B. had not got epilepsy. With that he prescribed some injections, drugs, and tonics, and departed. The only further communication they had from him was his bill.

The specialist, I should add, was an intelligent man, high in his profession. He must have known about "release mechanism" fits, which presumably he would have called functional, or hysterical. Discussing them with his colleagues, he might even have been willing to concede the possibility of their emotional origin, had he known about it. But what he was not prepared to do was to make any attempt to differentiate between them and what he would have described as real, or organic fits, in his treatment. And I have no doubt he is still prescribing injections, drugs, and tonics, in all similar cases—though the injections, drugs and tonics will now all be different, as he is a man who strives to keep abreast of the latest fashions.

Which brings me to the second significant point. It so happened that B.'s particular release mechanism took the form of a fit. If he had had a different type of personality, or a different constitution, or a different environment, might it have taken a different form? Might it have made him physically ill, or mentally ill in a different way—causing him to suffer a black-out, perhaps, with loss of memory? If the symptoms were from a clinical standpoint functional, as in this case, the actual form they took might be incidental. If illness is the personality's way of quitting the arena when emotional stress gets too much for it, by whatever escape route is available, the difference between mental and physical illness may be relatively unimportant. That neuroses and psychoses appear to be on the increase may simply be because the advance of medical science in the physical side has stopped up so many knot-holes that, increasingly, people who want to take advantage of the release mechanism which illness affords are forced back on functional, or neurotic symptoms.

This is not to suggest that the physical side of illness is

irrelevant or unimportant. Injury to the brain can cause insanity; so can some genetic factors, as yet not fully understood. Still, even where there are strong grounds for putting the blame on heredity, the actual cause of breakdown may be less the hereditary taint than the fear of it. This is something that cannot be proved, but it is strongly indicated in such cases as that of Clifford Beers, described in his autobiography, *A Mind that Found Itself*. Beers had an elder brother who was struck down with a mental illness, at first thought to be epilepsy, and died:

> "Now, if a brother who enjoyed perfect health could be stricken with epilepsy, what was to prevent my being similarly affected? This was the thought that soon got possession of my mind. The more I considered it and him, the more nervous I became; and the more nervous, the more convinced that my own breakdown was only a matter of time. Doomed to what I then considered a living death, I thought of epilepsy, I dreamed epilepsy, until thousands of times during the six years that this disquieting idea persisted, my overwrought imagination seemed to drag me to the very verge of an attack."

Beers did not get epilepsy; but he did become suicidal, and eventually, for a time, insane; and it seems very probable that insanity can be self-induced in this way—or at least, that the unconscious emotional conflicts which exist in all of us may be concentrated or exacerbated by such terrified broodings and lead to psychosis. Fear of mental illness (which may be particularly strong) can perhaps help to produce it. But this is likely to become less of a worry, when the stigma and the terror of mental illness decline, as they are already fast beginning to do.

In any case, there is no reason to suppose that mental illness is in any way singular; it may well be, as I have suggested, only one of the ways in which the mind arranges to fall ill. How the mind makes its arrangements is something that has yet to be explored; research is still only around the periphery of that vast new territory which Freud began to open up for mankind.

But, reduced to its simplest terms, it is possible to get an idea how it works from the story of the pseudocyesis of the analyst's dog. Symptoms are the product of a want; a need. The wanting may not be conscious; very often it is directly opposed to what in our conscious minds we think we want (anybody who finds this hard to believe has only to think of his own struggles with his own vices, gluttony, or sloth or lust). But where it is deep enough, or strong enough, it can mimic symptoms with extraordinary faithfulness; and more than that, it can create real symptoms, by starting the chain reaction of mind and body which leads to illness.

3

IN THE CHEST—OR IN THE HEAD?

To the three diseases that are fairly widely considered to be caused by, or linked with, emotional stress—certain skin disorders, stomach ulcers, and asthma—three more ought properly to be added, though their presence in this category is less often accepted: heart trouble, diabetes and tuberculosis.

There should be no surprise over the inclusion of T.B. as a stress disorder. In the last century the frequency with which it followed emotional crises was generally recognized. In *Anna Karenina*, when Kitty contracts T.B., family doctor and specialist agree that behind it there is some emotional reason; the family doctor urges that treatment should consist of travel abroad, to help "the change of her habits and the disassociations from the conditions that serve to recall unhappy thoughts"; and the specialist agrees. The specialist also insists that Kitty should only drink the mineral waters he prescribes not because he thinks they will do her any good—"their virtue, in his eyes, consisted in their uselessness"—but to prevent her from chasing after the spurious cures then being hawked around for T.B.

In spite of its dangers, T.B. was considered an "interesting" disease to contract in the nineteenth century, particularly for decorative young ladies like Elizabeth Barrett.

> "There was pain," Flanders Dunbar remarks, "but there were compensations. She was spared exposure to most of the paternal rages . . . she had a good deal of care for the first time of her life. She had what was a great boon in a family of that size—a room of her own . . . under the circumstances, there was

nothing for the poor woman to do but cling to her symptoms. Her emotional system had been unequal to the strain put upon it by her environment. The body succumbed, but in doing so selected a set of symptoms which could give some relief to the emotions."

It required only the impetuous love of Robert Browning, and the prospect of escape from her family, to release her from her twenty years of invalidity; at forty she married, at forty-one she was scrambling over hillsides, and at forty-three she bore a healthy baby: "She didn't need her symptoms any longer."

It can be argued that Elizabeth Barrett's illness was "functional," or that it was wrongly diagnosed; but hers is only one of countless cases where the onset or course of T.B. has been observed to reflect emotional crises. I have come across a number of instances, the most striking being when an acquaintance of mine left his wife. She got T.B. so badly that her doctors asked him to come in for a reconciliation just before she died; and to console her, as he thought, in her dying moments, he spoke of renewing and rebuilding their life together when she recovered. She did, so rapidly that had it been a vision of some saint of her church that she had seen, rather than her husband, miraculous intervention would have been considered the only possible explanation. Nor is this exceptional; every doctor who has been connected with T.B. establishments can recall remarkable recoveries of this kind, so much so that Sir William Osler, who retains the reputation of having been one of the greatest of all medical teachers, asserted that the fate of the tuberculous depended more on what they had in their heads than what they had in their chests.

The profession, however, ignored him; for they had come to regard T.B. almost as a plague. There was good reason for this: when unleashed among primitive communities—say, the Red Indians—or among people living in slum conditions, it became the most destructive of all diseases. Not until the 1930s did the discovery of new drugs for use in T.B. treatment, coupled with a widespread improvement in living standards, begin to bring it under control. Understandably, it came to be believed that T.B. could not be attributed to emotional difficulties; it must be the result of an infection—an impression confirmed when the T.B. bacillus was discovered, and when drugs were at last found by which the bacillus could be destroyed.

The emotional aura surrounding T.B. did not disappear, but it took an entirely different form; from having been thought "interesting" T.B. came to be regarded as sinister—unmentionable, even. To this day, in some circles a person who has—or has recently had—T.B. may still be made to feel that he is regarded with something of the uneasiness that people feel about a leper. When Gilbert Harding, the British television performer, fell ill in the winter of 1956, although he continued to write his weekly newspaper column from and about his sick-bed, he did not disclose the nature of his illness until he was allowed out of hospital; only then, under the headline "I WILL NO LONGER HIDE THE TRUTH FROM YOU" did he admit what had been the matter with him. The trouble was, he complained, that people who had it, and even people who had been cured of it, were still being shunned by colleagues, friends, and employers "as if they were carriers of some dreaded disease".

The impression that the bacillus is the only cause of T.B. is still general. But almost everybody in civilized communities is a host to the bacillus, and is consequently infected with T.B., at some time or other—acquiring a limited immunity. Normally the effects are so slight that they are not even noticed. The theory that the bacillus is responsible, then, does not explain why some people who are infected get ill, and others do not; nor why some who get ill die, while others recover. The suggestion that in some cases the bacilli are particularly virulent has not stood up to investigation; the answer appears to be in the individual's capacity to resist.

This may be the result of his heredity, of his constitution, or of his circumstances, or of all three. Members of certain tribes who are not normally exposed to T.B. do not acquire immunity young, and are particularly susceptible if they are exposed to it; undernourishment, and bad housing, can also help to create the surroundings in which it flourishes. But these explanations, though valid, do not explain how and why T.B. selects and strikes down individuals in other circumstances; and recent investigations are tending to confirm Osler's opinion that the search should be directed to the patient's head—or perhaps it would be closer to say, his heart.

In the 1930s George Day, an English doctor, was struck by the frequency with which T.B. patients had been involved in unhappy love affairs; and he helped by his work to arouse interest in the possibility that T.B. might sometimes be connected, as the Victorians had assumed, with broken hearts. His work encouraged the National Association for the Prevention of T.B. to sponsor an investigation into the subject at the end of the Second World War: "although a connection between the psychology of the patient and the course of the disease has always been assumed by thoughtful physicians," it declared, "this knowledge has tended to remain the personal possession of the doctor, and has not to any extent been made the subject of modern research." To remedy the deficiency, the Association asked Eric Wittkower to conduct research for them; and its results are set out in his *A Psychiatrist Looks at T.B.*

Wittkower concentrated on what he felt to be the real problem; not why so many people contract the disease, but why so few develop it, and why of those who develop it some are killed by it, while others recover. The differences had usually been accounted for by variations in their physical resistance; a number of attempts have been made to find out if some people are constitutionally predisposed to develop T.B., rather than others, and why; but from such research no positive conclusions had emerged. But there had also been Day's suggestion, that emotional disturbances often precede, and possibly precipitate, the onset of T.B., and that the illness may be a means of flight from frustration or from responsibility. With this view Wittkower eventually found himself, after a study of some 300 patients, in broad agreement.

His conclusions were that the outstanding common feature of the personality of T.B. patients was an inordinate need for affection. Sometimes the individual would show it by parasitic attachment to his family, or to an individual member of his family; sometimes he would go to the other extreme and ostentatiously express distaste for dependence—refusing to admit a need for it, though the need was palpably present. "There are, no doubt, many patients in whom the development of active T.B. is adequately accounted for by exposure"; Wittkower wrote, "there are others who for reasons inherent in their personalities expose themselves to situations which lower their resistance; and there are still others in whom one cannot help but feel that emotional stress in adult life has reactivated a primary infection which might otherwise have remained dormant." The existence of some mechanism whereby infection is reactivated by emotional stress does not exclude the possibility of people getting T.B. for other reasons, but it helps to explain, in many otherwise incomprehensible cases, why the illness strikes, or why the patient relapses—though not why the illness should be T.B., rather than anything else: a problem, Wittkower thought, which required further and much deeper research.

The weakness in Wittkower's work, as he himself admitted, was that his experiment was done without "controls": it was not carried out at the same time on ordinary people who did not have T.B., to show in what way, and to what extent, T.B. patients are different from other patients. An attempt has since been made to remedy this in the investigations carried out in Scotland by Dr. D. M. Kissen. Characteristically, his work received no publicity in the British press; though it was referred to in *Time* magazine.

Kissen began by recalling (*Time* added corroborative detail about Mimi of *La Bohème*) that emotional distress has been advanced as a reason for tuberculosis since the days of antiquity; but no scientific investigation with controls had been carried out to check whether the belief had substance (in fact Wittkower and many others who worked in this field did not believe the use of controls was feasible). Consequently, Kissen thought, the belief that a common personality trait in T.B. patients is their "inordinate need of affection" might merely reflect the fact that the world is full of people who have an inordinate need of affection—don't we all!—so that it may be characteristic of other diseases as well as T.B.

Dissatisfied with what he felt was too casual an approach, Kissen determined to carry out experiments which would satisfy two requirements: they would use controls, and they would, as far as possible, deal with the patients' emotional lives on the basis of established facts rather than on subjective judgements about their supposed emotional needs. This he did by investigating patients attending a diagnostic chest clinic for the first time. As these patients included, in addition to those who were later to be found to have T.B., people who were suffering from other illnesses (or from no illness at all), the non-tuberculosis group were used as the controls.

Kissen was here himself being unscientific; patients who have not, but think they have, lung trouble of any kind might conceivably share a similar emotional make-up with T.B. cases; they are not necessarily a representative cross-section of the community. It would not have been wholly destructive of the Day-Wittkower theory, if Kissen had found that the emotional background of his controls did not differ much from that of the T.B. cases. But as it happened the divergences were very great, revealing a striking statistical relationship between certain emotional situations and the development of T.B.

Kissen provided all patients with a simple questionnaire asking for information which he thought was as nearly factual as, in the circumstances, such information on the subject can be:

1. Have you had any unusually severe emotional stress or strain, for example a bereavement?
   or prolonged illness of a close relative?
   or difficulties or serious disagreement with your family?

2. Did you have a happy childhood?
3. Did you have any severe emotional upset in childhood?
4. Has there been any divorce or marital separation in your immediate family?
5. Have you had any unhappy love affairs?
6. Have you any sexual problems?
7. Have you any religious problems?
8. Have you any worrying difficulties in your work?
9. Have you had any frustrated desires, hopes or ambitions?
10. Have you had any other strains or upsets or worries not mentioned above?

Naturally such a questionnaire can itself be criticized for looseness of wording; almost every question begs another. But at least it gave patients an opportunity to provide a certain amount of concrete evidence, as well as a general picture of their emotional condition—or at least, what they thought was their emotional condition.

All patients were asked to fill in their answers while awaiting X-ray examination. Where Kissen found information he considered significant he asked them to expand these answers orally and recorded the details; but he made sure that the investigation was over and done with before the X-rays were taken—even before any clinical examination had been made, or their medical histories examined—in order that there could be no risk that he might be swayed in interpreting their answers, by prior knowledge of what was the matter with them.

In all, 267 patients were investigated, of whom 88 were subsequently diagnosed as cases of pulmonary T.B., the remaining 179 being used as the control group. Severe emotional stresses were found to have preceded the onset of illness in 65 per cent of the T.B. cases; only in 26 per cent of the others.

"The type of emotional factor characteristically preceding the onset of T.B.," Kissen explains,

> "although at first sight including a variety of life situations, could be grouped under the broad heading 'Break or serious

threat of a break in love link', using the term 'love' in its spiritual sense and not in the sexual meaning—indeed sexual factors were conspicuous by their absence. More than 90 per cent of the emotional factors came into the group described which was typified by the high incidence of 'Break or serious threat of break in a romance, engagement, or marriage.' "

Other broken love links were caused by bereavement, break within the family for various reasons, and enforced separation due to circumstances. On this evidence, Kissen argues, it is clear that deprivation of love and affection play an important part in the onset of T.B.—confirmation in rather more concrete form of Wittkower's belief that T.B. patients have an inordinate need of affection, and are suffering because they are deprived of it.

Kissen then went on to the next step, which was to try to ascertain by a similar experiment whether this particular personality trait is peculiar to T.B. A smaller selection of patients was taken, but the questions put to them were much more searching. The incidence of "deprivation of affection or broken love link" was found to be 100 per cent in the cases which were subsequently diagnosed as T.B., as compared with 16 per cent among patients who were found not to have T.B. Deprivation of natural parental affection was also found to be significantly higher in the T.B. cases, than in the controls:

"the frequency with which the characteristic life situations involving the 'break in the love link' occurs in association with the characteristic personality trait 'inordinate need for affection' in cases of pulmonary T.B. suggests that both are highly important factors in the onset of the disease . . . the combination of the two characteristic psychological factors leaves the door wide open to the development of pulmonary T.B."

In a further investigation Kissen examined whether emotional stress is one of the factors predisposing T.B. patients to relapse. The same questionnaire was given to all patients attending his clinic; those who were found to have relapsed were the subjects, and those who had not relapsed, the controls. The answers of 194 patients were used; 73 of them had at some time relapsed. He found that 75 per cent of all the patients who relapsed suffered from some severe emotional stress after their recovery from the initial illness, and before their relapse; and only 12 per cent of those who suffered severe emotional stress following their recovery did not relapse. Or, putting it another way, 80 per cent of all patients who suffered severe emotional stress after recovery from the initial illness subsequently relapsed; of those patients who did not, after recovery from the initial illness, only 14 per cent relapsed. The type of emotional stress characteristically preceding relapse—in over 90 per cent of cases—was again shown to belong to the "break in a love link" group.

If these findings prove to be representative, Kissen argues, our ideas on T.B. will have to be reoriented:

> "The removal of patients to a sanatorium for treatment involves not only a break with the family for the patient, but a broken love link for other members of the family, especially children. It may well be that, varying with the psychological state of the patient, and the psychological state of the family, some patients would be better treated at home and some in hospital . . . the psychological danger to young children in removing them from their parent is so great . . . that they should be treated at home unless there is very strong reason for not so doing. Indeed young children, whatever their illness, should where possible be treated at home."

This is a point worth making; because the tendency for many years has been to consider only the assumed needs of the patient. Often it is in the patients' interest that they should be sent to isolation hospitals—not, as was once assumed, because of any particular virtue in the magic mountain air, but because it removes them from the stresses which have contributed to their catching the T.B. But even when the patient has no family to worry about, there is still a need, if the Day/Wittkower/Kissen thesis is accepted, to make a thoroughgoing investigation into their individual emotional circumstances, before deciding what is best for them. The precipitant of T.B. for one patient may be an accumulation of home and office stresses, in which case removal from his environment may be exactly what he needs; for another, the precipitant may be deprivation of affection by a loved one, for which the real need may be reconciliation, if that is possible, with the person concerned—as in the case I have referred to, where the husband's reappearance at what was thought to be the death-bed side turned out to be the cure.

Kissen's findings are open to criticism from two sides. Statisticians can reasonably object that his experiments were conducted under conditions which were far from being strictly scientific; and that he was himself forced in the end to use some of the loose descriptive phrases ("deprivation of affection") that had been the ground for criticism of earlier research. The objection from the other side is more complex: that Kissen, in trying to pin his subjects down to facts, was ignoring the most important fact of all—that the most serious emotional stresses arise out of feelings of which the patient is unconscious, and which he cannot, therefore, relate or answer to a questionnaire.

Neither of these objections can be sustained to the point of dismissing Kissen's findings. If, for the sake of argument, it is conceded that there may be a connection between T.B. and unhappiness in love, the connection cannot be scientifically computed, because "love" and "unhappiness" are not scientifically measurable; they can only be estimated by the rule-of-thumb, subjective methods Kissen used. And these methods did not ignore the possibility that the most serious emotional stresses may be unconscious. He was not concerned with the nature of the stresses; his object was to consider the physical reaction of people to certain situations—a legitimate field of inquiry, even if it does not go deep.

What may well turn out to be true is that broken love links are not themselves the cause of T.B., but that the broken love links and T.B. are both reflections of some emotional immaturity which causes people to put too great a dependence on their relationship with others—a personality trait arising, possibly, out of unsatisfactory family relationships in early childhood, which have had the effect of preventing the child from growing up into an emotionally-weaned adult. We all know that some people are unhappy-love-affair prone, just as we know some people are accident prone; and it is possible that this type of personality is particularly susceptible to T.B. It may be that further research will even find a link between the T.B. which arises in conditions of poverty, overcrowding and malnutrition, and the T.B. which arises in conditions of what might be called emotional malnutrition: find it, perhaps, in some common factor of over-excitation of minds and bodies denied adequate outlet and fulfilment.

But this is speculation—something which, in time, researchers may be able to assess. In the meanwhile, the need is to explore the road along which Osler pointed. Not that the emotional aspect needs sole rights over research: there is no suggestion that broken love links can be blamed as the sole cause of the disease. Jerome Hartz, of Johns Hopkins University, has summarized the new viewpoint:

1. the mind is affected by toxic conditions;
2. bodily states are influenced by the patients' emotions and vice versa;
3. emotional problems in tuberculosis are the result of cultural and socio-economic conditions which have affected the patients' lives.

"Any severe stress," he argues, "internal or external, may be sufficient to tilt the balance in a given individual away from immunity and toward active disease." Hartz's estimate of the relative importance of emotional stress is lower than Kissen's; in his view, the proportion of sanatorium patients which will be found to have had either the onset or the course of their disease significantly altered by emotional stress is about one in three. Presumably the proportion varies in different countries and according to the type of society from which patients are drawn.

Whatever the differences, the likelihood is that it will be found that the success of the invading bacilli is not the cause, but the reflection of some weakness in the individual; a weakness which may be related to hereditary, constitutional, cultural, or environmental circumstances, but which in many cases appears to be closely connected with the onset of emotional stress. In such cases treatment by drugs and rest and even surgery may still be required; but they will not by themselves—except occasionally by chance—restore the patient to full health; to achieve that, the nature of his emotional illness must also be diagnosed, so that he may be given whatever treatment is appropriate to his needs.

*

Odd though it is that the significance of the deprivation of love in relation to T.B. should not be more widely known, it is even harder to understand why there should be so much resistance in the profession to accepting the closeness of the connexion between heart trouble and emotional stress. The intimate connexion between the heart and the emotions is revealed constantly in everyday experience; it is so obvious as to be taken for granted. We know how the heart's beat is affected by tension; how it begins to beat faster in moments of excitement; how it pounds disagreeably just before it is our turn to perform in public; how it seems to miss a beat following some shock. Common sense alone would suggest the hearts of people who suffer from chronic tension may well get disorganized by the extra strain that is being put on them—just as a tense driver wears out a car more quickly than a calm one.

But though doctors realize that emotional stress may precipitate heart failure, they usually (according to the three Cincinnati doctors who contributed the chapter on heart disorders to Wittkower and Russell's *Recent Developments in Psychosomatic Medicine*) consider that:

> "such an association occurs only when the stress is that of some dramatic and catastrophic life experience (such as the sudden death of a significant person, narrow escape from accidental death, etc.). Because of the relatively infrequent occurrence of such events it has been assumed tacitly that psychologic stress only infrequently constitutes a significant clinical factor in the course of the patient with structural heart disease. However, psychoanalytic studies clearly indicate that life events, which appear on the surface to be routine and 'bland', may, by virtue of their conscious and/or unconscious linkage with previous unresolved life problems, be specifically stressful for the individual."

In a study of 230 patients with high blood pressure in their clinic in Cincinnati—the authors continue—emotional stress was very frequently found to have operated as a precipitating factor; and in long-term observations on about half of these patients, the coincidence of stress with definitive changes in the course of the disease could easily be observed. The severity of symptoms was closely related to the severity of the emotional stresses; conversely, during times when patients were emotionally stable, the intensity of the disease abated. "There can be no doubt," the authors concluded, "that there is, in patients with hypertension, a linkage between emotional stress and the vascular mechanism of hypertension; and that life experiences that are specifically stressful for the patient may lead to discharge or activation of the hypertensive mechanism, and be reflected by changes in clinical and physiologic status."

The Cincinnati experiment is only one of many such, undertaken in different parts of the world. In London Dr. John Hambling, of St. Bartholomew's hospital, conducted interviews with patients, recording their blood pressure changes while the interview was in progress. Listening to a Mrs. B., he found that her blood pressure varied between 120 and 130 while she was discussing her illness and her marriage; rose sharply nearly to 140 while she described her obstinate, self-pitying and restrictive mother, who had opposed her marriage; dropped again below 130 when she described her memories of a pleasant holiday at the seaside; and rose to 150 when the suggestion that her mother might die was discussed (she admitted that she felt her mother would be better dead).

Similar instances could probably have been multiplied, but Hambling felt some risk was attached to such interviews, in serious cases. Still, he noted a number of other instances where changes in blood pressure were related to the changing life circumstances of patients; and his studies led him to believe that although there is no specific personality type which is blood-pressure-prone, there are characteristic traits of personality; the common denominator being suppressed anger, which appears to be the emotional component of all blood-pressure sufferers. Weiss and English agree in their textbook that the common feature of blood-pressure cases seems to be the presence of emotional tension due to chronic repressed hostility. "The inhibited aggression (chronic rage) seems to bear a definite relationship to hypertension; and if it can be relieved by means of psychotherapy anxiety is diminished and blood pressure is often lowered."

Confirmation of this view has come from a curious experiment conducted by Dr. M. L. Miller. Miller argued that if blood pressure was the result of repressed hostility, it should follow that patients in mental hospitals with types of insanity in which hostility is inherent—depressed, self-accusatory patients, and paranoids who think everybody is conspiring against them—should show higher blood pressure than patients whose insanity makes them complacent or self-satisfied—people who think they are Napoleon, or Cleopatra. And so it proved; so much so, in fact, that after confirming his hunch by testing the blood pressure of a preliminary group of mental patients, Miller felt confident enough to interview a second group, and to write down his prediction after each interview of what the patient's blood pressure would be. He then compared his prediction with the actual blood pressures, as recorded on a machine; and the results were highly significant statistically.

Experiments by Franz Alexander in Chicago have led him, too, to believe that the chronic inhibited aggressive impulses associated with anxiety influence blood pressure; and his explanation is that civilization requires a degree of control over aggressive and self-assertive tendencies for which some people cannot find an outlet. Their chronically inhibited hostile state may therefore become a source of permanent stimulation of the heart "as if the inhibited organism were constantly in preparation for a fight which never takes place". He points out that whereas the disease is extremely rare in the African Negro, it is common in the American Negro; and the explanation may not be geographic, but cultural—based on the difficulties which the American Negro finds in making his social adjustments. Alexander is careful to stress that emotional stress does not cause high blood pressure; only in combination with physical factors do emotional conflicts produce the symptoms.

Blood pressure is only one aspect of heart trouble; but research which has been undertaken into other aspects tells much the same story. Reporting on a ten-year study of 100 young heart disease patients in the *American Journal of Medicine* (March 1958) Henry I. Russek and Burton L. Zohman of New York claimed that too much attention had been paid to the attempt to trace heart disorders to such matters as sedentary living and bad eating habits, while ignoring the effects of the social and economic stresses of modern life. Over 90 *per cent* of their subjects, they found, had been under unusual occupational stress just before the heart attacks occurred; and they concluded "it would appear that undue emotional strain associated with job responsibility is far more significant in the etiologic picture of coronary disease than heredity, or a prodigiously high fat diet."

In his *A Psychosomatic Approach to Medicine*, too, Desmond O'Neill describes experiments conducted to determine the relationship between emotional tension and cardiac efficiency. Eleven patients were chosen who had symptoms such as palpitation and dizziness, but no ascertainable organic disease; sixteen with these symptoms, and with organic disease; and eight normal people as the controls. All the subjects were given both a physical and a psychiatric examination, and then required to take exercise, the functioning of their hearts being measured before, during and after it. The controls showed fewer emotional changes, and the variation in their tolerance to exercise was less than the heart patients. Among the patients with organic disease, a close relationship was found between their tolerance to exercise, as measured by the appropriate instruments, and situations of emotional stress; and the same was true of the patients with heart symptoms but without organic disease. It was found that the capacity to endure exercise without distress could be improved if, before taking it, a patient was able to ventilate his feelings; whereas if before exercise the patients' anxiety or resentment was increased by an interview, the same exercise would be too much for them.

In other words, the close connexion between the emotions and the heart which is observable in everyday circumstances is paralleled in illness. To a limited extent, this is recognized by the profession; doctors normally recommend patients who come to them with heart trouble to take it easy, the "taking it easy" including the avoidance of emotional as well as physical strain. But what is often not realized or not admitted is the possibility that emotional stresses may be the main reason for high blood pressure, or for a "stroke". The body's tolerance to physical strain is normally remarkably high: the reason why people often get a stroke apparently as the result of over-exertion may be not because the exertion itself was too much for them, but because they happened to exert themselves at a time when their tolerance to effort was impaired by some emotional stress. Treatment in such cases need not consist of "take it easy"; it should be directed to discovering what caused the emotional stress, and deciding how best to avoid its recurrence—particularly where there is no organic defect to worry about.

When the links between mind and body are so very obvious, as they are with the workings of the heart, it is reasonable to assume that because symptoms are familiar, and easier to mimic, there will be a high proportion of patients presenting symptoms of heart trouble to their doctors which have no organic basis, but which none the less exist, and have consequently to be labelled hysterical, or functional, or neurotic. Weiss and English confirm that in spite of the enormous increase recently of heart trouble, the majority of patients who have symptoms do not have evidence of organic disease; and Flanders Dunbar has noted evidence that heart trouble is emotionally infectious—that exposure to contact with somebody suffering from heart disease appears to increase the chances of bringing on symptoms in the observer, either immediately or at some later date. This may help to account for what has been considered as the hereditary aspect; where there is "heart" in the family, particularly where the circumstances are dramatic or tragic, the disease may be "catching".

★

The way in which emotional changes are reflected in changes of the functioning of the heart are obvious for all to see; not so the way in which they are reflected in the quantity of sugar in the bloodstream—which helps to explain why resistance to classing diabetes as a stress disorder is strong in the profession. Yet again, there are good common-sense reasons for understanding why a connexion between the sugar level and emotional stress exists. Primitive man had certain defence mechanisms which went into action as soon as he was faced with a threat. In civilized man the mechanisms survive, and they are still called upon when he faces threats to his security and prestige. One of the physical features of this mobilization of the body's resources to meet an emergency is the mobilization of sugar in the bloodstream. Consequently, as Weiss and English argue, it is strange that the likelihood of a connexion between stress and diabetes has not been more quickly recognized: "it would seem that fears and threats of which the patient is not wholly aware could, by the very nature of their unconscious energy, act as a chronic stimulus to the insulin-producing mechanism, and hence might have something to do with the development of true diabetes".

Yet to this day diabetes is commonly treated as if the failure of the body to produce sufficient insulin to enable the body to absorb and make use of sugar were unaccountable. The whole emphasis has been on the replacement of the missing substance—rather than on the search for reasons why the body has stopped producing it; and such research as there has been on that subject has concentrated largely on the physical aspect.

That this attitude should still persist is extraordinary when it is realized that—as Flanders Dunbar puts it—tests have been able "to measure the power of emotion in terms so tangible as ounces of sugar". One experiment she relates showed that a diabetic's passing of sugar rose alarmingly, though there had been no change in his hospital treatment, when he heard that his business was about to retire him. And long before such experiments had been carried out on humans, W. B. Cannon had succeeded in producing diabetic symptoms in cats, by inducing fear and anxiety.

That this applies to humans has since been confirmed by experiments in many countries. In America, Hinkle and Wolf made physical observations on diabetics during interviews in which they introduced topics known to be charged with special emotional significance to the patient; his blood-sugar level was observed to drop sharply at these times. In England, Joan Walker found that in a study of 200 diabetics, emotional stress often occurred in significant relation to the course of the illness:

> "The type of emotional stresses recorded are commonly the illness or death of a near relation, a broken marriage, concern over children, financial or business worries. A prolonged period of worry is more common than a sudden devastating shock, but the odd dramatic episode does occur. More often it was found that there had been two types of stress which were

coincidental, or closely following one another. One hardship occurs, and then something else happens which is the proverbial last straw."

As with T.B. patients, research in the long run may show that the "last straw" is not as important as it may seem; there is "last-straw proneness" as well as broken-heart, and accident, proneness. The last straw, too, may be only the precipitant of symptoms stemming from some hereditary or constitutional. weakness. But whatever the combination of causes may be, there is very much more to the management and control of diabetes, O'Neill concludes, than mere prescription of insulin and diet: "the patient with diabetes, like every other patient, is a person; and his loves and hates, hopes and fears, have a profound effect upon his illness".

4

THE UNHAPPY MAN

THE disease which in recent years has come to offer the medical profession's most formidable challenge is cancer. Little is known about it: how it begins, or why it begins. It arouses something of the awe and alarm that T.B. used to arouse; in Britain it has even been customary not to refer to it by name in, say, newspaper reports about the illness of a celebrity, though this reticence now appears to be breaking down. There is little concrete evidence from research, of the kind I have been describing in connection with other diseases, that cancer is a stress disorder, but there is some; and a few distinguished members of the profession are convinced that a link between cancer and emotional stress exists. Yet doctors (if they are not believers in the stress theory) resent the suggestion that funds might profitably be diverted into research along these lines; except in Canada, very little such research has been done.

Of recent years the aspect of the subject which has received most publicity has been research into the statistical relationship between lung cancer and smoking—on the assumption that if such a relationship could be clearly established, it would give a promising line for research on the causes of the disease. The course which controversy on this issue has taken may most conveniently be illustrated by recounting the chief events in Britain after Dr. Doll and Professor Bradford Hill first published the results of the statistical inquiry they had carried out into the incidence of lung cancer among smokers; from the evidence of which they argued that a relationship between the two had been established.

Their report placed the health authorities in an embarrassing position. The extent to which smoking has come to affect the economic and social life of civilized countries is hardly calculable; were a verdict of guilty to be clearly established against tobacco-smoke as cancer-forming, the repercussions would be startling. Tobacco is one of the world's major industries; on its existence national finances have come heavily to depend; and as punitive taxation has not succeeded in turning people away from cigarettes and pipes, it is likely that in any economic emergency, the dependence of governments on smokers continuing to smoke will be increased. Against this, of course, has to be set the fact that most countries have to import tobacco, an expensive business; that smoking results in a great deal of costly damage, through fires; and that it creates annoyance and inconvenience to people who do not smoke. But on balance, the existence of the smoking habit has become one of the pillars of the Western world's economy.

The British authorities consequently felt no great enthusiasm for the Doll-Hill findings, when they first came out; the immediate reaction was to insist that further evidence was needed. Dr. Doll and Professor Hill went back to work, and in 1954 published the findings of a new set of investigations, confirming what they had found in the earlier investigation (the same conclusions had also by this time been reached by research workers in the same field in America and other countries): first, that there had been a great increase in the deaths from lung cancer since the first world war (when about 250 people died from it each year in Britain: by 1954 the figure had risen to around 15,000 a year); and second, that a statistical relationship exists between lung cancer and smoking; about fifteen heavy smokers, and five moderate smokers, die of lung cancer, to every one non-smoker.

The facts could no longer be disputed. But although a statistical relationship between smoking and lung cancer was established, no proof had been forthcoming that the relationship is one of cause and effect. Experiments were by this time being made in many countries in the attempt to establish that cancer-producing agents existed in tobacco, or tobacco smoke, or cigarette paper; to discover whether the cancer rate is different for people smoking cigars, cigarettes or pipes; and even to find whether people who use lighters are more (or less) prone to get lung cancer than people who use matches. But although it was claimed that cancer-forming properties could be isolated in minute quantities in cigarette smoke, and although skin cancer was produced in mice by smearing them with tobacco tar, nothing could be found positively to attribute lung cancer to smoking, beyond the presumption provided by the statistics.

The presumption was enough for some people, including an influential section of the medical profession. But smoking persisted; and in the absence of any certain proof that the statistical relationship was one of cause and effect, governments were able to continue to collect their revenue from smokers with one hand, while occasionally wagging a warning finger with the other. For the most part, though, people continued to smoke not because the final proof had not been established, but out of weakness—much as a believer whose religion warns him there will be a day of judgement may nevertheless continue to indulge in vice. Smokers rarely allowed themselves the luxury of thinking that either the statistical evidence or the interpretation of it were unsatisfactory.

Yet the evidence could have been interpreted in other ways. For example, even if it had been established that more smokers were dying of *lung* cancer, the difference between smokers and non-smokers in the total death-rate from *all* forms of cancer might still be small—a smoker might be more liable to get his cancer in the lungs, but less liable than the non-smoker to get it elsewhere. If this proved to be the case, it would suggest that smoking does not cause cancer; it merely helps to determine the site where cancer establishes itself—either because smoking is an irritant, or for some other reason.

Another argument, which received more attention, took cognizance of the fact that the death-rate in the country from lung cancer is lower than the death-rate in the towns: although some observers held this to be irrelevant—a reflection of the different incidence of smoking in town and country—others held it to mean that the search for a cancer-producing agent was on the wrong track; that smog, or diesel fumes, or some specifically urban irritant, might in the end be found responsible.

There were other peculiar and unaccountable features of the statistical relationship. A comparison of the sexes showed that lung cancer has been increasing more rapidly in men than in women; but the greatest increase in smoking during the same period has been by women—indeed, there is little to show that men now smoke more than they did when the lung cancer rate was low. Comparisons between smokers who inhale and those who do not inhale, too, revealed that the incidence of lung cancer is not, as might have been expected, higher among inhalers.

These points were made, and accepted or criticized; but it was only on rare occasions that anybody dared to cast doubts on the whole basis on which the research was proceeding. Permeating the whole atmosphere of the discussion was the assumption that there must be a "cause" of cancer, in the sense that there must be some unidentified biological or chemical substance which set in motion the mechanism by which cancer begins to spread. Only occasionally would a voice be heard protesting that this was not the right way to approach the problem; that the proposition "smoking is a cause of cancer" is meaningless because no single factor in isolation determines the nature of illness; that a person who smokes forty cigarettes a day may enjoy good health provided his life is relatively free from other sources of stress; whereas another individual, who smokes only twenty a day, but suffers from other stresses, may fall ill.

Indirect evidence in favour of the possibility that cancer is a stress disorder has since come from an investigation made by the American Tobacco Company, which revealed that though its employees in its nine factories smoke nearly twice as much as the national average, they nevertheless manage to live longer than the national average; and they have average, or below average, cancer rates. If cancer were simply the product of some irritant, say, in tobacco smoke, the rates for tobacco workers should be higher than the national average. Why are they not? There is one obvious possibility: that tobacco workers smoke a lot not because they suffer from stresses which drive them to smoking (as is often the case with smokers) but simply because cigarettes are easier and cheaper to come by in cigarette factories than they are elsewhere.

The idea that cancer may be a stress disorder has another small, apparently trivial, but conceivably significant piece of evidence in its favour. There is a type of tumour—admittedly benign, unlike cancer; but a growth, none the less—which can be cured by suggestion, and has been cured in this way for many a year, even by doctors who are indifferent or hostile to any other form of cure which is not in the textbooks: the common, unattractive wart. In hospitals and homes warts are usually treated by physical methods, by burning them off with some acid preparation; but many a doctor will vouch for the fact that their disappearance is often achieved more effectively, and with much less discomfort, by the application of old wives' remedies like dandelion juice, coupled with the assurance that this will cure them.

The success of treatment by suggestion has been demonstrated in the laboratory; H. J. Eysenck has described an experiment on two groups of children with warts, one of which received the orthodox medical treatment, the other being treated by suggestion. The suggestion

> "consisted essentially in drawing a picture of the child's hand, with the wart on it, on a large sheet of paper; and then, with a certain amount of hocus pocus, drawing circles round the wart and reducing its size on the picture day by day until the wart had completely disappeared in the picture"

—curious though this procedure was, it proved distinctly more effective than the orthodox treatment.

Hypnotism has also proved useful in dealing with warts—as

in the remarkable case of the "rhino boy". And this evidence, slight though it is, can be taken as suggesting that tumours are related to conflicts in the mind; and that cancer and smoking may be related not as effect and cause but because both are symptoms of deeper-lying causes. One suggestion that has been made is that cancer is the result of a misdirected emotional drive, which has turned the individual's life force into a self-destructive force (the process being unconscious, often being utterly at variance with the patient's conscious desires). This could be attributed to some heavy sense of guilt, long repressed, manifesting itself in, say, somebody who has ambitiously climbed to the top of his chosen tree, but has gained no real satisfaction from his success. In such cases the appetite we call ambition may turn on a man and destroy him through the mechanism of cancer, whereby the host sustains and nourishes its own destructive guest.

Again, we are up against the difficulty of the lack of scientific evidence; but there is no lack of support for the belief that the course of cancer can be altered by the patient's mental and emotional reactions to his illness. Other things being equal, once cancer gets beyond a certain stage there is no physical means of stopping it; if treatment or operations are no longer possible the patient is doomed. But time and again apparently inoperable or "incurable" cancers have stopped spreading: in some cases for no apparent reason; in others—or so the individuals themselves believe—through will-power or faith. No doctor who has had anything to do with cancer would deny that imponderables can occasionally alter the course of the illness, where all known physical treatments have failed.

A striking plea for a new approach to the understanding of cancer was made recently by Sir Heneage Ogilvie, K.B.E. Consulting Surgeon to Guy's Hospital. Putting forward the thesis that the human body is composed of colonies of cells, Ogilvie remarked that colonies, like empires, age; and the first indication that they are past their zenith is an increasing unwillingness of the group to take part in the general affairs of State:

"At 48, the individual cell groups tend to lose their corporate loyalty, to increase their numbers without any social need, and to make demands for nourishment which their neighbours cannot satisfy. The question 'why do so many of us get cancer after the age of 48?' has proved entirely sterile as a guiding principle of research. It is surely time that we posed and faced the real problem. 'We all have cancer at 48. What is the force that keeps it in check in the great majority of us?' "

In middle age, and often long before, growths appear; sometimes growths of a type which the profession call cancer in *situ.* Such a cancer may remain *in situ* for years, before suddenly invading the rest of the body—becoming malignant. Why? Ogilvie asked: what starts its Gadarene progress?

"Like most general surgeons, I have treated and watched many cases of cancer. Some were relatives; many were friends; others, coming as patients, died my friends. I have slowly come to frame in my mind an aphorism that can never be stated as such, because no statistics can be advanced to support it: 'The happy man never gets cancer.' I have often caught myself thinking about a colleague, 'So and so has started to look unhappy. He is either unhappy because he has got cancer, or he is going to get cancer because he is unhappy.' So run my thoughts, and I try to dismiss them. Then I notice he is missing from the next council meeting. Three months later I read his obituary in the *BMJ*. The instances where the first recognizable onset of cancer has followed almost immediately on some disaster, a bereavement, the break-up of a relationship, a financial crisis, or an accident, are so numerous that they suggest that some controlling force that has hitherto kept this outbreak of cell communism in check has been removed."

In suggesting that happy men are captains of their cells and masters of their fate, Ogilvie admits, and that they are thereby immune from certain disease, he is "sending up a provocative balloon that any real scientist could shoot down". The most ardent believer in the stress theory of disease would be inclined to treat with caution the suggestion of such close links between cancer and unhappiness—except the obvious one, that a man who knows he has cancer is unhappy; and one which is less obvious, but possibly also relevant, that the development of cancer and unhappiness may both be reflections of some deep-seated emotional crisis.

Belief in the influence of emotional stress, too, does not preclude acceptance of the possibility that there are many other physical influences. As Julian Huxley has shown in his book on cancer, statistical evidence which has been collected reveals a very wide range of suspects, against some of whom the evidence is very strong. Habits of diet, for example, appear to affect the issue in many parts of the world. It seems probable that in cancer—and, indeed, in many other diseases—the body is capable of being made more disease prone, or more disease resistant, by an enormous number of genetic and environmental factors. The presence of some substance in a national diet may increase the number of deaths from cancer. But this does not mean that the substance, whatever it is, is the cause of cancer; it means merely that it is a contributory factor which, other things being equal, increases the chance of a person developing the disease; what actually precipitates the disease remains unknown.

The belief of Ogilvie and a few other distinguished members of the profession that the precipitant may arise from a link between unhappiness and cancer, should be enough to promote research along these lines; especially as research teams in America have recently been reporting observations, which appear potentially significant, concerning the personality characteristics of cancer patients. One group, reporting in the journal *Psychosomatic Medicine*, gained the impression "that the very development of cancer in man might conceivably result from the physiological effects of long continued inner stress which has remained unresolved by either outward action or successful adaptation".

They point out that the profession has clung to the idea that the patient is a non-participating bystander, for all he can do about cancer; but this belief is palpably untrue, as the numerous cases where cancers have stopped developing or have disappeared, for no apparent reason, cannot be accounted for by the stock excuse of "wrong diagnosis". On the contrary, they claim that it is now possible to relate the speed or slowness with which cancer advances to personality characteristics, by standard tests. If so, researchers need to switch their attention from the tumours to their hosts.

5

ACHES AND PAINS

OTHER things being equal, stress disorders might be expected to reveal themselves most commonly and obviously in everyday illnesses, like coughs and colds, headaches, and miscellaneous pains and twinges, and it is easy enough to assume, from personal experience—from watching friends and relations and office colleagues—that this is so. But it is not easy to produce concrete evidence. There is little to show that colds are directly related to emotional stress. But the absence of proof need not mean no link exists; it may be found that a cold is, or can be, the mechanism by which individuals work off an accumulation of minor stresses—including difficulties arising in the office or at home, constitutional predisposition to colds, and infection from somebody else's germs.

The same may be true of influenza. The term " 'flu" now covers a multitude of diagnostic sins, and it is commonly attached to an illness with no specific characteristics but with some of the usual non-specific symptoms of unwellness—fever, aches, running nose, sore throat—by patients themselves who like to be in the fashion; particularly if the fashion has a slightly esoteric ring about it, as in the epidemic of Asian, or Asiatic, 'flu. A characteristic virus for this disease existed but it may legitimately be doubted whether the virus was always, or even usually, the cause of the illness. Its presence in the body may simply have been a symptom—the excuse which was used unconsciously in finding a way for the body to be ill—an unusually good excuse, as so many people caught it that nobody was likely to hint that they were malingering. How badly patients were affected could also be ascribed not to the venom of the invading virus, but to the extent of their need for illness—for a period of withdrawal: and this need may have been the product of an accumulation of different stresses over a period—not to any single episode.

With headaches—or so my own experience, at least, suggests—the link with a single episode is often more direct. I had an indication of this recently in Seattle, when a group of us were entertained by two of the residents who had never met us before, but who had earlier allowed themselves to be cajoled or bullied by some local organization into promising to give "American Home Hospitality" to visitors from other countries when they arrived on tours sponsored by the State Department, or by other bodies. Our hosts, a man and his wife, had entertained in this fashion once before; and we gathered it had been rather boring and difficult because of linguistic and cultural barriers. In the afternoon before they were due to entertain us, both of them got splitting headaches—independently: he at the office, she at home. Naturally there was no proof that their headaches were caused by suppressed irritation, on their part, at having to entertain us, but it struck me as a possible explanation; when I mentioned this later, I was interested to find that it had struck another of the group, too. He had been reminded that both he and his wife regularly got headaches when confronted with certain social duties which irked them—so regularly, that they had long since recognized and laughed over the link.

The existence of such links has received some confirmation from research in New York. Dr. Robert Marcussen has described how it has actually been possible to induce headache experimentally by putting subjects into situations of emotional stress. "The cycle of accumulating rage, resentment and fatigue leading to vascular headache can be interrupted at various points by various means and the appearance of the expected headache prevented. Vascular headache can on the other hand be precipitated in susceptible individuals by introducing pertinent stress in a setting of accumulating tension." If the evidence is accepted, Marcussen argues, it is no use trying to treat headaches by any standard method; what is required instead is treatment which will help the patient readjust his existence, so that he does not overtax himself emotionally.

In an article written in conjunction with Harold Wolff, Marcussen has also suggested that a common personality factor in migraine sufferers is that they are tense and driving, rigid, ambitious, and perfectionistic; as a result, they tend to take on more work or responsibility than they can carry; and because they cannot carry it, they become resentful and unsettled. Where this is the background of recurrent headaches, the obvious need is for the family doctor to know about it; he should be trying to get his patients to understand themselves, or at least to adjust their lives to avoid certain situations of stress. To fob them off with palliatives is lazy, and may be dangerous. But it is comparatively rare for a doctor to follow this trail, beyond giving vague advice to his patients not to overstrain themselves—advice which is often useless, because they are wholly unaware of the nature of the stresses that are upsetting them. They may blame their job when it is not the work itself, but the *tempo* at which it has to be undertaken, or the feelings which fellow-workers arouse, that really worry them.

Two people out of three who suffer from headaches, Wolff has asserted, "can be greatly helped by any physician who is interested in human problems, and willing to spend a minimum of time in reviewing them with him"; their trouble is not "sinus" or anything of the kind (the once very fashionable "cure" of chronic headaches by nasal operations is now out of favour), but emotional stress provoking physical reactions through its effect on the blood vessels in the head—a variation of the mechanism of blushing. Just as a blush may either be directly related to some event, or may appear to have no direct connexion with events until investigation eventually reveals some deep-seated sense of guilt, so a headache may be related to stresses we can recognize—having to see somebody we do not like, or do something which irritates us—or it may have causes which we will have to probe more deeply if we wish to uncover, and thereby to banish, whatever stress may be responsible. In any case it is unlikely that the immediate stress—the impending visitor, or the chore which has to be finished—is anything more than the precipitant; to avoid a visitor or a chore may be a simple way to avoid the pain, just as aspirin is a simple way to alleviate it; but what is usually needed is something more radical, if we hope to find out why frustration, dissatisfaction or tension should manifest themselves in these irritating, if usually minor, symptoms.

The connection between headaches and stress has been suspected for many years; it was noted in the 1920s by F. G. Crookshank who would have some claim, if justice were done—along with Weiss and Wittkower—to be called the father of the stress theory of disease in its present form: certainly most of his beliefs are rapidly being verified by research. A point he made which was well in advance of his time was that the headache of convenience need not be "functional". Crookshank detested the term: a doctor, he complained, who used it usually realized that he was using it as a let-out—as a synonym for "not-diagnosed"—and consequently he tended to vent his annoyance on his patients whom, he felt, were pestilent knaves for bringing along unaccountable symptoms so destructive of his self-confidence. "Every person who is ill," Crookshank insisted, "is ill psychically as well as physically"; a headache caused by annoyance is not necessarily imagined; it may be as real as a headache caused by a blow.

The hypothesis may be put in a different form: a good actress on the stage is perfectly capable of simulating grief so well that the grief becomes real (for the time being, at least); its reality is attested by the fact that she weeps real tears. In the same way, the actress may be capable of simulating real annoyance at not having been given enough applause to satisfy her vanity so well that the annoyance becomes real; its reality is attested by the fact that she gets a headache—a headache which, if she could be subjected to the appropriate tests, would be found to have its physical symptoms within the skull, just as her stage grief had its physical symptoms, coursing down her cheeks.

Migraine, Crookshank contended, is real; it has a physical basis, which can be discovered, analysed and described; but it is none the less a symptom of some emotional disturbance—usually, he suggested, of repressed rage and humiliation felt in the face of some problem which appears insoluble. Migraine sufferers, he thought, actually "derive some satisfaction out of demonstrating how well they behave under adverse circumstances, hampered as they are by their own ill-health, and the bludgeonings of fate".

The difficulty in accepting this theory—as I mentioned earlier, in connexion with the way fellow-journalists seemed to want their illnesses—is the improbability of anybody wanting to have a headache. But except in the case of hysterical illness, the "wanting" is rarely near the surface of consciousness: we may eventually become aware that certain symptoms, such as headaches, tend to attach themselves to certain unpopular duties, but usually the existence of the link is not recognized, and is indignantly repudiated if it is brought to our attention. Yet it is just as likely that a man should want to be ill unconsciously while consciously he is desperately anxious to be well, as it is that a man should want to lay off women, or drink, and yet be unable to do so, even when he is aware that he will get no pleasure from them but, on the contrary, may be consumed by guilt.

This contradiction between conscious and unconscious desires is a clue to the workings of the mind in illness. All of us are compelled by circumstances to do things we do not want to do. Sometimes we are aware that we do not want to do them—but often we are not, because we have got into the habit of doing them, and habit, as the Pavlovians have demonstrated, dies very hard. If we have been conditioned by habit to be somebody whose way of life, deep down, dissatisfies us, because it is worrying or frustrating, symptoms may arise which reflect our inner dissatisfaction with that way of life.

Such symptoms are as old as history, and have long been given colloquially suitable names: "housemaid's knee" or "clergyman's throat" or "writer's cramp". The knee, the throat and the fingers give trouble, because they are the points at which the physical strain is greatest; but they give no trouble to the housemaid or the clergyman or the writer who is satisfied—who is on terms with his work; on the contrary, the knees and throats and fingers of such people become stronger than ever. It is when we cease to be absorbed by what we are doing that we begin, deep down, to be bored or dissatisfied with it (and with ourselves); and it is then we develop symptoms which are, in a sense, designed (though we are not aware of it) to make it impossible for us to carry on.

The variety of such symptoms is endless. "Clergyman's throat" might now be renamed "broadcaster's throat", so common is the drying up, the tensing of the muscles, the tickle, before going on the air or on television. Pianists develop rheumatism in their fingers; so do typists. Sportsmen are particularly prone, sometimes even lending their sport's name to an illness, as in "tennis elbow". But such popularizations are now out of fashion; the tendency instead is to speak of "fibrositis"; and what was once plain backache became first, lumbago, and, later, "slipped disc".

It is often possible to demonstrate the existence of a slipped disc clinically, but most fibrositis sufferers have no such consolation; they have no recognizable organic symptoms. The term has long been so freely used to cover undiagnosable pains that J. L. Halliday wondered whether any organic trouble really existed. Writing just before the Second World War, he recalled that rheumatic pains had once been considered nervous in origin; and he thought this interpretation deserved to be resuscitated—fibrositis, he suggested, ought to be renamed psychoneurotic rheumatism, the term to include muscular rheumatism, neuritis, and lumbago, as well. He also believed that the rheumatic condition tended to occur in certain personality types; that the pain was precipitated by emotional events; and that recovery might follow simply from change of emotional situation. Some patients "developed a clear fibrositis with its specific features and physical symptoms, when they were suffering from unexpressed emotional tension; and as these patients found peace of mind and relaxation, this fibrositis syndrome disappeared". There is nothing surprising in the idea that a tennis player should develop pain in elbow or wrist when he is suffering from some emotional tension; nor that his trouble should materialize in swellings, or other symptoms; nor that these symptoms should disappear when the cause of the tension is removed. (It is also possible that the symptoms may be removed by physical means, such as by massage; but the presumption must be that they or other symptoms will return unless the cause of the tension is also removed.)

After the war, Franz Alexander reached similar conclusions about rheumatoid arthritis: "a conspicuous feature of this disease —its capricious course, its inexplicable remissions and relapses— points to emotional conflicts as partly responsible". The disease, he believed, is related to an unconscious rebelliousness and resentment which has been increased by the vicissitudes of life, and which can be precipitated by events which tend to increase feelings of guilt or hostility; and the general psychological background is of a chronic but inhibited hostile aggressiveness aroused by being thwarted by other persons, or restricted by personal inhibitions.

Prejudice against the idea that backache is related to the emotions remains strong in the profession; the argument is still commonly heard that although medical science has not yet reached the stage when it can give much assistance in the diagnosis of rheumatic complaints, the time will soon come when they will be traced to specific physical, rather than emotional, causes. Some negative support was lent to this theory by the results of an investigation which the British Empire Rheumatism Council carried out in 1950; 292 rheumatism patients were compared with 292 "controls", and no significant difference was found between the patients and the controls in the number of psychological precipitating factors preceding the onset of the disease. This line of research was therefore abandoned by the Council. But the experiment was unsatisfactorily conducted. The people who examined the patients and the controls were not qualified in the highly skilled work of taking case histories to find unconscious stresses. All that the experiment showed was that emotional precipitants of the simple type found by Kissen in connexion with T.B. are not present in rheumatism: that the links, if they exist, do not lie so near the surface.

For a time it was thought that the discovery of cortisone had given a more definitive rebuff to the stress theory. Its early results were astonishing: patients lost their symptoms; cripples were able to get up and walk; and the mental symptoms commonly associated with the disease—depression and instability—vanished. But soon the enthusiasm for the drug waned. It often temporarily removed the symptoms, but it did not cure. Some patients did not respond to it at all; others soon became resistant; and on others it produced a variety of unfortunate side effects which, though usually temporary, were extremely unpleasant—some physical, like the flaring up of other diseases; some mental—particularly in those patients who had a poor record of emotional adjustment. Recently a detailed investigation sponsored by the British Medical Research Council reported that "the introduction of cortisone has not materially affected the prognosis of patients developing rheumatoid arthritis for the first time. Secondly, in such cases there appears to be little difference between the therapeutic effect of aspirin and cortisone; but in the long term management of the disease, at least during the first four years, a medication with aspirin is more often likely to prove satisfactory than medication with cortisone".

How, then, to account for the startling effects of cortisone, when it was first tried? The effectiveness of the treatment may have lain not in the drug but in the circumstances in which the drug was administered. Health, like disease, can be catching: patients who really believe that a drug or a doctor is going to cure them may catch health in the same way that patients who really believe in a faith healer, or in going on a pilgrimage to Lourdes, or in the curative properties of some saintly relic, or in Lydia Pinkham's Pink Pills, may benefit from them. It is not even necessary for doctors or nurses to say "Lucky you! here's a new wonder drug!" (though obviously this may be effective, too); the stimulus may come from an unspoken belief in a treatment's efficacy, which can create an atmosphere in hospitals that engenders confidence in the patients.

This possibility is now recognized in the profession, so that when new drugs are tested, it is customary not merely to have "controls"—patients who think they are getting the drug, but in fact are getting a neutral imitation—but also to ensure that neither the doctors nor the nurses or anybody else connected with the giving of the drug knows which patients are getting it, and which are getting the imitation; so that there can be no chance of the donors' enthusiasm communicating itself to the recipients, thereby helping them to get well.

Once again, though, it must be emphasized that even if cortisone had fulfilled its early expectations—to the extent, say, that penicillin has—the stress theory would not thereby be contradicted. Where physical symptoms have arisen out of emotional disturbance, it may be possible to remove or alleviate them by physical means; and it is often desirable to do so. What has usually to be decided is whether removal of the symptoms is enough; often it is necessary to go back further, to find what gave rise to them, to prevent them from returning. And in some cases, where a symptom reflects a deep-rooted want, or need, on the patient's part, it may be useless or even dangerous to try to remove it.

A typical example of symptoms arising out of deep unconscious desires (or fears) are those which relate to procreation. It is not necessary to accept the Freudian thesis to realize how strong, how difficult to regulate, and how "loaded" with guilt feelings the sexual instincts can be; rare is the man who never suffers from nervous incapacity, and the woman who never suffers from nervous frigidity, in making love. Just as a man's feelings of guilt, too, may be reflected in mimicked venereal disease, so may a woman's. Yet the literature on the subject of inflammation of the vagina still treats it exclusively as if it were a question of tracing some infection.

The elimination process is hardly less emotionally loaded than procreation. Nature's eccentric economy in using the same channel for spermatozoa and for urine has something to do with it, but normally it is probably a relic of childhood training in continence, that makes the bladder respond to emotional stress; given the knowledge that a lavatory is accessible, we may not require to use it for hours; should we suddenly find ourselves unable to use it because, say, we are attending some formal banquet, we may be in some discomfort after a few minutes—unless we are lucky enough to be kept distracted by the company or the speeches.

Women may suffer less often from this particular affliction, but emotional stress affects them in other ways. Researchers have examined menstrual and menopausal troubles in the light of the possibility that they are stress disorders. Irregular menstruation is very common in women under stress; Desmond O'Neill cites one investigation where it was found that in a series of women without stress symptoms, attending a London hospital clinic for routine medical care, irregularity was rare—it was present in only three; but of a series of forty women attending with stress disorders such as headache, asthma, and kindred ailments, of comparable age and social class, twenty-two had irregular periods. In America J. C. Donovan, investigating menopause, came to the conclusion that the woman who seeks medical aid does so because she is emotionally upset; so that the doctor who has to deal with her ought properly to ask himself, "of what anxiety are these the symptoms?"

Specific symptoms have also been traced to occasions of stress; a British doctor, at first unable to account for the irregular bleeding from the uterus in one woman patient, eventually discovered that it occurred in every instance on the birthday, or day of death, of one of her sons; all three sons had been killed in the R.A.F., and shortly after that her husband had died. Recounting this story, O'Neill remarks that it should be studied by everyone who has to deal with such problems, "since it shows how readily the diagnosis may be made by the doctor who is willing to listen, whether he has special psychiatric experience or not".

*

It would be possible to prolong the list of stress disorders almost indefinitely, for there are few symptoms which cannot in some people, and on some occasions, be related to stress. For example, I have not dealt with disorders of the thyroid, though they are very commonly associated with stress; according to Dr. Theodore Lidz of Yale, "the intimate reciprocal relationship between thyroid function and the emotional state of the individual is apparent from clinical observation . . . increase and decrease in thyroid secretion distort emotional equilibrium and affect mental functioning, and thyroid hyperactivity produces instability; but there is ample evidence that emotional disturbances often play an important role in the etiology and exacerbations of hyperthyroidism".

Another stress disorder which I have barely mentioned—with one of the closest, though least understood relationships between stresses and symptoms—is illness of the senses: sight, and hearing, particularly. The refusal to take this into account angered W. S. Inman, an eye specialist, in the early 1920s, when he observed how often eye trouble accompanied what he considered to be neurotic symptoms of headache, giddiness, sleeplessness, and anxiety. When he investigated the "scientific" basis on which eye troubles were then (and to a great extent, still are) treated, he found the most ludicrous discrepancies, the same type of treatment often being advised on the basis of contradictory sets of figures. Relatively little has been done, though, to follow up the course of inquiry he suggested, nor has there been much investigation of how often deafness has its origins in emotional disturbance. It is possible that the phrase "none so blind as those who will not see" may have a more literal meaning than its coiner intended; some people appear to lose their sight (or their hearing) because they need (though they are not conscious of it) to escape from doing whatever it is they have to do. Curiously, there has been much less resistance to the idea that people can be struck dumb by emotional shock, and cured, by the same process; indeed more than one popular film has been made on the subject. Yet the idea of being struck blind, in spite of innumerable examples from Saul to the present-day, is grudgingly accepted; and the idea that people may lose their sight gradually owing to chronic stress is hardly considered in treatment of eye disorders. Yet there are many indications that these disorders are not necessarily of physical origin—even when they appear to be. Halliday cites the case of an investigation carried out in Britain in 1921 into "miner's nystagmus". The committee brushed aside the suggestion that it might be due to anything but physical causes, coming to the conclusion that deficient illumination was responsible. New standards of lighting were laid down, but in the Scottish mines the incidence of the disease increased five-fold in spite of the better light in the years that followed—1922-30. Halliday suggests this may have been related to the uncertainties in the coal mining industry in that period; and the possibility should not be ruled out that certain diseases can be emotionally catching among groups who are under similar social, cultural, or economic pressures.

But these are extreme cases; the commoner stress disorders of our time arise out of tensions set up by accumulating minor tensions at home and at work. In every business, particularly in big business, and in every department of government, they arise out of uncertainty and ambition—out of the struggle for security or promotion. At lower levels, on the factory floor, much research has been done into how these tensions arise, and how they can be modified or banished. It has shown some surprising results: for example, the discovery that attempts to introduce greater variety and flexibility into work, to break the tedium of routine, may be unsuccessful because it also breaks social groups and habits, thereby inducing insecurity. On a higher level—the stomach ulcer level—less is known; but it is obvious that stress disorders arising out of work tensions are widespread. They take different forms in different individuals—as they did in the newspaper on which I first worked. Many of us have our own built-in fuse wire, which burns out when stress loads become excessive; we may be a prey to colds, or to headaches; one woman may have pains associated with menstruation; another may suffer from some recurrent ache associated, perhaps, with a childhood accident. Many people who in childhood have had a severe sprain, or damaged a kneecap, find in later life, from time to time, that it returns in the form of pain and disablement which treatment cannot cure, though it may bring temporary relief.

But probably the aspect of stress disorder about which most needs to be learned are the diseases of childhood. Every doctor who has to deal with young children comes to learn that their illnesses are not always their own: very often they relate to the family situation. At a children's clinic, Desmond O'Neill has written, "it has happened to me several times that a child is referred with itching, and the itch, and perhaps the rash as well, has cleared without the child ever being seen at all; the mother is seen first, by herself, and she gets so much off her chest that the emotional temperature at home falls, and the child gets better and never comes to hospital after all". The importance of achieving a great understanding of how these "family" illnesses arise is not confined to improving the health of the children at home: it may also help to create a pattern of health—or of avoidance of ill-health—which will persist in later life, and enable individuals who might otherwise fall into a bad health habit—many do, as children, owing to their reactions to difficult situations at home—to learn the art of keeping well.

2

THEORY

I

STRESS AND DISEASE

FOR the past fifty years doctors have tended to confine themselves to two questions: what disease has the patient got? And, what is the remedy for it? In the light of the evidence which has been accumulating—and I have given only a fraction of it—they must, as Halliday urged in *Psychosocial Medicine*, ask three questions: why did this patient become ill in the manner he did? What kind of person is he, that he should behave in this way? And, why did he become ill when he did? In a few cases the answer to the first question may make the second unimportant; where, say, a man has stomach pains following, and obviously directly as a result of eating contaminated food. But in most cases of illness the second and third questions—what kind of a person is he that he should behave in this way? And, why did he become ill when he did?—are of real significance.

To answer them, four things have to be taken into account. First, the patient's physical constitution. People may be hereditarily predisposed to illness: sometimes to specific types of illness. Caution is required before assuming that madness or alcoholism "runs in the family" because in many cases children are psychologically conditioned: they can apparently be predisposed—or, in a sense, predispose themselves, as Sydney Beers did—to a disease which they are frightened of getting; their fear seems to help undermine their capacity for resistance. Still, the existence of inherited physical characteristics is so obvious that it is foolish to underestimate the importance of heredity in illness; and the way in which people's physical condition at any given time may make them ill, or weaken them so they are more likely to get ill—in the sense that a man who habitually drinks or smokes too much can get ill either directly or indirectly as a result of his excesses—is so obvious that there should be no need to emphasize it.

Second, the patient's personality. I have mentioned researchers who have been tempted to relate diseases to personality; they have produced evidence to show the existence of a link between people of certain personality types, and the illnesses they tend to catch—asthmatics suffering from "smother-love"; T.B. victims craving affection; blood-pressure sufferers bursting with repressed hostility; and so on. But recognition of personality types is still a highly subjective process; and, as all of us have repressed or suppressed emotions, the researcher finds it a little too easy to get the evidence he wants to fit his own theories. For the present it is as well to mistrust glib generalizations; but at least the theory that illness can sometimes be the physical symptom of an emotional conflict, as a blush is the physical symptom of the emotional sense of guilt, is a reasonable starting point for diagnosis. Although a great deal more work will need to be done before the nature of this link can be well enough understood to be used in prevention and in treatment, its possibilities ought no longer to be ignored; doctors should now be more prepared than most of them are to recognize that the individual's personality and emotional conflicts can have, and in a wide range of diseases do have, a decisive say in causing illnesses and in determining their course.

Third, the patient's environment. Research is gradually revealing the remarkable extent to which the answer to Halliday's last question, "why did he become ill when he did?" lies in the arrival of some environmental last straw. The straw may be trivial—an impending visit from mother-in-law—or serious—a gradual recognition of failure in life, or the break-up of a happy love affair; but great or small, the possibility that emotional stress may detonate an illness ought never to be ignored, in the way it still so often is ignored. For, if T.B. can be precipitated by broken love links, every doctor should know enough about the family situation of any of his patients who catch T.B. to judge whether the best policy is to remove them to isolation hospitals, to treat them at hospitals nearby, or to leave them at home; and if the commoner ills of life are symptomatic of stress the family doctor needs to watch all his flock, to be ready with his advice as soon as any of them show signs of being subjected to a heavier stress load than they can bear.

Fourth, the disease. The time has come when we should reorientate our thinking on this subject; as Crookshank put it, to blame microbes for causing disease is like blaming bullets for causing war; what has to be found is why the war broke out. And the number of diseases in which it is possible to be sure why it broke out is small. Where everybody who has eaten the cakes at a certain café has fallen ill, it is reasonable to expect that their food poisoning will be traced to some contamination at the café; but this kind of illness, though common, is not the doctor's chief problem today. In few of the cases which confront a doctor can he be confident of identifying the cause. Diagnosis now consists mainly of recognizing the invaders, not in explaining how they have come to break through the body's defence system, which normally has shown itself capable of repulsing them. Nevertheless this act of recognition is important, particularly in those numerous illnesses where the cause, once they have started, is of little relevance to the immediate treatment. Doctors do not stop to ask themselves why a haemorrhage should have started, before staunching the flow of blood; if they do, the patient might bleed to death before they get round to treating him.

Constitution (inherited and acquired); personality; environment; and disease—all four interact in illness, and all four need to be considered in diagnosis and treatment. And the part played by emotional stress needs particular consideration because the ways in which it can influence physical symptoms are only now beginning to be appreciated. Some indication of the variety of forms this influence can take was given by Wittkower and Russell, in their work on skin diseases. They suggested that:

symptoms may be wholly induced by emotional conflict;

the emotional conflict may be the most important single reason;

a normal manifestation (e.g. blushing) may occur too easily, and become chronic;

emotional disturbance may precipitate virus or other infections;

emotional disturbance may aggravate virus or other infections;

emotional disturbance may predispose an individual to infections;

emotional disturbance may increase the risk of exposure to infections (e.g. V.D.) or actually bring them on (e.g. by compulsive washing, leading to excessive use of soap or antiseptics);

a vicious circle of mind-body and body-mind aggravation may be set up (e.g. acne causing worry, and worry making the acne worse);

and so on (their list continues, but becomes more technical).

What is true of skin diseases is true of disease in general; and this means that, except for the purposes of immediate treatment where, say, it is necessary to deal with a haemorrhage, diseases ought not to be separated into different categories—physical or emotional; organic or functional; real or imagined. An emotionally-induced illness is just as real to the patient as any other illness. For a doctor to bluff or bully patients who feel physically ill but have nothing organic is as unwise, and sometimes as cruel, as to punish a child which bruises itself acting out its childhood fantasies.

Where the personality is sick, symptoms of illness are going to appear; whether they go down as organic or functional in the doctor's case-book is often a matter of chance. Many people (like the woman with the stomach troubles in Balint's case history) produce a succession of illnesses of which some are functional, others organic. Others produce a puzzling variety of apparently organic illnesses, in succession; in an investigation into absenteeism in New York in 1952, Hinkle and Plummer found not only that 25 per cent of workers had 75 per cent of all the sickness, but that many of the members of this 25 per cent group tended to have consistent records of sickness of all kinds, including injuries and operations, over a period of years (incidentally, the investigators also claimed to have discovered differences of personality between the 25 per cent group and the rest, the illness-prone tending to be dissatisfied and frustrated). In many individual cases, too, it has been found that the physical symptoms change with alterations in the patient's emotional circumstances. Wolff cites the case of a man developing colitis in a humiliating family situation. So long as he had the physical symptoms he seemed tranquil enough; but when his relations with his family deteriorated still further, his colitis disappeared, to be replaced by restlessness, depression and suicidal tendencies. In all probability the illness was fundamentally the same; only the symptoms which reflected it were different.

This is something the profession finds it hard to accept. Few doctors will admit that in *all* illness, the interaction of the four factors, constitution, personality, environment, and disease, should be taken into account; the tendency is to argue that this theory, so far as it holds good at all, applies only in a limited range of diseases. Few doctors are prepared to concede that diabetes or influenza may arise out of stress; and any suggestion that cancer may, arouses positive wrath ("you will only spoil your case", a neurologist friend told me when I was writing the articles on the subject for the *Spectator*, "if you cite cancer—people will assume you are a crank." To judge by one or two of the letters which came in afterwards, he was right).

In their attitude, doctors reflect as well as affect the climate of lay opinion. Most of us have accustomed ourselves to the idea that illnesses—other people's illnesses, that is—may be connected with their emotional states; but we tend to think of them as different from *real* illnesses. Yet if we pause to consider the problem, the absurdity of trying to maintain them as two separate categories of illness immediately becomes apparent.

An example can be taken from the study of accidents. I ought properly to have included "accidentitis", as Flanders Dunbar has called it, in my list of common stress disorders; that certain individuals are accident-prone has long been realized by employers of domestic servants, and has recently been verified statistically by investigations into accidents in industry. It is possible to relate accidentitis to all manner of abstruse theories about the workings of the mind, that it represents a death wish, or repressed anger, or regression to an infantile state; and undoubtedly unconscious motives are often present; but the simplest explanation, and one which all of us would recognize from our own experience, is that when we are worried about something our attention is apt to be distracted from whatever we are doing, so that we are more likely to drop a plate while washing up, or to fall down a flight of steps.

Imagine, then, two traffic accidents taking place: in both of which a pedestrian steps off the road and is run down by a car in circumstances which, to a policeman arriving on the scene, are identical; but where investigation will reveal an essential difference.

In the first accident, the pedestrian, worried about losing his job, annoyed with his nagging wife, and conscious of an unpleasant interview ahead of him, was so preoccupied with his own concerns that he stepped on to the street without looking where he was going, and was knocked down. The root cause, in this case, is emotional; he was suffering from accidentitis. But the symptoms—the cuts, fractures, bruises, are obviously physical and have to be treated as such.

In the second accident, it was the driver who was preoccupied with his worries, and who ran into the pedestrian. The shock to the pedestrian was profound; he began to dream badly, have headaches, and pains in his back where he was struck; but the examining doctors could find nothing physically the matter with him. Here, the root cause of the symptoms is demonstrably physical; but the illness itself is emotional—or, in the medical term, functional. The shock was responsible for producing symptoms for which no organic explanation could be found.

What is true of accidents is true of almost every form of illness. The interaction of emotional and physical states is close and complex; even the most "physical" of conditions can have emotional components—and vice-versa; though I have naturally been underlining the possibility that it is the hidden emotional causes which are often the real culprit, the converse is also often true. The stock example, always quoted by neurologists as an awful warning of the hazards of placing any reliance on psychiatrists, is of the neurotic patient who is treated for months by psychotherapy, and then dies of an undiagnosed brain tumour; the physical links in the chain of events leading up to illness are self-evidently important—as most writers on stress are at pains to show.

The complex way in which emotional and physical stresses act and interact, can be illustrated by another homely example: indigestion after a Christmas dinner. The natural tendency is to blame the last mince pie: and we may be right, in the same sense that a broken-backed camel would be right in blaming the last straw. But why should our digestion have taken us thus far—to the penultimate mince pie—and no further?

To answer that question, we have to consider all the food taken earlier, and the drink; not only the quantity of drink, but how it affects us. Our physical condition counts, obviously; and that depends partly on our heredity, partly on our upbringing, partly on the life we have led, partly on how well we celebrated Christmas Eve. Then there is our emotional state; whether things are going well for us in general, and whether the particular Christmas gathering has been a success, or been spoiled by some family row. Finally, there may be unconscious emotional disturbances of which we are not even aware—brought back, sometimes, by associations with a Christmas dinner during our childhood—or, perhaps, with some other childhood event. That some people experience intense feelings of guilt after sexual intercourse or drunkenness is generally known, and there is no reason to doubt that we can feel a sense of guilt after other kinds of excess. And—as guilt often does—it may materialize in symptoms which are, in a sense, a form of punishment.

*

The difficulty, in fact, is not so much in demonstrating that emotional and physical states interact, as in explaining why so few of us realize it. Explanation is the more difficult because nearly everybody does realize it to some extent. In America, particularly, there is a general recognition of the existence of stress disorders; it is even accepted by the courts—to judge by a recent case in Los Angeles; a wife testified that "her husband required her to travel with him, and because of his insistence she broke out into hives and became so ill that she was hospitalized at times"; she got a divorce on the strength of her testimony. But though recognition on this level is common enough, the stress theory of disease, as a general theory, is very far from being accepted; indeed it is hardly known.

I have already suggested some of the reasons why people are so slow to accept it; any change in the climate of public opinion of this nature is bound to be gradual, because habits of mind are hard to alter. Most of the arguments used against the stress theory of disease are tired copies of arguments that have been used against earlier revolutionary ideas. But some of the arguments which have been advanced against the stress theory are sensible; and it is worth seeing what can be learned from them.

The first is that the evidence that certain disorders are related to emotional stress is anecdotal. "Anecdotal" is a word which has come to have a derogatory connotation; it implies that the evidence is based on hearsay, or that, even if it is well attested, it has not been sufficiently strictly examined, sifted, and criticized.

This argument is justified, as a glance at the descriptions I have given of research shows. I do not mean those passages in which I refer to my own personal experiences and observations; these are certainly anecdotal, but their aim is not to prove a thesis, or even to provide corroborative detail, but simply to try to keep the subject on the level of ordinary experience, on the assumption that only when we can relate things to our own experience can we begin to understand them—for only then do they become part of ourselves, rather than remote impersonal abstractions. But most of the evidence which I have quoted is also anecdotal, because it has rarely been possible to conduct research into stress under conditions which would satisfy the scientist or the statistician.

It is highly questionable, though, whether scientists or statisticians could ever be satisfied, except by a type of research which is often irrelevant to human problems. They would like experiments to be conducted under laboratory conditions, to eliminate extraneous influences; but, as F. G. Crookshank argued, if this kind of "scientific" principle were generally followed it would mean that military strategists would have to "abandon all such purely literary exercises as the study of the Caesarian and Napoleonic campaigns, in favour of investigations of "what really does happen" during autumn manoeuvres on Salisbury Plain". Such ridicule had no effect. Even if laboratory tests could not provide the whole answer, the profession in effect decided, they would point the way; in time, the desire Sir Thomas Sydenham had put into words in 1769, that "all diseases ought to be reduced to certain and determinate kinds, with the same exactness as we see it done by botanic writers in their treatises of plants", would be gratified. But Crookshank was right. The mechanistic theory was based on a fallacy: it was itself unscientific, because no exact assessment of the effect of our emotional states on physical symptoms is possible: emotional states cannot be measured. Anger can be detected by various signs; and some of them are measurable—pulse rate, colour of face, shakiness of hands. But no two people react the same way to anger—some go red in the face, others white; some become more violent, others grow strangely calm. In any case, how can suppressed, or repressed, anger be measured? Anger, in fact, is "anecdotal". So is love. And most of us would believe the poets who tell us about love, rather than listen to anybody telling us that, as there is no scientific evidence that love exists, it cannot be recognized as a clinical phenomenon.

The other charge against the stress theory, or some aspects of it, is that it is notional. "Notional" is another word that now has picked up a derogatory connotation; it implies that the researcher's findings are based less on the facts he has uncovered than on his preconceived theories, or notions—the implication being that he has used only those facts that fit his theories, or that he has twisted the facts to suit them.

This is a real risk in all research, but particularly in investigations into unconscious mental and emotional processes, because it is so easy to interpret observations according to the observer's viewpoint. In every fat man, the saying is, there is a thin man trying to get out; in every character there are contradictions; and when psychologists dip down further, into the remoter regions of the unconscious mind, the chances of their being able to find precisely the characteristics that fit their theories are very great indeed.

But this is only an argument against accepting such theories uncritically. It is legitimate to be sceptical of some of the assertions which have been made that certain personality types are particularly prone to catch certain diseases; but this is not to say that the whole theory that disease can be related to emotional stress is false. Even if, say, the whole of the Freudian thesis were to be set aside, and all the reports which have emanated from Freudians on the relationship of illness to unconscious emotional conflicts rejected, the stress theory would not be undermined. Indeed, it is arguable that it would be stronger, for such is the resistance to Freud and all his theories that the medical profession might find it easier to accept the theory if all reference to him (and all mention of words beginning in "psycho") were cut out.

*

I have been referring to a "stress theory of disease" without offering any definition of exactly what it is. It is not a single unified theory so much as a complex of ideas; it might better be called a way of thinking about disease—Hippocrates' way, which was generally accepted until the end of the nineteenth century, when it was replaced by the mechanistic beliefs which still hold today. Basically, it rests on the belief that mind and body are a unity; neither can be affected without affecting the other. As soon as the mechanistic idea took charge, however, the natural tendency of the Hippocrateans—such few as continued to preach the old doctrine, like Georg Groddeck in Germany and Crookshank in England—was to concentrate on the anti-mechanistic evidence: i.e., on the evidence that could be found to show how emotional states affect the body. And this trend has continued until the present day. Although, as we have seen, stresses can be of many kinds, it is normally of emotionally induced stress that doctors are thinking when they use the term "stress disorder".

Naturally much of the work that was done—and still is being done—into the links between mind and body in disease has been by Freudians. The first, probably, to set about research systematically was Eric Wittkower in England, and later at McGill University in Montreal. He demonstrated in 1928 how the flow of bile was affected by emotional changes, and then went on to work on many other forms of mind-body research on skin diseases and on the relationship of emotional stress and T.B.; and though his work has never had the public recognition he deserves, he will in due course be recognized as the real founder of the school of research methods of which the experiment on "Tom" is the most striking example.

But perhaps the most significant advance towards a general theory of the relationship between stress and disease has come out of the work of a man who was not a Freudian: Hans Selye, an Austrian, who went to the United States on a research fellowship in 1931, and who, like Wittkower, eventually settled down in Montreal; becoming Director of the Institute of Experimental Medicine and Surgery at Montreal University. His theories have also remained little known to the public in spite of an occasional write-up in the popular press; but in 1956 he published a survey of them designed for lay reading, *The Stress of Life;* and his work may turn out to be the most influential contribution to the study of medicine since Freud.

When Selye reached the clinical stage of his medical studentship, he was struck by the realization that most patients, no matter what might be their illness, had certain symptoms common to the fact of being ill. They felt ill; they looked ill; their tongues were coated; they had vague aches and stomach disturbances and fever; and so on. These "non-specific" symptoms seemed important to him; but he noticed that they were quickly passed over by the professor in charge, who concentrated upon the specific signs which would help in the diagnosis of the disease which the patient had contracted; signs that, compared to the non-specific symptoms, were few and inconspicuous. This surprised Selye:

> "Even now—thirty years later—I still remember vividly the profound impression these considerations made upon me at the time. I could not understand why, ever since the dawn of medical history, physicians should have attempted to concentrate all their efforts upon the recognition of *individual* disease and the discovery of *specific* remedies for them, without giving any attention to the much more obvious 'syndrome of just being sick'. I knew that a syndrome is usually defined as 'a group of signs and symptoms that occur together and characterize a disease'. Well, the patients we had just seen had a syndrome, but this seemed to be the syndrome that characterized disease as such, not any one disease."

Some years later, after he had qualified and begun to do research, Selye was on the track of what he believed to be a new undiscovered sex hormone which, injected into rats, produced certain symptoms. To his disappointment, he eventually realized that the symptoms were being produced not because of a hormone, but by the poisonous effects of the injections. But disappointment changed to surmise when he began to look at the results of his experiments from a different angle: could it be, he asked himself, that there is such a thing as a general, non-specific reaction of the body, to poisons—to damage of *any* kind?

> "As I repeated to myself 'a syndrome of response to injury as such', gradually my early class-room impressions of the clinical 'syndrome of just being sick' began to reappear dimly out of my subconsciousness, where they had been buried for over a decade. Could it be that this syndrome in man (the feeling of being ill, the diffuse pains in joints and muscles, the intestinal disturbances with loss of appetite, the loss of weight) were in some manner clinical equivalents of the experimental syndrome . . . that I had produced with such a variety of toxic substances in the rat?
>
> If this were so, the general medical implications of the syndrome would be enormous . . . everything we had learned about the characteristic manifestations of disease, about the specific actions of drugs, would be in need of revision."

From this time, Selye devoted himself to a study of the "syndrome of just being sick"; its symptoms, and how it develops —its dynamics. He experimented with different kinds of poison; he subjected rats to heat, and to enforced exercise; and always he found the syndrome. Confident that he was on the right track, he then cast around for a way to describe why people suffer from the "syndrome of just being sick"; the reason, he asserted, is simply, "stress".

It is not easy to define stress because it is something which we normally are aware of only through its effects—through the symptoms arising out of it. It should, strictly speaking, be kept distinct from strain, and from tension: by analogy, when two tug o' war teams "take the strain" just before they start to heave, the rope is then in a state of tension, and the effects of the tension on the rope—the wear and tear arising out of the contest—are the symptoms of stress.

Although we are all under strains of various kinds, which keep us constantly in a state of tension, we do not necessarily show stress symptoms because—unlike the tug-of-war rope—the human mind and body are constantly working together to make the necessary, often automatic, adjustments—breathing more deeply to replenish oxygen, sleeping when tired, eating when hungry, and so on. It is only where the strains imposed are excessive (where a man swallows a dose of poison for which no antidote is available) or unexpected (where a boxer is unprepared for a blow) or prolonged (through, say, overwork) that serious symptoms of stress actually appear.

The idea is not new. Selye himself traced it back to Claude Bernard, who over a century before had described how the body contrives to maintain itself in a state of equilibrium, by means of a built-in homeostatic mechanism which enables it to deal with all the strains it is normally called upon to meet. But just as an office thermostat cannot cope with temperatures outside the range for which it is designed, so may severe, unexpected or prolonged strain upset the body's normal homeostatic equilibrium; and illness results.

Selye elaborated on this theory. The body, he argued, copes with strain in three stages: first an alarm reaction, like a call to arms—a partial or general mobilization of the body's defenders when an invader threatens; second, the stage of resistance and adaptation, when the defenders come to grips with the invader—germ or poison—and either repel him, or seek to secure an acceptable armistice (as when a foreign body which cannot be ejected is sealed off, so that it gives no further trouble); and finally, the stage of exhaustion. No living organism can be kept permanently at alarm stations; if there is too long an exposure, or the enemies are too powerful (something life eventually imposes on everybody), the capacity to resist and adapt is lost; and death follows.

From this thesis, Claude Bernard's idea of health and disease re-emerges not as a static condition (even if a battle is lost, and a man loses a limb, he is not thereafter considered "ill", though he may be disabled), but as a dynamic condition; as a ceaseless struggle by the body to preserve equilibrium. The body may be likened to a factory which employs automation. There is always a risk of things going wrong; grit may get into bearings, a rotor arm may fracture, a gasket blow out. The whole machine is constantly being subjected to wear and tear. But in normal circumstances the symptoms of wear and tear—say, a falling off in oil pressure—are relayed to the machine's nerve centre, and the appropriate counter-action—replenishment with oil—is taken automatically. Where the action cannot be automatic, a warning light or noise tells the engineer or electrician what is wrong, so that he can replace the faulty part.

So it is with the body. Normally, our homeostat keeps our bodily mechanism running smoothly; where there is an invasion of enemies, hostile microbes, they are usually dealt with so expeditiously that we do not even know of their existence (tests often reveal that people have had T.B., or polio, without knowing it). In most cases, though, symptoms of the struggle appear, in the form of pain or irritation—the warning that a struggle is in progress; there may be nothing much we can do directly about it, but we can avoid other stresses in order not to distract the defenders from their immediate aim; much as an engineer lowers the revs of a machine until the oil pressure is back to normal. In some cases, it may be necessary for our bodies to have a part removed, or replaced, or reset, where there has been an accident, or where the body's defenders have failed to cope satisfactorily with invaders. But provided the machinery is sound, and the "brain" of the machine is functioning properly, alarms are met automatically with the appropriate response, without the need for external intervention.

The treatment of disease, then, is not simply a matter of fighting the body's external enemies with antidotes; it is chiefly a matter of assisting the body to make the appropriate homeostatic responses to whatever threats it is called upon to face. What drugs should be designed to do is to assist the body in its process of adaptation, rather than to remove or assuage symptoms,

"We are beginning to realize", Selye says, "that the purpose of medicine must not necessarily be directed against what is the immediate cause of disease . . . it is to encourage, to try to complete, to perfect, certain natural self-defensive mechanisms of the body." But it is also necessary to find out why they are not working properly—why the efficient working of our homeostats has been disturbed. And research is gradually revealing why our homeostatic balance is thrown out—why the body's response is either inadequate, or inappropriate.

The response may be inadequate for simple reasons, the most obvious one being that the body does not carry big enough guns to meet the threat. There is a point at which injuries, or burns, or the effects of poison are too much for the healthiest organism. But if Selye's evidence from animals is found to have relevance to human symptoms, the body's capacity to deal with hostile microbes may also be inadequate because the patient is suffering from unnecessary stress, which reduces his body's ability to put up its usual fight.

When somebody is taken ill with the symptoms of poisoning, and traces of the poison are found in his body, it is normally blamed for his symptoms. His illness, he is told, is caused by it. But this does not dispose of the question, why did the body's homeostatic mechanism fail automatically to deploy its defenders in sufficient strength to save him from its effects? Selye sought an answer to this question by experiments on rats, and later on other animals. He subjected them not simply to varying doses of poison, but also to varying degrees of stress—including "frustration":

> "In such tests, the animals are forcefully immobilized, so that they cannot run around freely; this causes them to struggle, and to become very angry. A rat wants to have his own way, just like a human being, and does not like to be prevented from doing what he wants to do. I thought this kind of frustration and struggle would come about as close to the most common stress situation as we can come, in rats."

By an ingenious device Selye was able to study the effects of frustration on the rats' tissues. He found that the resulting stress does not necessarily excerbate a disease condition; when rats were injected with some relatively weak irritant and then subjected to frustration, it actually helped them to throw off the effects of the irritant. But where the irritant with which they were treated was strong, frustration had precisely the opposite effect; it aggravated the irritant's effects, and the rats died.

The process evidently resembled that put forward by Arnold Toynbee in his "challenge and response" theory in *A Study of History*. A certain degree of environmental challenge, Toynbee argued, is necessary to produce the qualities that enable a tribe or a nation to establish its supremacy; it is as if the need to master rude nature, or tough neighbours, creates the strength and spirit which leads on to the establishment of nations and empires. Where there is no challenge, there is no response; the people live indolent lives. Where there is too great a challenge, they are crushed. This thesis, it can be argued, applies also to human beings. A limited amount of pressure acts as a stimulus, rallying us, so that we become stronger than we normally are. Stress is not, then, inherently harmful: indeed, as Selye insists, without it there would be no life. But if it is too great, or if severe emotional stress affects us at a time when we are under other physical strains, it may be destructive.

Looked at in this way, the nature of stress disorder immediately becomes clear; and so does the reason for the confusion which has arisen owing to the belief that germs and viruses are *the* cause of illness. Ideally, our homeostatic mechanism would deal with any germs, viruses, or poisons, within reason, that invade the body; and normally it does. But if we happen to be suffering from severe frustration (or some other emotional or physical stress) at the time the invasion takes place, the homeostat may be unable to cope; the invaders are allowed to establish themselves, and we fall ill. One doctor, finding the germ present, pronounces that the germ is the cause. Another doctor, recognizing the fact that it was the frustration that precipitated the illness, calls the stress the cause. Both, in fact, are causes. Neither the germs alone, nor the stress alone, would have made us ill; but the two of them coming together proved too much for us.

For prevention and for treatment, then, the need is to keep both in mind. A sick man may be relieved either by a drug which destroys the invading germs, or by psychotherapy which helps him to get over his emotional stress. What is important—and this is where Selye's work, when it is more widely accepted, is going to be of extreme value—is that doctors and patients should realize that illness is not exclusively physically, or exclusively emotionally, induced; it is produced by the interaction of germ and stress. Treatment should depend on the circumstances and needs of the individual patient: not simply on the nature of his symptoms.

Although this theory is not inherently improbable—it might reasonably be called applied common sense—it has met with strong and sometimes rancorous opposition, ranging from charges that Selye's work was unscientific, to the usual (and often justified) warning that the symptoms of frustrated rats are not necessarily the same as the symptoms of frustrated humans. But Selye has since found it possible to reproduce in rats the symptoms of specific disorders (closely paralleling human symptoms)—rheumatic fever, diabetes, arthritis, and heart trouble. In one of Selye's recent experiments:

> "rats were treated for five days with highly active cortisone derivatives. This in itself produced no evidence of cardiac damage. However, when these animals were subsequently strapped to a board (a frustrating experience which leads to nervous excitement and struggle) large patches of their heart muscle underwent acute disintegration, and all the animals died within a few hours. Animals not pretreated with these hormones withstand the same frustrating experience, without difficulty. . . .
>
> All these observations have recently been confirmed in the primate (rhesus monkey); this suggests that man is likely to

respond similarly under comparable conditions. Attention is called to the fact that, in its microscopic features, the cardiac damage produced under these conditions in experimental animals is quite similar to that seen in men who die from an acute cardiac accident as a result of exposure to stress."

When Selye's experiments on animals are set beside other research on the links between emotional stress and disorders of the human heart, the case for the stress theory appears overwhelming.

*

Selye's work has also helped to clear up some muddled thinking on the subject of symptoms, which has led to much unnecessary suffering, and wasteful forms of treatment, in the past few years. During the second stage of the body's reaction to invaders—the stage of resistance and adaptation—the body becomes a battlefield. And naturally, though some of the symptoms we are accustomed to associate with illness are the signs of the invasion, many of them are simply the signs of the battle—the equivalent of the carnage, smoke, and dust of the battlefield. They may actually be indications that the battle is going well for the defenders. To some extent this has been generally recognized by the profession: boils, for example, are known to be a sign that the body's regulatory mechanism is working, if not to the extent of preventing symptoms of poisoning, at least to the extent of sealing poison off so that it cannot do much damage. But in many other cases the distinction between the symptoms of illness and the symptoms of homeostatic reaction to invaders are ignored, or misunderstood.

In practice the distinction is often difficult; a doctor finds himself in the position of the leader of a squadron anxious to drop his bombs where they will do the invader most harm, but unable to distinguish between friend and foe in the confusion of battle. This is why in some illnesses it may be best for the doctor to do nothing, except prescribe rest, to give the defenders the opportunity to succeed on their own. But the temptation is often to treat the symptoms of the struggle as if they were the disease itself—particularly in those illnesses with the suffix "-itis" —gastritis, tonsilitis, colitis, neuritis, and many more—where the inflammation is really a sign that the battle is on; that the defenders are fighting; that the homeostatic mechanism is working.

Far more than we realize, symptoms are homeostatic. Tears, for example, are normally a symptom of emotional disturbance; crying represents a physical way of releasing tension. They are unsightly, a nuisance, and sometimes painful; but they may be a necessary outlet, for the person crying.

Nobody would deny this in the case of babies, who are actually slapped to make them cry as soon as they are born, in order to start them breathing; and whose crying subsequently gives notice to whoever is in charge of them that they are hungry, cold, wet, or uncomfortable. A baby that cries is a nuisance; a baby that could not cry would be a menace. There is reason to believe that in some cases the inability to cry deprives adults, too, of a useful emotional release. I have mentioned how it has been found that attacks of asthma cease, when the sufferer bursts into real tears; and Flanders Dunbar's suggestion that asthma may be a substitute for weeping, carried on from childhood. If so, tears and asthmatic wheezing may both be symptoms arising from the same causes: yet the one is regarded (except where it becomes excessive, or chronic) with comparative unconcern, while the other is treated as a disease.

There would be some justification for making this distinction if asthma were the unnatural, and tears the natural, response to an emotional conflict. But is it not possible that an asthmatic's wheezes, and many other symptoms which are treated as illnesses, are in fact signs, as tears are, that the body's self-regulatory mechanism is working; painfully, perhaps, and unnecessarily—but working?

So great has been the preoccupation with symptoms that this possibility has often been overlooked. The only surprise is that tears have not themselves been regarded as requiring medical attention. Crookshank once sarcastically asked why "some hard-boiled and orthodox clinician does not describe emotional weeping as a 'new disease', calling it paroxysmal lachrymation, and suggesting treatment by belladonna, astringent local application, avoidance of sexual excess, tea, tobacco, and alcohol, and a salt-free diet with restriction of fluid intake; proceeding in the event of failure to early removal of the tear glands". Grotesque though the suggestion may seem, it closely parallels what orthodox clinicians have been doing for other types of physical response to emotional disturbance.

★

In reaction against the stress theory, the argument is increasingly heard in the profession that the theory is only a fanciful elaboration of something that has been known all along; that it is, and has long been, standard medical practice to try to keep people who have some physical illness from emotional or physical stress; there is no need for elaborate experiments on rats to show that a man who has some germ or poison in his system is likely to recover more slowly if he is physically or mentally exhausted. This is true; but what the profession as a whole has not realized is the *extent* to which emotional stress creates the bodily situation that enables germs to flourish.

The way in which emotions influence the working of the body is still not fully understood, but it is clear that what we think of loosely as "personality" has a very close connexion with it through the endocrine system—through the work of the ductless glands, particularly the pituitary gland. Our important internal organs, pituitary, thyroid, liver, pancreas, adrenals and gonads are interconnected; if anything goes wrong with one of them others are affected, and so is the personality; and if anything goes wrong with the personality, it upsets the body's homeostatic balance and may throw the glands' workings out of order. So close is the connexion that it is usually difficult to decide which is the culprit. The profession has been trying to maintain that it is normally a physical upset, reflected in emotional symptoms, rather than vice-versa; but the findings of Selye, Wolff and others have now made this position impossible to sustain.

That the body's homeostatic mechanism should be subject to a great extent to the mind's dictation is not repugnant to common sense; it is the mind, after all, which has to relay the signals upon which the body is required to act—"blink", "run!", "sleep!", or whatever they may be. What is repugnant to many people is the idea that their automatic responses may be inappropriate because their minds are giving the wrong signals; so that their bodies either fail to react to dangerous situations, or react powerfully when there is no real danger at all. What, Selye asks

> "could possibly be the use of responding with inflammation to something harmless like a plant pollen, which cannot multiply or invade anyway, and which is not damaging to tissue? Yet some sensitive persons react to such plant pollens with the inflammation which we call hay fever. You may say, perhaps nature knows best; perhaps inflammation has a protective value even here. After all, who could tell whether the nasal tissues of a sensitive person would not be destroyed by such plant pollens if there were no inflammation? This is not so, and we can prove it. If a hay-fever-sensitive person is first given large doses of anti-inflammatory cortisone, contact with plant pollens will not cause inflammation in his nose; still, under these conditions the nasal structures are not damaged."

On examination, the reason why we get hay fever (or other such disorders due to the body's responses being inappropriate) is simple enough. Man happens to be so constituted that he reacts not only to the actual existence of danger, but to the threat of danger, as represented by certain symbols—loud noises, blood, shrieks, sudden movements, shadows. Soldiers new to the front line duck automatically whenever they hear a bullet whine overhead, even though they have been told by their instructors that, as bullets fly quicker than the speed of sound, they will never hear the one which is going to hit them. And it is not difficult to show that the body makes the same kind of mistakes; it reacts to threats or symbols of danger, as well as to danger itself.

In his *The Nature of Stress* Wolff quotes a number of examples of how such threats or symbols can call forth bodily reactions little different from those which are caused by actual assault; one experimenter has shown that blood vessels can behave in a strikingly similar way when a patient is subjected to a sham blow (provided, of course, that he is not aware that it is going to be a sham blow), as when he is actually struck. The same experimenter went a step further, and measured the effect on the blood vessels of emotional conflict. Conversing with a patient who had presented himself because of "hives", he suddenly introduced a painful family topic, and was able to induce hives in the same way, presumably, he had been able to induce symptoms by means of the sham blow. In other words, Wolff concludes, "the stress accruing from a situation is based in large part on the way the affected person perceives it", his "perception" not being use of eyes, but depending on many things, including his heredity, childhood background, life experiences, and social and cultural habits.

Wolff's thesis that "the common denominator of stress disorders is reaction to circumstances of threatening significance to the organism" is also interesting in that it helps to explain why disease varies in different parts of the world, and in different stages of civilization. Where disease arises out of a wrong response on the part of the body, the nature of the mental or emotional processes which have made it wrong will vary according to the difference of the environment. Wolff cites the case of the Hopi Indians. Among them,

> "In recognition of the ominous nature of snakes, it is decreed that one may not tread on the track of a snake.

Whoever offends will experience sore ankles and legs. Should one by accident or necessity tread on a snake track, the Hopi culture deals with the crisis through the medicine man, who has a traditional procedure of neutralizing the untoward effects of the breach. Among the younger Hopi, however, who have been more exposed to the alien influences of United States schools, missionaries, moving pictures, and radios, belief in the medicine man and his power is weak or absent. Yet the taboo concerning snake tracks persists. The young Hopis who are unfortunate enough to step on snake tracks often experience pain in the ankles, for which they have at their command no satisfactory therapeutic procedure."

We, who worry over inumerable minor superstitions, are in no position to laugh at the Hopi Indians; but we can learn something from their dilemma. Our homeostatic mechanisms are up against not simply the pressures of home and job, the strains of everyday life: they are up against the influences of the culture in which we are reared, the religion in which we believe. It is no use, therefore, our doctor telling us to avoid stress: for many stresses are so much a part of us, so built in to our way of life, that we cannot see them, or cannot recognize them. Our illnesses, and our reaction to them, are imposed on us, to a great extent, by our environment—using that word in its widest sense.

In any civilization, then, and in any strata of a civilization, it should follow that disease is likely to take different forms; and this is a matter of common observation. The differences are commonly attributed to economic rather than psychological circumstances; often rightly, as typhoid is likely to be found in regions where sewage systems are elementary. But there can be cultural and sociological reasons too. In the 1930s Henry Sigerist suggested that in every epoch certain diseases push themselves into the foreground for sociological reasons, so that they can come to be regarded as representative of their time; the plagues of the Middle Ages; the venereal disease of the piratical

Elizabethans; the "luxury" diseases, gout and dropsy, of the eighteenth century; the love-sick diseases, such as T.B., in the romantic era; the neuroses and stress disorders of the present day. Societies, it can be argued, get the diseases they deserve.

This thesis has recently been taken further by the linking of cultures to specific diseases; notably by Arthur Guirdham. In his *A Theory of Disease*, he points out that the remarkable variations in disease patterns in different parts of the world often correspond to the different attitudes which the people concerned hold about life and death. An absolute primitive faith in some religion, he suggests, be it Catholicism or Communism or Seventh Day Adventism, affords some immunity from neurosis, particularly when it is linked, as it often is, with the social stability that is sometimes induced by extreme poverty, where the individual is so preoccupied with his toil that he is not engaged in the pursuit of social advancement.

The liberal, Protestant, Anglo-Saxon communities, on the other hand, with their lack of stable religious certainty, and their constant struggle to keep up with the Joneses, are more susceptible to certain stress disorders, neuroses and stomach ulcers. Although it will be a long time before such speculation can be put on any scientific basis, the general thesis is reasonable: that disease is to some extent the reflection of the civilization in which it occurs, and of the culture of the individual. And this in its turn may have considerable bearing on treatment; it is not too much to suggest that a working knowledge in sociology and anthropology will in time be regarded as an indispensable prerequisite to entry into the profession.

Such theories may sound fanciful: for the present it is perhaps best to concentrate on the simpler aspects of the stress theory; what it can do to solve the everyday problems posed by disease. And the first thing it can do is to make us abandon the mechanistic idea of illness. This is not to deny the importance of the discoveries about germs and viruses; it is simply to state that they are rarely "the" cause of illness. They are around us all the time: some people, in fact, are actually carriers of, say, typhoid, having the germ but not the disease. If the microbe is always with us, Selye asks:

> "and yet causes no disease until we are exposed to stress, what is the "cause" of our illness, the microbe or the stress? I think both are—and equally so. In most instances disease is due neither to the germ as such, nor to our adaptive reactions as such, but to the inadequacy of our reactions against the germ."

Selye goes on to recall that even Pasteur—the protagonist of the importance of the germ as the disease producer—recognized in the end the importance of the *terrain*—the soil in which the germ has to take root before it infects; on his death-bed he admitted "Bernard was right: the microbe is nothing; the *terrain* is everything."

*

The *terrain* is everything; and it is time that we got to know more about those aspects of it which are little understood; in particular, the workings of the mind. This is a subject which is made harder to discuss by the fact that to most of us, "mind" is largely synonymous with consciousness. But the mind is also an automatic telephone exchange, to which the nerves are constantly sending signals which are immediately relayed to the interested parties; so that every time a blow (or the threat of the blow) is reported, the appropriate (or sometimes inappropriate) instructions are issued, without our being aware of it, though what we think of as our reflex actions make us aware of it as soon as they happen. Nor should it be hard, considering the mind in this sense, to realize how easily things may go wrong. Just as telephone wires may get crossed, or blown down, so our own internal information system may be disrupted; and it is a reasonable hypothesis that the cause of the breakdown may sometimes be emotional stress.

Admittedly we know from our own experience that this

cannot simply be a question of emotional and physical strains accumulating, straw upon straw, until the breaking point is reached. Some strains cancel others out. In the presence of external threats the symptoms of internal emotional disturbance—neuroses—often disappear. A Jewish doctor during the war found that while his patients were awaiting deportation or death, a high proportion of asthmatics lost their symptoms; of thirty asthmatics being treated during the war-time siege of Budapest twenty-seven lost their symptoms, only three growing worse. A common experience of psychiatrists during the London blitz was that their neurotic patients who suffered from unspecified worries and fears lost them when—and, in a sense, because—they had something real to fear.

Selye's rats, when they threw off the effects of small doses of poison more quickly because they were subjected to frustration, were behaving as human sometimes do. Traditionally, the Victorian hero who was unlucky in love became an explorer in central Africa, finding balm in the hardships and hazards of safari; the capacity of the individual to deal with threats whose nature he understands, even when they are terrifying, is remarkable. History abounds with cases of people who, when they have had to suffer fearful physical or mental torture for a cause or an ideal, have been so buoyed up by their beliefs that they have appeared almost to be immune from suffering. Even where he has no such consolation, an individual can cope with a remarkable load of stress provided he knows what it is, and faces it. It is stresses the cause of which—sometimes the existence of which—we are unaware, or which we misinterpret, that are hard to handle.

It is hard, though, to assess the importance of unconscious emotional disturbances in creating stress—simply because they are unconscious. Sometimes they lie very deep; often the discovery of what is thought to be the cause of a neurosis may turn out to be only the removal of the top layer of a concealed emotional conflict, as in a case once related to me by a social worker. It concerned a young girl who was living in London during the blitz. One night she went out when the sirens sounded to the Anderson shelter with her family—all except her grandmother, who decided to take a chance and stay in bed. The house was hit by a bomb, and the grandmother was killed. Shortly afterwards the young girl developed neurotic symptoms. Not unnaturally they were attributed to the effect on her young mind of the shock from the bomb, and it was assumed that they would wear off. But they persisted, and grew worse; so she was taken to a psychiatrist.

The psychiatrist had already observed that the incidence of neurosis in his patients had actually been reduced by the blitz. It was at least possible, he thought, that the bomb was not itself responsible—it might be that the shock was the detonator of the child's neurosis, and that the real trouble would have to be looked for in the death of the grandmother. Did she love her grandmother very much? "Oh, yes!" So that was it . . . a simple matter of deprivation of affection! This was explained to the family (who were asked to try to make up the missing affection) and—as far as such things can be explained—to the child; and the psychiatrist hoped that all would be well.

But the child's neurotic symptoms grew worse; and the psychiatrist was finally forced to realize that his diagnosis must have been too superficial. So he began to get the child to talk; and eventually he unearthed a deeper cause of her worry which she had previously repressed. Apparently she had not loved her grandmother. She had hated her grandmother with all the concentrated loathing of which a small child is capable. And every night, she had added to her spoken prayers the unspoken wish that God would smite her grandmother with a thunderbolt. The child was too young to know what a thunderbolt was; when the bomb fell, it seemed to come as a direct answer to her prayers. It was impressed upon her by her family, however, who were in complete ignorance of her feelings, that she ought to feel real sorrow at her grandmother's death. She was told, too, that her grandmother had gone to heaven—where, presumably, she would learn about the prayer that had been offered nightly for her destruction by a thunderbolt. The child's terror could then easily be understood; and the psychiatrist had no difficulty in finding a way to assuage it.

Owing to the rules of our social existence, many powerful emotions are also felt by adults—fear, aggression, guilt, lust—which cannot find expression and relief. The mind has a mechanism whereby such impulses can be repressed; but they may manifest themselves in time in other ways—in neurosis, or in mental or physical illness. And not only do such unconscious conflicts add to the total quantity of stresses to which the individual is subjected; they are qualitatively the most important of all stresses, because the victim, being unaware of processes which are unconscious, cannot regulate them.

This is another reason why it is unwise for doctors to say about the stress theory (as some of them do) that it is merely applied common sense—that they have always realized their patients must avoid unnecessary stress. Where their stress arises out of an emotional disturbance the reasons for which they do not understand, they cannot avoid it; it is no use telling them to avoid it, or to "stop worrying!" because the worry is a symptom: they can no more stop worrying to order than they can stop feeling hungry to order. Nor is it any use the doctor trying to prove to them they have nothing to worry about, for unconscious worry is not about anything—not, at least, about anything in the outside world; it may plague us even when everything is outwardly fine.

The symptoms of unconscious disturbances take many negative forms: anxiety, frustration, tension, lassitude, depression; or they may appear in the more positive syndromes which we think of as actual illness; the psychoses and neuroses. Sometimes the illness acquires physical symptoms either through mimicry (hysteria) or through starting up certain bodily processes for which the doctors, finding no physical cause, call functional. But often the unconscious disturbance does not start the process. Something else starts it; microbes; or irritants; or an accident. Normally our homeostats would be able to deal with the situation;

the appropriate warning would be flashed by the nerves (or whatever outpost first perceives the invaders) to the mind; and the appropriate forces would be despatched by the mind to deal with them. But if the mind is distracted by unconscious disturbances which it has failed to master, it may not be able to gather sufficient forces; or it may give wrong, confused orders; or it may even—though this is only conjecture—welcome the enemy, in some cases, in an act of what amounts to unconscious suicide. Valuable though the stress theory is, then, it takes us only a part of the way; before it can be fully employed for the benefit of humanity, we will need also to know more about the workings of the unconscious mind.

2

THE UNCONSCIOUS MIND

ONE of the chief obstacles to the acceptance of the stress theory of disease lies in resistance to ideas about the power of the unconscious mind: ideas usually thought of as Freudian, though some of his followers have developed variants of their own. I do not want to become involved here in the battles between the different schools; if in this chapter I deal mainly with Freud's teaching it is not because it affords the best explanation of the relationship between mind and body—it is at least arguable that Alfred Adler had a better grasp of the links between emotional stress and physical symptoms—but simply because Freud was responsible for the new concept of the mind; it was he who first explored and began to chart the unknown territory of the unconscious, and even if it should be found that some of his reports need drastic revision, it would still be Freud that we would have to thank for providing us with a key to the understanding of the human personality.

I said earlier that the word "mind" is still normally used as synonymous with consciousness; in our everyday affairs, we relate it to thinking, rather than to feeling; but we know it works on a level of which we are not conscious; as an automatic telephone exchange, receiving reports from the nerves and transmitting instructions back. Where the resistance tends to come is to the idea that there is a third force in our minds, which is neither automatic nor conscious; and one which plays an important, sometimes a decisive part in shaping our personalities.

One reason why it is difficult to visualize this third force is that most of us grow up taking our minds for granted. Considering their overwhelming importance to us it is remarkable how we continue to use the words "mind", "awareness", "feeling", "thinking", "knowing", "will", "memory", "imagination", and many more in a way which, when we come to examine it, is incredibly casual. Presumably this is because introspection is considered a rather unsuitable pastime for children; the idea of psychology as a school subject remains faintly ridiculous. It has even been resisted—it still is—at undergraduate level, on the principle that a degree ought to be obtained in some "proper" subject first. Not until many years after leaving my university was I aware of how much valuable research had been done into such obviously important subjects for a student as how to get the maximum benefit from reading for examinations—how to take notes; how often to stop for rest or recapitulation; and so on.

Because we take our minds so much for granted as children, it is normally difficult to recall later what we thought about them—what we would have said at any given age if somebody asked us what we meant by the word "mind". There was certainly some confusion between mind and "soul", or "spirit", among those of us who were brought up Christians. The nearest I can get to explaining it is to say that we grew up thinking of the mind as a clearing house, which received and registered impressions from outside (through the senses) and from within (from instinct, memory and imagination); and passed them for inspection to the soul. The soul transmitted its instructions back; and the mind, through the application of reason, worked out how to put them into practice. But as the soul was not something we could visualize, even in the imagination, it tended to get left out of the reckoning—except, perhaps, in the form of conscience; I suppose we thought of twinges of conscience as the soul's way of reminding us of its existence. Normally we thought of our minds as directing our actions, and our behaviour.

Every day we were constantly being faced with decisions; we "made up our minds" one way or the other, and took action—or, if we failed to take it, we attributed our failure to lack of will-power. Ideally, "soul", "mind", and "will" ought, we would have agreed, to work as a unity; but sometimes the mind would let us down—make a wrong diagnosis—through ignorance or obstinacy; and sometimes the will would let us down, out of weakness. Still, we were never in any doubt that both mind and will should be within our control.

For example: although it was obvious that difference existed in innate ability, some boys being cleverer than others, it was assumed at schools that everybody ought to be able to reach a certain minimum standard in class; and that if anybody fell below it, he deserved punishment. All of us were assumed to be capable of learning our lessons, catching a ball, sitting still, and obeying the school code; none was conceded the right to plead individual incapacity, unless it was so great as to take the boy out of the main stream of school life—post-polio paralysis, say, or blindness. Short-sightedness, even when it virtually incapacitated a boy from playing games, was regarded with little sympathy; games might be compulsory for a boy who could scarcely see the ball he was supposed to hit, or kick. The prevailing attitude to anybody who could not accommodate himself physically or mentally to school standards was still reminiscent of the episode in *The Way of All Flesh*, where Theobald Pontifex tells his small son Ernest, aged four, to say "come"; when the boy, unable to sound a hard "c", continues to say "tum", his father hauls him out of the room, thrashes him, and sends him off to bed. At my own schools, inability to pronounce letters, or stammering, were more commonly dealt with through the ridicule of the other boys; but Theobald's basic principle was generally accepted: that we all ought to be able to have control over ourselves, our speech, our limbs, our sexual urges, our memories; and the older we grew, the more firm that control was expected to become.

This could be justified, and was, on the grounds that the

outside world is no respecter of individual frailties; that a boy who had not learned to control himself before he left school might expect short shrift afterwards. As the dispensing of justice in the courts is based on the assumption that everybody is expected to be responsible for his own actions, this school training, it could be argued, was very necessary. At home, too, the principle was inculcated that we could and should exercise self-control over the whole range of normal activities—except one. Illness it was conceded, is not normally within the control of man.

★

The point at which a man might be considered so ill that he would cease to be a responsible citizen was admittedly never quite settled. Everybody agreed that a psychotic—a lunatic—could not be held accountable for his actions; if he escaped and committed murder, he was returned to his asylum: not hanged. But a psychopath—a man who had no obvious mental disorder, but who could not or would not accept the moral code of the community—would sometimes be put into an institution, for a crime; sometimes into a prison. The fact that he might be just as incapable of controlling himself as a lunatic did not necessarily save him from the gallows. As a rule he was treated as if he was responsible for his actions, because the community tends to impose its own ideas of responsibility into legal and medical practice; there might be individuals who could not readily be fitted into either category, mad or sane, responsible or not responsible for their actions; but the principle, it was felt, should be maintained that the two categories existed.

This is still broadly true today. Courts normally decide on the basis of medical evidence which category a man is in; they do not admit that he may not fit exclusively into either. Exceptions have been sidling in, by legal backdoors; "blackouts" are now a recognized, though often a suspect, way of accounting for the occasional unaccountable escapades of otherwise respectable company directors. But it remains generally true that every adult is held accountable for his actions, unless he is certifiable, or obviously mentally defective. The idea that we are masters of our own minds provided we are well is one of the foundations of the country's social structure. Only if we are demonstrably ill is the rigour of the law relaxed; for illness is considered to be outside our control.

This legal concept of responsibility is reinforced by religious teaching, which emphasizes that it is within our choice whether to be saint or sinner; and it is reflected in ordinary life by the obstinacy with which most of us cling to the assumption that people are aware of the motives for their actions. Few of us even bother to make any colloquial distinction between "hypocrisy" in its conscious and in its unconscious senses. We assume that hypocrisy is deliberate yet in many cases—Dickens's Pecksniff is the classic example—it is impossible to tell how far the process is conscious; all of us, when we reflect, know some people who are aware and some who are palpably unaware of the fact that they are humbugs, frauds, and even crooks—like kleptomaniacs. Within the family circle we make the distinction between thief and kleptomaniac, between conscious and unconscious fraud; but when we read about somebody brought up for shop-lifting whose lawyer pleads kleptomania, we tend to think the plea is spurious; and to this day, except when the defendant is so well off that theft for ordinary motives can be ruled out, the law tends to share our opinion.

Until the workings of the mind are better understood, and possibly even then, the legal concept of individual responsibility will inevitably remain; all that can be done to modify its rigours is a greater humanitarianism in the acceptance of pleas of extenuation—which may be justified by the growing weight of evidence revealing the extent to which punishment, so far from preventing, actually helps to increase, crime. But though the legal position cannot be changed, there is no reason why we should continue to accept a theory of the mind which is utterly at variance with reality. In our relationships with other people, and still more, in our attitude to ourselves, it has become necessary to examine the new theories of the mind which have arisen out of Freud's work.

★

The conscious mind, according to the Freudian thesis, resembles the cap of the iceberg, beneath which lies the great hidden bulk of the unconscious, swayed by as yet uncharted currents; some of which may carry us, perhaps uncontrollably, into latitudes where reason melts away. But we find it hard to admit this: to realize that most of the time, when we think we are exercising our powers of reason and deciding consciously where to go and what to do, we are in fact only rationalizing—seeking to justify taking the course which our unconscious minds, carried by these currents, are steering for us. Nor do we realize that the more subtle and refined our intellect is, the more ingenious and the more misguided our rationalizations can become.

I do not propose to go into Freud's theory of the unconscious, or the other theories which have sprung up since, except where they are relevant to the problem of stress and disease. The essential point is that the mind is one, just as the iceberg is one: the unconscious is not a separate institution from the conscious. Yet, in a curious way, the relation of the unconscious mind to disease is easier to grasp if it is at first considered as a separate entity; because most of us find it much easier to accept the possibility that something alien to us, something hostile, is responsible for illness—or for other characteristics in ourselves which we dislike, or regret, or fear—rather than admit that we are ourselves responsible. This is presumably the reason why illness, particularly mental illness, has long been attributed to the machinations of malevolent spirits, or devils. Witch doctors accuse evilly-disposed persons of casting spells which cause illness; religious healers effect cures by driving out demons which, they say, have taken up residence in men's bodies, or minds. In primitive communities, the shock treatment of witch doctor or healer may work—far more quickly and effectively, often, than the cures of civilization. But, as the parable points out, the cure is often temporary; seventy times seven devils return to replace the seven devils which have been cast out. The parable represents one of the great truisms of medicine—that cure is not enough, unless the reason can be found why the illness began, so as to find out how to prevent it from beginning again: and it also provides a bridge between the old theory of disease—possession by devils—and the new—possession by our own repressed feelings of guilt. The devils return after they have been cast out because they know the residence suits them. In effect, the host is inviting them back—though he is not aware he is doing so, and may regard them with horror. If this is accepted, it becomes less difficult to accept the Freudian thesis that the devils are within us—are created by us; and may work against us.

Few of us realize, until we stop to think, how little we like ourselves. If we could keep a diary of all the occasions in a day when we have thought or acted in a manner unbecoming to our opinion of ourselves, we would find that we are lazy, gluttonous, and short tempered; that we are snobbish, arrogant, and rude. We might perhaps congratulate ourselves that our vices are rarely carried to a point where they cause serious pain,to ourselves or to others; but few of us could honestly deny, at the day's end, that there have been a score of occasions when we have failed to live up to the standards of the person we like to think we are, and like other people to think we are.

And this covers only the defects of which we are conscious; how many deplorable failings there are which we do not recognize, because we are not aware of them, can only be guessed from watching other people, in the office or at home, and realizing how little they really know about themselves; how many mannerisms, or attitudes they have, of which they are not aware, but which, we feel, they would be much better off without.

On reflection, all of us would have to accept that there is a part of us which cannot or will not accept the rule of our conscious minds. Why should it be rebellious, or unco-operative? So long as it was possible to believe in spells or in demons, the assumption was that the sufferer must have been wicked, or at least slack, to have let them take residence originally. But the demon theory has ceased to satisfy even those to whom it should be the natural explanation; few doctors would now tell a Christian patient that what he needs is not a prescription but a priest. In its place, Freud put forward his own theory: a theory calculated, on his own admission, "to offend the whole world and excite its resentment". What had been thought of as demons, he asserted, were in fact manifestations of our own repressed desires—repressed because we have been conditioned to regard them as wicked: and he went on to define these desires: "impulses which can only be described as sexual, in both the narrower and wider sense, play a particularly large part in the causation of nervous and mental disorders".

Freud was too rigorously and perhaps mistakenly honest with himself to evade the issue by using some less loaded word than "sexual", even though it meant not merely that he was misrepresented—he was prepared to accept this as inevitable—but that he was misunderstood. He insisted on it; and there is little point now in shuffling around with politer versions. Briefly, what he asserted was that children growing up into civilization are inevitably subjected to intense emotional stresses of a kind not experienced by primitive children. The child of civilization has to recapitulate thousands of years of evolution during early childhood, and to face the existence of taboos which prevent him from expressing his natural impulses, some of them very strong—as the roar a baby lets out when it is thwarted shows. There can be no question that some of the most intense of these impulses are sexual, or have sexual implications—such as the fantasies which children often have about their relationship with each other and with their parents. Yet indulgence in some of the strongest and pleasantest of his pleasures, as the infant soon becomes aware, is forbidden. In others he is expected to conform to the household's routine requirements rather than to gratify his own strong impulses; he must learn to adapt his feeding times and his bowel movements to suit his mother's convenience;

and when he seeks erotic satisfaction he is punished—sometimes to the accompaniment of what may seem to be terrifying threats.

It is not necessary to explore further, as Freud went on to do, the common childhood wishes and fantasies, to realize the feelings of a child when he finds that some of his most ardent desires are considered naughty, wicked, and that the people he most loves, his mother or his nurse, may appear to take away their love if his wickedness persists. So great is the shock, Freud suggested, that the child does not merely suppress such desires, in the sense that we restrain ourselves from doing something we would like to do, but know we shouldn't; he may repress them—push them out of sight into an unconscious region of the mind which cannot be reached through the exercise of memory—not, at least, by any of the ways in which we normally exercise memory.

The distinction is vitally important. A suppressed feeling can be recalled and felt, at will; a repressed feeling cannot. And in the transition from infancy to childhood—when we realize that some of our strongest desires are naughty, wicked, leading to hell fire—we are apt to collect a cellarful of repressions which cannot be examined, until we can find the cellar key.

The chances of this happening are likely to be increased if infancy and early childhood are disturbed by unhappy or unstable family relationships. A child is so utterly dependent on his parents that he naturally can be subjected to great emotional conflicts when his relations with them, or his parents' relations with each other, are disturbed. If he is unable to express his feelings for fear of parental disapproval, or for lack of parental love and understanding, he is more likely than a happy child to be unable to cope with the conflicts consciously; and more likely, therefore, to repress feelings of guilt, arising out of his desires. In the comparative lull that follows when he has succeeded in adapting himself to society's demands, usually after his fifth year, these repressions may lie dormant; but they tend to flare up again at puberty, when his adult sexual life begins, or in adolescence, when he is about to be launched into full adult life.

It is not only children who are capable of repressing feelings which are too much for them. Soldiers who are terrified on the battlefield often suffer a kind of amnesia which enables them to forget what they saw and felt at the time. But the really deep repressions stem from the conflicts of infancy and early childhood; and repressing them does not get rid of them altogether. They continue to give trouble in a variety of ways by a process which appears to be analogous to the law of conservation of energy; just as in the physical world no energy is ever lost, so in the personality there is apparently no loss of emotional energy. If it cannot be relieved directly (in the sense that we relieve our emotions by laughing or crying) or indirectly (in the sense that emotional energy can be diverted or sublimated into different channels) it will find ways to make its presence felt: and these manifestations may be unpleasant, disabling, and sometimes destructive.

Among the commonest ways in which repressions reveal their existence are neurotic symptoms: compulsive actions (Christopher Robin justified his determination to walk only on the squares of the pavement by explaining that bears lurked in the areas, waiting to carry off anybody who walked on the cracks; some grown-ups feel compelled to follow his example without the comfort of his rationalization); phobias (the "I must make sure that the gas really *is* out" impulses, which drag us out of bed in the middle of the night to go down to the kitchen to make sure we have turned it off—perhaps more than once in the night); foolish but invincible superstitions (the mumbo-jumbo we feel compelled to enact, though we don't really believe in it, after breaking a mirror, spilling salt, seeing the new moon through glass, or making a boast); and ineradicable fears (of mice, of spiders, of elevators, of undergrounds). Many of these cases, whether we produce some justification for our action ("it really is not safe to walk under ladders"), or justify them simply as personal quirks of character, or regard them simply as ingrained habits—which, of course, they often are—point to the emotion arising out of some repressed conflict, which has adopted this roundabout and unsatisfactory way of obtruding into consciousness; the straightforward way being barred by a mechanism which Freud considered as a form of censorship, imposed by the personality to save itself from having to face the monsters of its own deep.

At this point I must emphasize once again that Freud's theory is not necessarily the correct explanation of neuroses: the idea that there is a law of conservation of emotional energy is "notional", not a scientifically observed fact. And there is a strong and growing school of thought which leans away from Freud to the Pavlovian theory. To the Pavlovians, as I have said, neuroses are bad habits which have been learned and which, given the discovery of techniques, can be unlearned. Thus, Christopher Robin's refusal to walk on the cracks between paving stones is a natural and indeed almost universal childhood game (hopscotch is the refined version); and it is not unnatural that a child's mind, ever ready to create its own fantasies, will provide him with the rationalization that if he does walk on a crack, a bear will eat him. Such fantasies in time get handed on to other children by nurses or parents, or in books of fairy tales; and they may take on a much greater significance to a nervous child than for normal children. The nervous child may grow up still fearing to walk on the cracks (though the mechanism of repression may mean that he does not understand how the fear arose); or the phobia may spread into different forms; or his fears may arise at moments of stress. In any case, it is not necessary (the Pavlovians argue) to grope around in his unconscious mind for the cause of his fears; it may be a simple matter to recondition him, so that he is no longer worried by stepping on cracks (or whatever form his phobia takes); just as it was easy to recondition the child who was induced to hate rabbits, and then induced to like them again.

But this does not explain why the child was nervous; why he suffered from, and later repressed, strong fears about walking on the cracks. True, the reason when it is found may turn out to be trivial: the combination, perhaps, of a day on which the boy was particularly keyed up, with a nursemaid sensing it, and teasing to the point of terror. The actual episode to which a repression may be traced back is often trivial; it is not the episode itself but the feeling aroused in connection with it which matters. If the feeling is ignored, to recondition somebody—to get rid of his neurotic symptoms by a refinement of the means whereby Pavlov conditioned dogs—is to risk inflicting on him the fate of the man in the parable; fresh devils will see their opportunity; and a new set of neurotic symptoms will develop.

This, at least, is the Freudian argument. My own feeling—though it looks as if it will be some time before ways are found to test both theories fully and fairly—is that both may be right, according to the case. Some neurotic symptoms are learned habits, which can be unlearned; others are symptoms of repressed conflicts, whose source needs to be uncovered if they are to be satisfactorily exorcized. I shall be discussing this in relation to treatment; for the moment it is enough to say that, violently though the arguments run between them, both sides agree that the reason for emotional stress can be unconscious, because the original conflict from which it arose has been repressed. The existence of repressed (as distinct from suppressed) feelings is easy to demonstrate; under the influence of certain drugs a man can be persuaded, just as he can under hypnotism, to recall and "act out" events which he has managed to shut out of his conscious mind—showing that the memory is there, though amnesia has censored it from consciousness.

The reason for this censorship, Freud thought, is that the conscious mind cannot bear conflict beyond a certain point. Suppose a child has a powerful desire of the kind I have described in the case of the London girl who wanted her grandmother destroyed by a thunderbolt: the conflict between this and another powerful wish—to be loved by her family—may put too much of a strain on her mind for her to bear; and repression is the safety mechanism by which she relieves herself when the strain becomes unbearable. Unfortunately the mechanism is not reversible, in the ordinary way. We cannot later recall our repressed conflicts, at will, to examine them and realize how irrelevant to our adult lives the terrors of childhood really are. Consequently they tend to continue to build up inside us, leaking out in the form of neurotic symptoms; which may be mental or physical.

To counter the argument, even commoner in his time, that emotional stresses could not give rise to physical symptoms, Freud pointed out that the sexual function itself is not exclusively physical. He recognized, too, that a variety of physical symptoms, or what appeared to be physical symptoms, could arise; neurotic headache, or backache, he argued, can be an early substitute for some repressed fantasy or memory. And, just as an irritating grain of sand is enveloped by the oyster in mother of pearl, so an accident may set a neurosis under way; a man who is knocked down at his work may begin to display symptoms which are identical with those which he might expect to have as the physical consequence of his injury.

Freud, however, was not very interested in the physical symptoms of neurosis; it is only recently that some of his followers have taken his theories and applied them to disease as a whole. Yet this is not, when it is examined, an unexpected development. If, as is generally accepted, a neurosis can manifest itself in the form of chronic anxiety, and if it is further accepted that worry affects the workings of the stomach, then it would be surprising if some neurotics did *not* have stomach troubles. Where confusion has arisen is in the assumption that stomach troubles can be classed as neurotic only if the patient shows other neurotic symptoms. But just as the incidence of neurosis is observed to decline when there is something that people really need to worry about, such as bombs, so a man who has neurotic symptoms arising out of inner anxiety may lose them when he has something that he really needs to worry about, such as an impending stomach operation. And this helps to explain why so often people appear to *need* to be ill. Where there is worry, they *do* need to be ill; they are grateful for real symptoms —little though they enjoy the pain or discomfort they may bring—because their presence provides an excuse for their anxiety—so much so that they may even stop worrying.

This is something few of us care to admit to ourselves. Understandably, we do not like to feel that there is an unconscious part of us which may be busy trying to make us ill when in our conscious minds we may want very much to be well. And at first sight, it appears grotesque that we should want to have a painful or disabling illness. There are two possible explanations. One is that the unconscious mind, not being capable of reason, does not look very far ahead. Like a child faced with alternatives, it tends to choose the one which offers it prospect of immediate satisfaction or relief; and actual physical illness may bring relief more effectively than mere neurotic symptoms. A nervous, bad-tempered, crotchety man is a nuisance to himself as well as to his family, his acquaintances, and his fellow-workers: if he can substitute for his neurosis something that appears to be a real physical illness, he may become an object of sympathy.

A physical illness too, may remove a man from the environment in which the symptoms of his repression can pester him. Anyone who suffers from some deep-rooted sense of inadequacy, of inferiority, is likely to suffer most from such symptoms when he has occasion to feel inadequate in real life—about his job, or his wife's fidelity, or his bank balance, or whatever it may be. But the need to worry about his personal inadequacy may cease, for the time being at least, if he is ordered to bed by his doctor, because he can tell himself it is not his fault that he is away from the office; what happens to his job or his bank balance is consequently out of his control. And if the unconscious mind is capable of choosing between one type of physical disease and another as skilfully as it does in cases of hysterical illness, where patients so often contrive exactly to mimic the symptoms of an organic disease, it is not inherently improbable that he should somehow be able to produce the symptoms he needs in order to make sure of being ordered to his bed.

This type of self-induced illness gave rise to the use of the term psychosomatic; which, for a number of reasons, I have been avoiding. To begin with, it means very different things to different people. In the medical profession it is sometimes used to describe physical disorders which arise out of repressions; but more commonly, to cover the whole range of stress disorders, where mind and body, psyche and soma, interact. But some doctors object to its use in this way, because it has become loaded: people, they argue, tend to concentrate on the psyche, and neglect the soma (some doctors have even tried to popularize somato-psychic, to redress the balance). Colloquially, too, it has picked up a misleading connotation; I have heard it used in America as a synonym for bogus (the implication being that the patient with a psychosomatic illness only thinks he's ill). In Britain the word is little used.

The most serious of these arguments against the use of "psychosomatic" is that it is loaded. The assumption is often made when it is used colloquially that the mind is the cause of illness, and the body only the purveyor of symptoms. "Stress disorder"—though this term, too, can lead to confusion—is better because everybody knows that there are many different types of stress, mental and physical, internal and external. Consider the case of cancer. To call cancer psychosomatic sounds absurd, because, as I have said, there is a tremendous weight of evidence accumulating revealing the links between genetic and dietary and environmental factors and the cancer rate, not only in humans but in animals. But such biological stresses do not necessarily cause cancer; they only add to cancer proneness—just as the irritant Selye injected into rats did not kill them; some other element was needed before the poisons became destructive; and that may be emotional stress. The interaction at that stage is indeed psychosomatic: but this is not to argue that the whole disease is emotionally induced.

In other cases, illness may have its roots in repressions. The part which the unconscious mind plays in illness is much greater than most of us realize. The extent to which repressed feelings manifest themselves in symptoms is determined by many other things—particularly by a man's environment; where he is in stable surroundings, with a good job, a happy home, and no serious worries, repressions may have no more effect on him than an occasional minor illness, and a few amiable mannerisms; but where he is in unstable surroundings, with a job he is afraid of losing, a nagging wife, and no pension coming up, his repressions may make his life miserable for himself and for everybody around him by making him a chronic, querulous invalid.

Yet though the extent to which repressions can lead to illness varies according to the individual and his circumstances, they have a disproportionately large influence compared to other stresses, because we are unaware of them. Man has a considerable capacity to face and overcome a stress he knows about; he cannot face, and is reluctant even to admit the existence of, an enemy within his own personality which he cannot see. It is at this point that understanding of the stress theory becomes helpful. I have said that most of us are prepared to concede, when we stop to think, that there are within ourselves personality traits and feelings which we dislike, or cannot understand: small compulsive habits, weaknesses, and fears. We cannot but admit that these come from a part of our personality which is, temporarily at least, outside our conscious control; and it is not very difficult to think of this as adding to the total of the stresses imposed by constitution, environment, and disease, to make us ill.

For the time being, then, it is reasonable to concentrate mainly on the discovery and removal of known causes of stress, many of them external, until the mechanism of the unconscious mind is better understood. It will be objected that this is evasion; that we ought all to face the fact that we are really at the mercy of our repressed guilt feelings; and it is these on which treatment should concentrate. But a lesson may be learned here from Freud's own technique of analysis. Analysts realize that a patient should not be faced with the realities hidden in his unconscious mind until his conscious mind is fully prepared for them: that is (in practice) until he realizes them for himself. It is not the slightest use an analyst telling his patients after a few sessions what is the matter with them—that A. has repressed sexual desires for his mother; or that B. has a repressed feeling of hatred for his father. Any such explanation is meaningless to patients until the feelings themselves have been revived, and released from repression's bondage; if they are not worked out of our systems in this way, even if we believe in the truth of the analyst's verdict, our acceptance will be only on a superficial level; it will not help us. More probably, we will refuse to accept the verdict, because it is so grotesquely out of line with what we have always consciously believed about ourselves. This, in fact, is what happened in the case of Freud's theories of the unconscious mind, and its sexual content; the public was not ready for them, and either accepted them uncritically without understanding them, or rejected them with contumely.

All of us have come across innumerable examples of the tendency to accept a theory on one level, while remaining resistant to it on another; it is particularly common in relation to illness and stress. People commonly announce acceptance of the theory while remaining hostile to its application in practice; or deny the theory while accepting its practical application. One example arose while I was engaged on this section, when I happened one evening to be in the company of some actors after a performance. We were discussing the work of a talented actress who on several occasions had fallen ill shortly before important first nights. Was this, somebody suggested, psychosomatic? No! said an actor who knew her well, in tones of rebuke: definitely not! People had been suggesting this; but at long last the doctors had found what was physically the matter with her, and were treating it; so all the gossip about "psychosomatic" had been shown to be misinformed.

The actor's attitude was significant in two ways. He was an intelligent man, with more knowledge of the subject than most: and he accepted the existence of illness arising out of emotional stress. Yet he was prepared to accept the doctor's verdict that if a physical "cause" were found, the existence of any emotional element in the illness could immediately be discounted; and he talked as if the suggestion that the illness was the result of emotional stress was in some way offensive to, or humiliating for, the actress. This attitude is widespread, and will remain so, because of our reluctance to admit that we are in any way responsible for our own illnesses. But the stress theory of disease offers a way whereby we can begin to realize the importance of the emotional side of illness without being asked to believe that the stresses are self-induced—for stresses, obviously, are of many kinds, external as well as internal.

This is not to suggest that the evidence of illness being self-induced should be ignored. It would be unwise for the actress, for example, to rest content with the assumption that the cause of her illnesses had been discovered. If her trouble was only physical, why should it always have materialized shortly before important first nights? It may not be necessary to go deeply into the emotional background: a simple enough explanation is, stress. Impending first nights provide that emotional last straw which carries her past her capacity to offer resistance to illness: the physical weakness in this case is her fuse wire, which burns out before stress carries her beyond the limits of her endurance. On the other hand, the mere additional worry which actors and actresses naturally feel before a play opens is not normally the cause of illness: on the contrary, it can act as a stimulus, providing the dynamic by which they overcome their nerves, so that though they often have minor symptoms, headaches or throat troubles, these are kept within bounds, and disappear when the real test begins on stage. Where this normal process of adaptation is not functioning properly, the chances are that some inner tension is responsible; and if it persists in giving trouble, it may be necessary to dig deeper to find where the tension began.

The decision whether to dig deeper, or merely to rearrange the patient's existence so that his sum total of stresses do not reach unmanageable proportions, is one that can only be taken according to the nature of the individual case. But whatever the decision, the fact should be faced that emotional stresses of which we are unconscious are a contributory factor in illness. And because they are unconscious, it is often useless and sometimes unwise for a doctor to question a patient about them. In the case of the doctor I met in Italy, he had no other alternative, because he did not know his patients; but a family doctor should know all his flock well enough to be able to tell if they have worries without asking; and also to be able to disentangle the reasons why they think they are worrying from the real reasons (naturally he may not be able to discover what the real reasons are; but he should at least be able to discount some of the false ones). In other words, the profession today needs men who are not merely skilled as physicians, but men who are also acquainted with their patients' personalities and environments—with the nature of their family and office life. It is on its capacity to provide patients with this service, rather than with chemists' prescriptions, that the future of the profession is coming to depend.

*

To recapitulate, before I go on to consider treatment. First, the stress theory would not be demolished even if Freud's theories of the unconscious mind were shown to be nonsense. The distinction between psychosomatic and stress disorder is at the best of times tenuous; and it is not surprising that the two terms are coming to be used synonymously. This is unfortunate, as everything with the prefix "psycho-" is loaded with mistrust, and misunderstanding—particularly of the fact that the diagnosis "psychosomatic" does not mean that the illness is caused exclusively by emotional disturbance which is what the term has come to imply in its colloquial usage. Emotionally-induced illness is, in correct terminology "psychogenic"; psychosomatic does not imply, or *should* not imply, that illness is *caused* by emotional stress—only that physical and emotional causes co-exist.

The only reasonable attitude to take is that at present, not enough is known about the interrelationship of mind and body in illness ever to be dogmatic about causes. The doctor who tries to relate every symptom to emotional stress is consequently just as misguided as the doctor who thinks exclusively in terms of microbes or chemical reactions as sole causes. The warning the Baron de Charlus gave to Marcel Proust still holds:

> "There are maladies which we must not seek to cure because they alone protect us from others that are more serious. A cousin of mine had trouble with his stomach; he could not digest anything. The most learned specialists treated him with no effect. I took him to a certain doctor . . . he guessed at once that the trouble was nervousness; he persuaded his patient, ordered him to eat whatever he liked quite boldly and assured him that his digestion would stand it. But my cousin had nephritis also. What the stomach can digest perfectly well the kidneys cease, after a time, to eliminate, and my cousin, instead of living to a good old age with an imaginary disease of the stomach which obliged him to keep to a diet, died at forty with his stomach cured but his kidneys ruined."

Our desire to divide illness into watertight compartments, physical and psychological, is still very strong; the way things are going, "stress" will soon develop the same connotation: it will be assumed to be the equivalent of "emotional stress" whenever illness is being referred to. Emotional disturbance very often is, as we have seen, a link in the causal chain, sometimes a vital one; but it is never the only cause. Much of the value of the stress theory is lost if it is confined to this one sense.

Second, stresses, as we have seen, arise from many things: constitution, environment, and personality; Selye's rats did not die solely because of the irritant injected into them, or solely because of the frustration from being tied down, but from the interaction of the two sets of tension. So it is with humans. The stress theory exists to lead us away from the single-cause idea of illness—away from the attitude of mind in which people can assume, as the actor assumed, that if you can find some physical cause it is *the* cause, the only cause; that all other stresses are irrelevant. The treatment of stress disorder can only satisfactorily be undertaken by somebody who knows his patients as individuals; knows the strains that are placed on them by their work, their home life, and, if possible, their emotional difficulties. It is with patient-centred treatment in mind that the medical profession should be judged when the question is put: how far can it provide the service to the public which the growing prevalence of stress disorder requires?

3

TREATMENT

I

DOCTORS

How far is the profession equipped to deal with the problem of stress? Obviously, hardly at all. The whole trend has been in the direction Sir Thomas Sydenham pointed, nearly two hundred years ago; the emphasis now is on the disease, on the symptoms; not on the patient. Medicine is still being chopped up and apportioned between the specialists' camps; and increasingly, men who enter into general practice find themselves compelled (as often as not by the patient himself) to act less as doctors than as sorters—doing work similar to that done in the post office, when mail is put into appropriate boxes or bags. If the illness is trivial, the doctor/sorter selects the appropriate trivial, simple drug—often, in effect a placebo, designed only to make the patient feel something is being done for him. If it is serious, the doctor/sorter passes him on to the appropriate specialist, who proceeds to diagnose, and prescribe for the disease without having the least interest in or knowledge of the patient's environment, or personality: indeed, often the specialist bothers himself only with the symptoms which concern his speciality, without considering the patient's physical condition in other respects.

In the section which follows, I propose to examine the alternatives which confront people who are ill; and to discuss why, in its present form, the profession cannot hope to provide a health service which is relevant to the treatment of stress disorders. In practice the profession is not divided up into mutually exclusive categories; a psychiatrist must be, and a psychoanalyst usually is, a qualified doctor; some doctors who are not qualified psychiatrists use psychotherapy, or hypnotherapy. But for simplicity's sake I have made an arbitrary division between the various faculties; and I have also included a section on "healing" because, though it is not a formally recognized branch of medicine, its practice is widespread, and it ought not to be ignored.

*

At present, only a tiny minority of doctors make any serious attempt to understand, let alone practise, medicine in relation to the stress theory of disease. The overwhelming majority do not know their patients well enough, and would not normally think in terms of stress disorders if they did.

The existence of this strong bias in favour of the physical approach is occasionally denied; but the facts speak for themselves. The management of medicine on national and professional levels remains largely in the hands of physicians, surgeons, and representatives of the other important specialist branches. In medical schools, training continues along the familiar physical lines, anatomy, physiology, biochemistry; students hear little about the stress theory in the ordinary curriculum (except in introductory lectures to courses, when even the most hidebound of physicians is occasionally heard to talk about the need for treating patients as individuals and not merely as bodies; advice not usually heard again in the course).

A glance at the medical journals will suffice to show how negligible is the extent to which patients' minds occupy the time of the profession. Until the middle 1950s it was uncommon to find articles even on mental health, let alone on psychosomatic aspects of medicine; since then the position has improved, but writers have only recently begun to mention the term psychosomatic without putting it in inverted commas, and explaining what it means; and nine-tenths of the articles still deal exclusively with physical matters. The shelves of medical bookshops afford further evidence, crammed as they are with studies of physical symptoms and diseases, in many of which no mention is made of the possible effects of emotional stress.

Doctors either refuse to admit that these facts conclusively prove their lack of sympathy with the stress theory, or they justify their resistance by arguing that the stress theory should not be accepted without much more evidence; continued reliance should be placed in the meantime on mechanistic principles until the stress theory is proven—which, they think, it may never be. They point to the remarkable achievements of research in bacteriology, surgery, anaesthetics, pharmacology, and so on; they insist that though there may recently have been a slowing down of the *tempo*, notable results will again be forthcoming; and they cite penicillin and other drugs as evidence that the advance is by no means halted.

Even where emotional stress appears to be a cause of illness, they argue, research may in time reveal that it is in fact only a reflection. This is certainly important in assessing the relative influence of physical and emotional stresses in cases of, say, an overactive thyroid. The physical trouble in this case may exist without the patient being aware of it; he may merely have been aware that he felt excessively tired. But suppose he reads about the symptoms of thyrotoxicosis in a magazine: all of a sudden, he realizes that he may have an actual disease. This will be an emotional shock, from which he will still be suffering when he visits his doctor; and the doctor, if he takes only a superficial view, may attribute the illness to the shock, rather than vice versa. But to admit this is no more than restate the proposition that diagnosis should never exclude any possible cause of stress, physical, environmental, or emotional.

It is understandable that the medical profession should have been reluctant to accept any new theory of disease in the absence of evidence; but this attitude can no longer be sustained. In view of the evidence provided by Wittkower, Wolff, Alexander, Selye and many others, it is clear now that the real mistake was in attributing "scientific" accuracy to the earlier interpretation—that diseases could be traced to a single physical cause; what was actually being found and called the "cause" was often no more than the last link in the causal chain. To attribute the catching of diseases to the presence in the body of the patient of a virus is as foolish as to attribute the scoring of a goal to a football boot, without taking into consideration the foot which is in the boot, the player whose foot it is, and the circumstances in which he took aim.

*

Active resistance to the stress theory, however, strong though it is, is probably less decisive than apathy (taking the form either of a disinclination to consider it, or of the feeling there is no real need to do anything about it) in preventing it from achieving more general recognition.

The apathy assumes ingenious methods of self-justification; notably in the argument that the need for a doctor to consider the effects of emotional stress is only professional common sense writ large; "my dear man, in my job you have to be a psychologist; I can assure you I was using what you think you've just invented before you were born". But this is superficial. Doctors do indeed use psychology in their dealings with disease, but as a lubricant rather than as a fuel. They use it when they give a placebo to that pest Mrs. Smith, pretending it is the latest wonder drug; or when they assure her husband that he is right as rain, not because they think he is, but because they know his real trouble is his wife. Often, too, doctors arrive by trial and error at certain principles which (they might be horrified to find) Freud also reached, through his researches into the mind. But it is still comparatively rare to find a doctor who has studied psychotherapy or the stress theory.

The fact that the "it's only common sense" argument is increasingly often heard is really a sign of how little Freud's work is understood. To give a single example: most doctors would consider it "common sense", if they discovered what was the reason for the emotionally disturbed state of a neurotic patient, to tell him. Usually they would be wrong to do so. It is one of the hardest tasks of psychotherapists to restrain themselves, when they believe they have discovered the reason for certain neurotic symptoms, from telling the patient; yet to do so is often a mistake, because that is something the patient must learn for himself. As Leland Hinsie argued in his book *The Person in the Body*:

> "the psychotherapist should not reveal to patients what he thinks may be the mental meaning of the symptom. Often the beginner is greatly tempted to give a hint. Do not do it, for doing so may, and frequently does, hamper the course of treatment. It cannot be emphasized too strongly that successful therapy does not depend on your insight into the hidden factors of the psychosomatic disorder, but it does hinge upon the understanding that the patient derives from the simple facts that *he* has given to himself, and you".

In any case, the number of doctors who even try to understand the emotional troubles of their patients is small; partly owing to the dominance of the physical concept of disease, which makes them seem of little importance; partly on account of increased specialization, which has discouraged general practitioners from placing so much reliance on their own opinion, and led them to forward patients to specialists more often, and more quickly; and partly owing to the growing gap between doctors and their patients—few practitioners now share their social lives with their patients, in the way that the family doctor once used to do. The result is that, at the very time when new trends in medicine are increasing the demands on the doctor's understanding of his patients as individuals, rather than as walking symptoms of specific diseases, he is often very far from possessing, or even wanting to possess, the necessary knowledge of them.

Doctors like to think of their work as a science, not as an art; most of them deliberately try to keep their relations with a patient impersonal, rarely encouraging him to talk—either because they think they have no time; or because they believe that even if they had time, they would be foolish to encourage hypochondriacal reminiscence; or—an increasingly common excuse—because they want to be on the safe side; they prefer to send the patient to a hospital for tests, or to a specialist for a second opinion. Once started on this round, the patient is further removed from any hope that his personality and environment will be understood. A specialist may occasionally prate of the need to deal with mind and body as a unity; but his whole habit and training prevent him from doing so, and usually he is speaking in the same way that politicians tend to speak of liberty—as a polite convention, no more.

Few specialists ever trouble to consider the emotional background of patients sent to them. And many actually ridicule the possibility of stress being an important factor: the profession has always tended to be not merely conservative, but reactionary, in its attitude to innovation. Innovators like Semmelweiss and Freud were assailed with ferocity which drove some of them to despair; even men who are now considered as archetypes of medical conventionality were as bitterly assailed when their ideas were young: Simpson, Lister, Pasteur, and Koch. If the hatred of new ideas, as has been argued, is in direct proportion to the need for them, the need for them in the profession is now strong.

With the profession, as with the public, habit of mind is largely responsible. Most doctors have grown up into a world of medicine in which research appeared to have discovered the physical causes of so many diseases that although no cause had been discovered for others, the discovery seemed likely to be just around the corner. As Alexander has put it, this is a typical manifestation of the inertia of the human mind:

> "the tendency is to force more and more diseases into a causal scheme of infection, where cause and effect appear to have a comparatively simple relationship to each other. When the infectious or other organic explanation fails, the modern clinician is only too ready to console himself with the hope

that sometime in the future, after more details of the organic processes are known, the psychological factor, unwillingly admitted, will eventually be eliminated".

There is some excuse for this attitude. Although for centuries the essential unity of mind and body in medicine was accepted, the success of the work of men like Pasteur and his successors not merely pushed it on one side; they made it look silly. What, after all, could the mind of the individual have to do with whether he caught hydrophobia? Once it was planted in people's minds that diseases were the product of an invading army of germs, finding their way into the human body through bites and cuts, through the lungs or through the mouth, and that these diseases could be controlled and perhaps eliminated simply by finding the appropriate antidote, hopes arose of the eventual total conquest of disease. For a time it really looked as if these hopes were to be fulfilled. Disease after disease appeared to render up its secrets as its germ, bacillus, or virus was discovered; and in many cases the appropriate antidote was found too. It seemed that the whole problem might be mastered, leaving only accident and old age as killers.

Within the last twenty years, however, the pace has slackened. The victories won by Pasteur and others against indiscriminate diseases of primitive society were not repeated against the more selective diseases of civilization. The results against these were by no means negligible: pneumonia, for example, was reduced from the status of a dangerous and often killing disease to that of (in most cases) a comparatively minor illness. But all too often the "wonder-drugs", as they came sarcastically to be known from the ecstatic write-ups about them in magazines, proved in the long run unsatisfactory. Nor did the disappearance of so many diseases seem to make for any substantial lessening of the numbers of people sick. Although hospital building proceeded more rapidly than ever, waiting-lists of prospective patients grew longer. Their illnesses were on balance less dangerous than those for which they would have been awaiting treatment before the time of Pasteur; but they were also more puzzling. Many of the sufferers had no diagnosable disease at all; others had a recognizable disease, but, when cured, again contracted it, or some other illness, a few months later.

Most of these patients have assumed they had some specific physical disease, which medical science should be able to detect, and for which there ought to be some known cure—helping to reinforce doctors in their assumption that such diseases are physical, and that there *is* some cure. Instead of beginning to doubt whether the lines on which it was proceeding were sound, the profession has simply stepped up its demands for still greater effort, and still more expenditure, on physical research. The results have been just good enough, or at least have appeared to be just good enough, to justify the effort and expense. Time and again new drugs, or refinements of old drugs, have been tested, with good short term results; a few, like penicillin, have confirmed expectations over a longer period. Always, research has seemed just on the brink of wonderful new discoveries. By the time one wonder-drug has been found in practice to have some disadvantages, or to have dangerous side-effects, some new drug has been ready to be marketed which seems to do its work better, and has—or so the advertisers boast—no side-effects at all. These new inventions and refinements constantly titillate any doctor who likes to feel he is up to date, and when they become publicly known, they create a vigorous demand from his patients, too; often to his embarrassment, as by the time they hear about a drug, he may have read in the medical press about its deficiencies.

The tendency to concentrate on the physical side, rather than the psychological, has been heavily reinforced by doctors' training in their student days. Philip Hopkins's description of his English medical training is true of most countries:

"There is too much detail in the teaching of physics and botany, whilst much of the time spent on zoology and chemistry could more profitably be used on a deeper study of human physiology. Of the present day subjects taught in the first year, the one of most use undoubtedly is chemistry, but little even of this is remembered by the average student by the time he is ready for his final examinations. When the student reaches the dissecting room far too much time is spent on the study of detailed anatomy; while the intricate and quite unimportant courses of various blood vessels and nerves are being followed and memorized (long enough, it is hoped, to satisfy the examiners) a great opportunity is being lost in the physiology department. In the two years devoted to the study of the structure and function of the body, reference is rarely made to the physiological responses of the body to emotions. The effects of the emotions of fear and anxiety on human physiology may become all too apparent to the candidate sitting any part of his medical examinations, yet they pass unremarked. Later, when in practice we see patients who complain of diarrhoea or micturition, our own earlier unpleasant experiences are forgotten, and we remain faithful to those specialists who guided us through the wards in our study of diseases and disease processes. We learned what effects diseases have on the body, and what symptoms they produce—but what brought about the disease itself remained all too often a mystery, unless some organism or other physical agent could be held responsible."

Hopkins goes on to relate how he found this type of training, useful though it might have been to a specialist in say, surgery, was utterly deficient for general practice. When he acted as a "locum" to gain experience, he seldom could pick out a disease which he recognized from the instructions of his teachers; his patients brought a multitude of symptoms which refused to conform to textbook patterns.

At the same time, the training in the psychological aspects of medicine remains meagre. Until recently, most medical students had only to take a short course of lectures in psychology, which was regarded as a joke (rightly, as it was always farcically out of date); and then, towards the end of their training, pay a few visits to a local asylum, where a psychiatrist (whom the students, again often rightly, took to be a pathological case himself) would show them a few schizophrenics and manic depressives, as a compère might introduce different turns at a variety show. The stress theory was never mentioned; psychosomatic symptoms ignored; psychotherapy hardly considered. The whole of the students' training was based on the assumption that medicine was a natural science based on the principles of physics and chemistry applied to the living body. Things have improved—but not very much. At universities, faculties of psychiatry have appeared; but the "natural science" principle still holds and the psychiatrists tend to keep aloof from the rest of the medical school. Most medical students become doctors with no knowledge of, and no interest in, the emotional aspects of health and disease; and most of them are intensely conservative, shying away from, or actively opposing, anything which upsets the almost mathematical precision of their work. "Disease plus remedy," they want to feel, "equals cure"; without the complication of imponderables like the patient's personality.

Nor is it easy for a student, even supposing that he does gradually build up an interest in patients as personalities, to pursue it. He can become a psychiatrist, but this in the main commits him to work in mental hospitals. The openings for a psychiatrist in general hospitals are few, and his status, if he obtains such a post, is low; he must accept the fact that he will be a line of last resort to whom patients are only sent when every possible physical test and treatment has been applied without success. And because medicine has become so compartmentalized, he is likely to find it difficult to do his work properly by going and talking to patients in general, to get to know them as individuals. If he is not careful he will be accused of poaching on the ground of the physician, the dermatologist, or whatever specialist has secured first rights on the patient concerned.

Both in teaching and in administration, the old-established specialists have built up their empires in such a way that it is very difficult for the psychiatrist to work except by carving out a similar self-contained empire for himself—which is just what, if he is any good, he should be anxious to avoid. Each empire has its own perquisites, its own rights, its own privileges—its representation on national, regional and local committees, its remuneration scales, its established jobs at universities—of which it is naturally the jealous guardian. Medicine in such circumstances tends to get ossified. No single speciality is anxious to step down to make way for a newcomer, even when the evidence of the newcomer's importance is overwhelming. The tendency is simply to squeeze the newcomer in on the fringes of the already over-crowded syllabus; and as, say, the anatomists insist that the time already spent on anatomy should continue to be spent on anatomy, the syllabus simply grows.

The anatomists can readily find their justifications—that it is essential for every medical student to receive a thorough grounding in the basic elements of his subject—just as excuses can always be found for continuing to teach the Classics (and preserving professorships of Greek and Latin) on the grounds that they provide good training for the mind. In medicine, each department has its own excuses. Each has its list of past triumphs; each, its new research triumph just around the corner. Inevitably, curricula get overloaded; courses lengthen, until the student finds it increasingly difficult to take up a book on anything but medicine; and the chances that he will grow into a well-rounded personality, capable of understanding people as well as symptoms, become remote.

To a greater extent than is realized, too, this ossification is encouraged by the examination system. For examination purposes, it is an obvious advantage if answers to questions can be marked simply as right or wrong. The task of the historian marking essays is naturally more demanding than the task of the anatomist marking answers on, say, the location and function of certain muscles. In such circumstances anatomists naturally resist the intrusion of the unknown factor of stress. It is much easier to point to toxins or microbes and attribute to them, and to them exclusively, the origins of a disease, than to admit that their movements may be stimulated, or precipitated, by the environment or personality of the patient in whose body they are found.

Wittkower has summed up the position:

> "In the past teaching has been focused too exclusively on the *impersonal* aspect of medicine and not sufficiently on the *personal* and *interpersonal* aspects which can, and should, be subjected to scientific investigation and made an object of teaching. This development is hampered by (1) Medical school teaching which concentrates disproportionately on matters of interest to the 'specialized' teachers without due regard for the needs of patients or students; (2) the erroneous premises that organic pathology is *the* fundamental 'science of medicine', that diseases are best described by syndromes of signs and symptoms, and that they are due solely or primarily to specific disease agents; (3) the frequent construction of the curriculum and the allocation of teaching hours by private treaty between virtually independent departments whose decisions are sanctioned by forty or fifty years of tradition."

As Wittkower goes on to say, some medical schools have made changes; a few have tried to introduce students to sociology and anthropology; at his own university, McGill, the second-year course is designed to integrate biochemistry, physiology and anatomy; at Boston University, students serve as family physicians in their last two years, making visits, and taking home calls; and other universities have a variety of similar programmes designed to relate medicine to life. But progress in this direction is slow, and the majority of medical students who are qualifying remain wedded to the old ideas.

It is fair to point out that this is not something exclusive to medical schools; it tends to infect all teaching faculties. The reason *laissez faire* continued to be taken seriously as an economic doctrine long after it had been discredited by events was that it could so nearly pass itself off as a science; to this day there are professors who try to teach economics as if it *were* a science, because their minds are so conditioned to thinking of it in these terms that they cannot teach it any other way, and because of the enormous convenience, for teaching purposes, of a subject which can be expressed mathematically, in formulae and in graphs.

The parallel between the schools of economics and of medicine can be carried a step further. The fundamental weakness of the classical *laissez faire* case was that it did not take into account the significance of an outside force: public confidence. At certain times, in certain circumstances, business men will react to, say, a falling off in demand by pulling in their horns: this may lead to fewer orders being placed; lower production; less employment; and a recession. But in the same circumstances, at another time, the same business men will react differently: they will intensify their efforts to sell, attracting more buyers, encouraging them to place more orders, so that production and employment expand, and a minor boom follows. What leads business men to one decision rather than the other can loosely be called confidence, and confidence is partly the result of some as yet little understood emotional contagion.

In the same way, what keeps a man well, or makes him better rather than worse, is often an emotional contagion. He may sense, in some way, that he can get well, or that people want him to get well, or that the doctor believes the new drug is going to help him get well. But it is impossible to assess the effect of the contagion in academic terms, for examination purposes—a fact which has influenced even those teachers in the various departments who are aware of the existence of more things in the relationship of mind and body than were dreamed of in the old curriculum.

Sometimes these teachers excuse themselves by saying that the only reason that psychiatry is not given a more prominent place in the curriculum is that knowledge of it has not yet advanced to a point where it can safely be incorporated; or that the lack of such teaching is no real disadvantage, because the curriculum as it stands provides an excellent foundation on which the student can build after he is qualified. But such arguments are really rationalizations. They are put forward because the teachers, all except the best of them, fear new ideas. So in practice, whatever they may say in discussion, they tend to continue to teach medicine as they themselves were taught.

★

It is also true, as Shaw unkindly argued in the preface to *The Doctor's Dilemma,* that the profession has a vested interest in disease—particularly physical disease.

> "That any nation," he wrote, "having observed that you could provide for the supply of bread by giving bakers a pecuniary interest in baking for you, should go on to give a surgeon a pecuniary interest in cutting off your leg, is enough to make one despair of political humanity . . . I cannot knock my shins severely without forcing on some surgeon the difficult question 'Could I not make a better use of this pocketful of guineas than this man is making of his leg? Could he not write as well—or even better—on one leg than on two? And the guineas would make all the difference in the world to me just now. My wife—my pretty ones—the leg may mortify—it is always safer to operate—he will be well in a fortnight—artificial legs are now so well made that they are really better than natural ones—evolution is towards motors and leglessness, etc. etc. etc.' "

Although Shaw's shock treatment may have woken up a few people into a healthy reappraisal of medical ethics, it also scandalized many others who felt from their own experience that doctors are not so calculating. Shaw's ignorance of the unconscious mind, coupled with his own vested interests in simplifying actions and motives for dramatic purposes, made him regard people (or pretend that he so regarded them) as if everybody is always aware of what he is doing, and why. What Shaw said is all too often true; but not on a conscious level. Doctors work for their financial vested interest through the very simple and widespread mechanism of rationalization, which translates disreputable unconscious wishes into respectable moral terms.

It is only when war is declared between two medical departments that rationalization is sometimes thrown aside and the struggle for power enjoyed for its own sake—for within the profession, jealousies between different departments occasionally lead to situations where they fight for their own interest and power much as trade unions and employers do, hardly bothering, in the heat of the battle, to consider the result of the struggle on the profession as a whole, or on the community. But normally doctors rationalize their feelings into respectability. Either way, the departments which have less power and prestige find it extremely difficult to get funds, either from charities or from the state, even when their need is most pressing.

A further trend towards vested interest arises in medical research. One reason why the change-over from physical to psychological research has been so slow is that ossification has set in, just as it has in teaching and in medical practice. Where there is money to spend, it tends to get spent along familiar lines; especially on research which gives results—positive or negative—which can be expressed in quantitative terms. This is often attributed to commercial self-interest, and indeed that is part of the cause; some of the drug manufacturers who do research might lose business if it were found that their drugs would be replaced by psychotherapy. But the real reason is that physical research gives results which can be objectively measured, where psychological research gives results which for the most part can only be measured subjectively; doctors can feel that a patient is "better"—less neurotic—but they cannot prove it scientifically. Taxpayers not unnaturally want to have value for money for research, and they appear more likely to get it from a laboratory—with its white-coated workers and its test tubes, all busy doing something—than from the psychotherapist or social worker, going out and talking with people; not even telling them anything, just listening, most of the time. Even if the people feel better, afterwards, they do not always thank the psychotherapist; they may not even relate their improvement to her visits; they may think it is due to that new pill they took for the first time, or the tonic the doctor recommended.

Researchers, too, like other members of the profession, have their unconscious mind on their vested interest; the more they promise, the bigger the research grant is likely to be. No doubt the latest quest for a "supervaccine", now being publicized will be the next project to have millions lavished on it. Within a year or two the preliminary results ("extremely encouraging") will be released; and then, from time to time, fresh examples of its potential value for different diseases will be given, keeping the public appetite whetted; until in due course some even more spectacular project is ready to begin. It is difficult to condemn any individual project, especially as a few have been strikingly successful. All that can reasonably be said is that the law of diminishing returns appears to be in operation; in relation to the quantity of money being poured into physical research, its results are becoming meagre.

*

I have left consideration of the commonest, and probably the weightiest argument against the general acceptance of the stress theory of disease until now: that, even if it is accepted, knowledge of the subject is still in its infancy; to avoid errors it is probably best for the profession to continue to treat patients along orthodox lines, until there has been much more research, and until agreed methods of treatment have been worked out.

This is a plausible argument, particularly when supplemented by the assertion that the profession, after all, is doing a good job—the overwhelming majority of people who get ill are cured. But this would still be true even if doctors did nothing except see patients, admit some of them to hospital, get their temperatures taken, and give them placeboes. Most diseases wax and wane regardless of treatment; if they did not, the human race would have been killed off long before it reached the stage in its development when the first doctor qualified. In any case, going to a hospital—even going to the doctor, if he is comforting or confidence-instilling—can itself often be therapeutic. It relieves part of the patients' conscious worries, and it takes them out of the way of the stresses which may have contributed to the onset of their illness. Most cures, at least in the everyday illnesses, are mainly due to a combination of natural recovery and release from stress.

Why not, then—a doctor might reply—leave things that way? What is the point of upsetting patients by filling them up with a lot of newfangled ideas, some of which psychiatrists do not fully understand, and others about which they disagree among themselves? Why not wait until you have the whole thing cleared up and then present it for inspection?

Unfortunately medicine is not like that. It is a process of trial and error in which the public as a whole—not just selected volunteer guinea-pigs—has to be the subject. There is nothing shocking in the idea; or, if there is, it is a shock which, like road accidents, we have got so used to as to take it almost for granted. All drugs and medicines on the market, great and small, are in the long run tested on the public; the complaint is not that they are so tested but that though the great majority now turn out to be either outright failures, or no better than the outmoded drug which they replaced in medicine's fashion book, huge sums of money are annually lavished on them which could more profitably be diverted to other forms of research.

The public, not the profession, will have to make the decisive move. The profession can present treatments—drugs, sedatives, operations—for the public's favour and make them fashionable; but it cannot easily make them unfashionable again. What the public wants—tranquillizers, vaccines, operations—dictates what the public gets, to an extent which most members of the profession will privately admit is alarming. Little can be done, therefore, until the public grows accustomed to and interested in the stress theory of disease. And this is not simply a question of proving by experiments that disease may be emotionally induced. Many people who know this already still rush off for physical treatment whenever they think anything is the matter with them. The only way to wake people up to what is wrong with medical practice as it is today is to refute the argument that little harm follows from a failure to recognize the significance of stress; that the practice of medicine is really all right as it is.

It is very far from all right. Current medical practice is extremely wasteful of human productive capacity. Thousands of the world's best brains are being kept busily engaged wasting billions of the world's money on research up blind alleys, and on treatment unrelated to patients' needs; and people are actually being encouraged to make themselves ill, thereby causing themselves, their friends and their relations unnecessary trouble and expense.

If the basic theory is accepted—that disease can be caused or precipitated by stresses, of which the most difficult to deal with arise out of the unexplored conflicts of the unconscious mind—then to continue to conduct research and to treat patients as if disease had nothing to do with their emotional make-up, is in effect to perpetuate disease. Again: this is not to say that a man who understands and accepts the stress theory is always going to avoid illness; awareness of the existence of unconscious conflicts does not necessarily help us to solve them—it may even make it more difficult for us to do so, if it leads us to concentrate our attention too exclusively on ourselves. But it should help us to realize when we are unnecessarily ill: that is to say, when our symptoms have been provoked by stresses that we can without difficulty avoid, with the help of a little understanding. And it is also going to help the profession to stop sending hypochondriacs on the weary round of unnecessary and costly examinations, tests, prescriptions, operations, which now take up so much of its time.

If what is wrong with many people is not that they are ill but that they think they are ill (which no doctor would dispute), this is largely because people have had their attention constantly drawn to the symptoms of individual illnesses, rather than to the basic causes of illness in general. The risk that a little learning in medical lore may be a dangerous thing for the layman is notorious; the patient who reads a medical dictionary is apt, like "J" in Jerome's *Three Men in a Boat*, to rush round to his family doctor with the news that he has every illness in the book, bar housemaid's knee. J's doctor, knowing his man, was able to prescribe

> "1 lb. beefsteak with
> 1 pt. bitter beer, every six hours
> 1 ten mile walk every morning
> 1 bed at 11 sharp every night
> —And don't stuff your head up with
> things you don't understand"

but the doctor of today often does not know his patients so well; and he sends them on to a hospital where they are not known at all, and where time, money and effort are spent in attempting a physical diagnosis of illnesses which are really the result of emotional stress.

There is a deeper sense too, in which the preoccupation with physical symptoms, now shared by doctors and patients, is wasteful and dangerous. In many of the world's philosophies and religions, especially those of the East, a belief is inculcated that health is a condition of unawareness of the self—particularly of the physical self. Conversely, a person who is aware of his physical self is sick. This belief is fairly widely held, though in a different form, in the West; widely enough to have been used as an argument against the technique of Freudian psycho-analysis which, it was argued, would encourage people to become morbidly preoccupied with themselves (this was being unjust to Freud; in theory, at least, analysis was designed to liberate people from such self-preoccupation, by finding the reasons why they were plagued with neurotic symptoms; introspection, in so far as it was encouraged, was designed to perform the same function as a purge—to bring up the poisons festering down below).

It might be suggested that unawareness of the self is a negative concept of health. But it need not necessarily be so. On the contrary, many great athletes have agreed that their most notable achievements have been made possible because they have gone into a trance-like state, in which they have felt as if they have been liberated from their bodies. According to Arthur Guirdham:

> "Dr. Lovelock informed the writer that when he won the mile in the Olympic Games of 1936 he ran without any sense of rivalry but with a visual image in his mind of himself moving not as fast but as gracefully as he was able. He had, in fact, realized the principle enunciated by Coué that the imagination is stronger than the will. His personality was merged and lost in an artistic projection of his own capabilities. He ran, in fact, as an instrument of art rather than as an individual and achieved his greatest personal triumph when his personality was submerged in the impersonal reality of artistic expression."

Roger Bannister has also described how, when he ran the first under-four-minute mile, he felt as though his body were being drawn along, as it were, apart from him. Even in sports where no great physical stress is imposed, the same experience has been noted; coming off the 18th green at St. Andrews after winning the 1957 Open Golf Championship, Bobby Locke told a TV interviewer (unless I misheard him) that he attributed his return to form that year to his recovery of his trance-state of mind which he had lost, for a while.

The archery by which Japanese Buddhists introduce aspirants to the mysteries of "Zen" is an extension of this principle; for the novices are taught that the right art is aimless—that the more obstinately one tries to hit a target, the more difficulty one will find in hitting it. Eugen Herrigel, an American professor of philosophy who took a course in Zen archery, found that he was required to forget himself completely; he must not even be conscious of loosing the bow string; it must loose itself. The apparent improbability of such a method succeeding is less great than it may sound to a sceptical Westerner, when we consider how frequently our aim is accurate on occasions when accuracy has not been consciously striven for—in throwing, say, crumpled-up pieces of paper into a distant waste-paper basket. And most of us can recall occasions when we have been possessed by some capacity normally beyond us, some power which has momentarily taken us out of our humdrum selves, and given us intimations of a genius we did not know we possessed.

A further way in which current medical practice helps to create illness is by starting or encouraging fashions of treatment. The extent to which we are susceptible to suggestion, particularly when we are unconscious that any suggestion is being made to us, is only now being demonstrated by research into advertising techniques; but there can hardly be doubt that suggestibility has played a large part in creating fashions of illness. I have already mentioned what perhaps is the most striking example; the increased incidence of appendicitis following the operation on Edward VII. Guirdham, pointing out that the incidence is now again diminished, suggests that "the contagion of suggestion within the medical fraternity" played a part in creating the fashion, as it did again after the first world war, when it became fashionable to attribute all manner of symptoms and diseases to the absorption of toxins from the bowel. Patients have an extraordinary capacity to induce in themselves the symptoms of fashionable disorders; to this day it is not uncommon for a patient to get pains in the region of his appendix; his doctor, suspecting there is nothing really wrong, dismisses it lightly as "grumbling"; but in time the patient becomes dissatisfied, and practically demands to have his appendix removed; and removed it is.

But very often there is no specific symptom of this kind. Rather, there are several symptoms: aches, feelings of lassitude, or worry, or irritability; constipation, perhaps—and a general feeling of unwellness—the syndrome of just being sick. To convert this negative unwellness into a positive disease, the sufferer goes to a doctor; and Balint has described what then happens:

> "When a patient comes to his doctor complaining—I leave the verb intentionally without an object—his attitude towards illness is still unorganized. What will happen in the future is determined partly by the nature of the illness, but partly—and especially so in chronic conditions—also by the doctor. What usually happens may be described as follows: the patient offers various symptoms to his doctor; the doctor, on the basis of his knowledge, experience and diagnostic skill, decides which of the symptoms should be taken seriously, and be treated, and which not. The 'illness' to which the patient and the doctor settle down is thus a compromise, acceptable to both. . . . The present state of medicine, with its emphasis on organic diagnosis and the corresponding neglect of psychological factors, prompts the doctor to organize illness around anatomical, or at least physiological—that is, around some concrete—pathology."

In other words, the patient is actively encouraged to regard the cause of his illness as physical; and in time this helps to make it chronic. A man with stomach trouble arising out of some emotional stress should, if the emotional stress is correctly treated, lose the stomach trouble. But if it is merely the stomach trouble that is treated, rather than the emotional stress, not only will he not be cured (though his symptoms may be relieved) but he will be encouraged to think of himself as a stomach-trouble-sufferer. And his very concentration on his symptoms may exacerbate them, as it did in the case of the woman patient "Mrs. D." in Balint's case history. As a result of her faulty treatment, Mrs. D. began to have an exaggerated awareness of her bowels: the awkward question arises, Balint says, "how much of this 'exaggerated awareness' is due to her intrinsic illness, and how much to her doctor's efforts . . . hospital surgeons performed four operations on Mrs. D.—all successfully—and so they closed her case, proudly improving their statistics. But what about the general practitioners? They had to go on attending Mrs. D., still suffering from exactly the same complaints as before or between the operations."

This is how much of the wastage of the present system arises. General practitioners are continually complaining of the amount of their time (and the public's money) that has to be spent on people they regard as hypochondriacs or neurotics—either people who think they are ill and are not, or people who are ill, but whose illness has no organic basis. But the time and money is spent mainly because these people have become accustomed to receive wrong—physical—treatment from their doctors.

Finally, it should be realized that there is a strong presumption, though as yet it is no more than that, that unresolved emotional conflicts may be partly responsible for certain destructive and killing forms of disease. To the extent that cancer is in time revealed to be a stress disorder, the work that has gone into the search for a physical cause will, in so far as it distracted attention and funds from research into stress, have been indirectly responsible for prolonging the ravages of the disease, and for allowing the deaths of people who, if the nature of the relationship between stress and cancer had been examined and discovered sooner, might have found how to live.

★

The present system, then, is bad for the patient. It is also bad for the profession. Even if the great majority of doctors restrain themselves from taking advantage of patients' infinite credulity on medical matters, it is certainly true that the present methods give every encouragement to dubious practices within the profession.

I have mentioned some of them: how many of the appendixes that have been removed in the last fifty years needed to be removed? In medical circles there are plenty of doctors—and many more nurses—who will jest that it is almost a matter of surprise when an operation reveals that an operation was really necessary. Some doctors hold that to remove tonsils is usually not only unnecessary but positively dangerous (in that they are sentry at the body's gate, whose job it is to give the alarm when something goes wrong; to remove them when the alarm sounds—except in serious cases—is as absurd as it would have been to shoot the geese who saved the Capitol, for disturbing citizens' sleep); yet tonsils are removed annually by the thousand.

Another disturbing sign is the growth of certain medical establishments, private hospitals and nursing homes, which scarcely bother to make even the pretence that they are anything but glorified medical hotels; their chief object being to profit from anybody who is rich enough and foolish enough to enter them. A friend of mine who went to one of them to have all his teeth taken out (because, unfortunate man, he fell into the clutches of a doctor who happened still to believe in that branch of the discredited auto-intoxication theory), was approached while still bemused after the operation, and almost persuaded to have his "slipped disc" operated on—he had complained of backache—while he was there; and it was only later that he discovered that the two doctors concerned were relatives.

Many other faults arising out of the present system need to be corrected; among them the wasteful system by which hospital beds are allotted to the various specialists, each feeling bound to take up his quota; the growing cost of routine physical tests to cover doctors against every legal eventuality, in case an action is taken against them for negligence; and the tendency to put people who are diagnosed as neurotics in hospital for observation and reassurance, thereby cosseting their neuroses, and often making it more difficult to help them. The cost to the community cannot be measured; it cannot even be guessed.

These things are incidental: the real damage is in the suffering created by a system which not merely offers mistaken treatment for disease, but creates more disease by doing so. The medical profession, as at present constituted, works like a gardener who mows a field of weeds, and then leaves them lying; the roots still in the ground, the seed free to be borne away on the wind, to bring more suffering later.

★

To be fair to the profession, its present difficult situation arises largely owing to the very success with which it converted the public to the physical theory of disease. It is now faced with patients who rely on drugs; a public mistrustful of psychotherapy. Many a doctor who would genuinely like to see the last of some of his patients, either because he is convinced there is nothing wrong with them or because he thinks they are neurotic, dare not recommend psychotherapy for fear of angering them.

The public's attitude to illnesses of the mind and of the emotions is largely compounded of ignorance and fear. "Mental" or "mad" still have an ugly sound; people who find it a matter for boasting if they have to go into a general hospital for an operation do their best to keep it quiet if they or any of their family have to go into a mental home. A suggestion that they ought to see a psychiatrist or psychotherapist still often carries to them the implication that they may be going mad. Still more unfortunate—it is probably the greatest single bar to a wider understanding of the nature of illness—is the popular use of the phrase "it's all psychological" or "it's psychosomatic" as a synonym for "he only imagines he is ill"—that he is a hypochondriac, or a neurotic. In such cases the general feeling is that if the patient is not aware that the illness is only in his imagination he ought to be made aware of it. Some doctors actually make a practice of telling a neurotic patient there is nothing the matter with him; they may even make a reputation for themselves as good, no-nonsense men, which is sufficient to compensate for the loss of any patient who leaves because he resents the implication that he is not really ill. But most doctors, either because they are reluctant to lose patients, or because they fear there may turn out to be some organic or "real" disorder, continue to try every variety of physical treatment, as well as tranquillizers and placeboes, rather than tell patients that it is their personalities which are sick.

2

PSYCHIATRY

Where a patient, or his doctor, finally becomes convinced that his symptoms do not arise from any physical cause, and where the symptoms are sufficiently unpleasant to require treatment, he is normally sent to a psychiatrist.

It is as well to understand, at this point, what the term "psychiatrist" does and does not mean. A psychiatrist is a qualified doctor; he has specialized in mental illness by working in a mental hospital, after qualification—though he may practice as a psychiatrist without having done so, and many a doctor has established fame and fortune for himself without formal instruction in the art. In any case, the specialist course in psychiatry is largely neurological in emphasis; it concentrates heavily on physical aspects of the brain, rather than on the mind. Not infrequently psychiatrists pay no more attention to their patients as individuals than other specialists do. The popular impression of the psychiatrist as a man who spends all day at the head of a couch, listening to people babbling about their early sex lives, is ludicrously wide of the mark; many psychiatrists pay little attention to Freudian techniques, and many actively dislike them (I met one in Louisville, Ky., whose room in the local hospital was festooned with pictures of celebrities in the psychiatric field: one was turned face to the wall—Freud).

The confusion is understandable, because most psychoanalysts—that is to say, men who practice the Freudian technique—are, strictly speaking, psychiatrists. They do not normally refer to themselves by that name; in England, when they use it, they tend to give it a sarcastic or reproachful connotation, as referring to men whose methods they consider retrograde; and for clarity's sake I propose in this section to discuss psychiatry in its physical sense.

For many years psychiatry was the dead end of the medical profession. It meant little more than police work, administering lunatic asylums. Little could be done to help patients. But recently there has been a marked change. This was partly due to the discovery (made long ago, but it took a long time to sink in) that insanity is caused, increased and prolonged by locking people up in wards, and confining them in strait jackets. When the open door system was first tried, staffs were horrified, but it has since abundantly justified itself, and most of the violence which used to be associated with insanity is avoided. The use of sedatives and tranquillizers has also helped.

But in addition to this change of attitude to the insane, another revolution has taken place in treatment: with the use of drugs, electro-convulsive therapy, and brain operations.

As I have already said, the use of physical treatments has a long history. Trepanning—the removal of part of the skull in order to relieve pressure on the brain—is of very ancient origin; so is the whipping or ducking of lunatics. Such treatment was based on results, not on reasoning; and it still is, at least in the case of electric shock. Many explanations have been put forward to account for it, but the real reason it is used is simply because, in certain cases, it has been found to bring relief. Even ducking, in a slightly different form, has been reintroduced, in experiments designed to test the effects on patients of sudden immersion in cold water.

Other treatments which have come into vogue consist of putting the patient into a coma, by insulin or other means; inducing him to "act out" his past terrors by questioning while he is under the effect of certain drugs; and operations on the brain. All these have been reported upon enthusiastically, at various times; all have proved disappointing as treatment in the long term.

It is impossible at this stage to strike a just balance between protagonists and critics, because judgement of the results has been so subjective: whether a neurotic is less neurotic is a matter of opinion, and in any case, it is not usually possible to tell whether he really is better, or whether his symptoms have been shifted elsewhere. What is certain, though, is that the original techniques produced some dangerous side effects. Many of those which were enthusiastically praised when they were first tried are now discredited—among them, insulin coma treatment. Some psychiatrists now mistrust electric shocks; and according to a speaker at the second international congress for Psychiatry in Zürich, the brain operation of lobotomy has been discredited in the case of one disease for which it was originally acclaimed—schizophrenia. Over the past fifteen years, he said, a study of 120 selected patients had shown that the 60 who underwent lobotomies were no better off than the 60 who did not.

Still, such methods have given some good results; and the latest to enter the field has perhaps been the most promising of all: the use of energizing drugs, which appear to be able to reawaken patients who before have been beyond the reach of any treatment. As a result the physical school is back in the ascendant; there are even psychiatrists who believe that in time all serious mental illness will be traceable to chemical and physical changes in the brain; and that these can then be reversed by the use of the appropriate drugs. Tranquillizers, too, have come to be regarded as treatment, not merely as a means to curb or quieten difficult mental patients. Psychotherapy is at a discount; something of the kind, it is conceded, may be necessary to help patients back to normal life after they have been cured by drugs or shocks or operations; but it is not, or not usually, to be regarded as an integral part of the cure.

There is no doubt that physical causes can create mental disturbance—not always unpleasantly, as the recent fashion for taking Mescalin has shown. In a self-confessedly biographical novel, *The Ordeal of Gilbert Pinfold,* Evelyn Waugh has described some of the hair-raising effects of miscalculation in the use of drugs—the drugs may not have been solely responsible, but obviously his consumption of them had some connection with hallucinatory experiences. A substantial proportion of the population of a French village went insane a few years ago, when the flour from which their bread was baked was contaminated with ergot; and a British Member of Parliament, Dr. Donald Johnson, has described in a book his experiences during temporary insanity due, he thinks, to poisoning of this nature.

But in such cases the source of the poison can be traced, or at least suspected; in most insanity there is no apparent reason why the brain should begin to degenerate; why its chemical composition should alter. Where organic changes are found, they are not necessarily the cause of insanity; they may be only a link in the causal chain, in the same way that the change in the texture of a man's stomach membrane, caused by alarm, may be a link in the causal chain leading to an ulcer. All that can be said is that though psychiatric states are related to physical states, the brain's chemical and electrical system presumably reflects personality changes, as well as creating them; the two elements, physical and psychological, should not be considered as cause and effect.

This is why the present emphasis on research and practice into physical psychiatry is a retrograde trend. In a sane appraisal of tranquillizers published recently in *Harper's Magazine*, Dr. Ian Stevenson points out that the value of the drugs is that they "suppress emotional resonance, as it were, rather in the manner of a piano's damper"; but this does not mean that they are enough in themselves:

> "Proponents of the physical approach to mental illness at first celebrated the introduction of these drugs as a confirmation of their point of view. But this was premature. They should have delayed the festivities. The word 'cure' ought to have no place in our praise of tranquillizers. A long sequence of causes underlies all mental illness. The tranquillizers interrupt one of the mechanisms in the production of symptoms, a rather late link in the causal chain. But they can do nothing to alter the more ulterior causes which have started and

sustained the stresses which strain the patient . . . tranquillizers will never replace psychotherapeutic experiences. They only make psychotherapy more feasible. And also more urgent."

This is not by any means exclusively a Freudian viewpoint; it is shared by many other workers in mental hospitals. Just before I began to write on this subject I was sent a copy of Paul de Kruif's *A Man Against Insanity*, a biographical study of the psychiatrist Jack Ferguson. I had long regarded de Kruif as one of the more regrettable products of machine-made American literature: the man who perhaps more than anybody else has helped to condition the public into belief in wonder-druggery. But this book was out of the ordinary run; still too slick for comfort, but written with the feeling of a man who has himself (as he explains in the course of it) been on the edge of mental breakdown. And the career he describes is extremely interesting, and moving.

Ferguson did not become a doctor until approaching middle age; and the effort took so much out of him that he became insane. His experiences as a patient in various mental hospitals around America started off an interest in psychiatry; and he explored and developed many of the physical methods then becoming fashionable—electric shock treatment, brain operations, and drug abreaction. Though essentially a Pavlovian, he gradually found himself being compelled to realize that psychological ingredients were necessary in treatment: that the patient's co-operation had to be won. This led him in time, when he found his patients were frightened of it, to abandon electric shock treatment: "it must do something bad to them, he thought, inside their heads". He grew critical, too, of brain operations; finding that although the cutting away of certain brain fibres may prevent the patient from becoming progressively demoralized, it also tends to destroy his morale—his character. Instead, Ferguson switched to what were then the new neurochemicals, and with these he had some spectacular results. But again, some ingredient was missing; and this, he eventually decided, was "tender loving care". His work, his treatments, his drugs all went for nothing, he saw, unless his staff realized that the new medicines alone were nothing much—"they only start up a mental awakening. By themselves they can't carry the patients along. The nurse attendants have got to pour in the confidence—they've got to wipe out the fear".

Partly this means that the attendants have got to assist in a Pavlovian process of reconditioning, helping patients to achieve the social habits necessary for life in a civilized community. But something more is required than mere reconditioning; somehow, the patients have to be made to realize that there is affection and love awaiting them not merely in the hospital, but in the world outside. Nine out of ten relapses, according to Ferguson, are due not to recurrence of mental illness but to inadequate provision of proper treatment and surroundings for discharged patients, or lack of love and care on the part of the relatives to whom they return.

The present hostility between the physical and the psychotherapeutic schools, then, is unnecessary; both have their part to play. There is no reason why, say, the study of the electrical activity in the brain, from which much is expected, should not be continued, giving us more knowledge of how chemical, electrical, and emotional activity interact—knowledge which can be used in treatment. But there are other convincing arguments against paying exclusive attention to physical treatment, particularly surgery, which should not be ignored; and one of them was expressed by Robert Lindner, in *The Fifty Minute Hour*, explaining why he refused to give it:

> "This I could not do, not only because I was then and still am reluctant to admit defeat until every possible therapeutic avenue has been explored, but because I could not conscientiously expose this patient (or, indeed, any other) either to the experience of such treatment, or to its possible negative effects. I am one of the more vocal antagonists of such 'heroic' measures as convulsive 'therapy' and the psychosurgical methods, believing most sincerely that they violate

every progressive canon of therapy, and convinced they do more harm than good, either immediately or in the long run. It seems to me the height of absurdity to blast or cut the very portion of the brain upon which both the individual's and the species' welfare depends, to say nothing of the fact that all our evidence points to the temporary nature of the cures achieved and the irreversible damage done to the personality thus treated . . . I could not, if there was any way to prevent it, consign him to the new kind of vegetable kingdom being created by so many of my well-intentioned colleagues."

Another argument is not so much against physical methods, as against their indiscriminate use. Ferguson abandoned shock treatment when he found patients were frightened of it; but not nearly enough research has been done into the relationship between the effects of such treatments and the patients' feelings about them. I was much struck by a letter I received following a review I wrote of Sargant's *Battle for the Mind*, in which I criticized the author's easy assumption that criminals might be reconditioned into good citizens by physical treatment of their brains. My correspondent had, she said, just been given electric shock treatment for depression, with good results. It affected her memory, she found, but this was more than compensated for by the fact, that "I found laughter coming to me quite easily again. At one time I had almost forgotten how to laugh. Music began to have meaning for me once more; and I found myself for the first time for several years really wanting to paint." She was favourably impressed by the treatment, but she added two qualifications. "I have thought a good deal about my experience. Such conclusions as I have come to are in no way original; but based, as they are, on purely personal reactions, they may be of some general interest. I feel sure that to accept the treatment voluntarily is a vital contribution to its success . . . and the treatment that one receives from the hospital staff plays an enormous part in, so to speak, conditioning one to receive the shock." In the letters that came in at the time from people who had had shock treatment—some in favour, some against—this was a point that was made sufficiently frequently to suggest it is becoming more widely known; that where treatment is ordered by a doctor without the patient's willing co-operation, it can later become a focus for resentment, and lead to the deterioration of the patient's prospects of recovery.

The chief argument against the physical approach to psychiatry, though, is that it still concerns itself too much—as does ordinary medical practice—with symptoms, rather than with the needs of the patient. This is not always the psychiatrists' fault; they are compelled by circumstances to deal with patients whom they do not know, and have no time to get to know; the tendency is inevitably to apply whatever type of physical treatment has proved, or they believe has proved, satisfactory with similar symptoms in the past. Although many psychiatrists have a knowledge of, and an interest in, non-physical methods of treatment, and although many of them are aware of the way mind and body react in creating symptoms, both physical and emotional, few of them, even if they want to, can find the time to apply their knowledge in individual cases; and that is why psychiatry, as at present generally practised, is of little value in treatment of stress disorders.

3

PAVLOV'S WAY

WHILE dealing with neurosis I referred to the school of thought which has grown out of Pavlovian and Behaviourist teaching; and though, for some reason, it has not attracted as wide attention as it deserves, it may secure more adherents among doctors when they understand it better, as it reflects an attitude of mind to neuroses which is quite compatible with their own. It also provides an apparently feasible alternative to the Freudian theory—which the profession is certain to welcome.

In his book, *The Dynamics of Anxiety and Hysteria*, H. J. Eysenck sums up the differences between the two schools of thought:

> "according to Freud, there is a 'disease' which produces symptoms; cure the disease, and the symptoms will vanish. According to the alternative view, there is no disease, there are merely wrong habits which have been learned and must be unlearned".

Eysenck goes on to quote evidence of the cure of symptoms of bed-wetting, writer's cramp, alcoholism, stammering and tics —symptoms which are fairly definite, so that whether they are removed can be established without reasonable doubt. He goes further, and claims that tests have shown not merely that the conditioning method can cure symptoms, but that they can improve the general health of the patient, without leading to any kind of "symptom substitution"—a patient cured of bed-wetting by conditioning does not necessarily develop a stammer or a tic.

Pavlovians have no basic quarrel with physical psychiatry; they merely complain that electric shock treatment and brain operations have been rushed into practice without their value being demonstrated in a fashion acceptable to the statistician, by experiments conducted on a rigorously scientific basis, with controls. With the Freudians, however, they wage a more vigorous polemical warfare, their argument being not so much that the Freudian thesis is wrong as that it is "notional", not susceptible of proof; whereas their own conditioning methods are.

Take the case of bed-wetting in children. The Freudian treats it as a symptom of some unresolved unconscious conflict, whose origin needs to be uncovered if the conflict is to be resolved; the Pavlovian argues that even if the origin of the conflict can be traced to emotional stress, continued bed-wetting is usually simply a continuance of a habit, and all that is required in most cases is to change the habit. "Psychological treatment", Eysenck explains:

> "follows the simple Pavlovian paradigm of conditioning. The child is provided with a quilted blanket embedded in which are electric leads connected with a strong battery and a bell. This blanket is put underneath the child; when he begins to urinate, the blanket is quickly saturated and the fluid makes electric contacts which complete the circuit, and cause the bell to ring. The child wakes up, ceases to urinate, and toddles off to the toilet to finish his uncompleted business. This is repeated a number of times and . . . through the repeated pairing of strong bladder pressure and the ringing of the bell . . . the child is conditioned to wake up to the experience of the expanded bladder".

The great majority of bed-wetting cases, the Pavlovians claim, are abolished quickly, safely, and finally by this conditioning technique; and its use is now fairly widespread in America, where the quilted blanket is marketed under brand names.

If the Pavlovian interpretation of neurosis is correct, conditioning certainly offers the simplest form of treatment. And it is not improbable that habits are often learned in time of stress, which cannot so easily be got rid of when the stress is past. If shock can turn a man's hair grey overnight (this has been disputed, but most of us have had experience of shock disintegrating, at least temporarily, a person's appearance) it is not surprising that shock can create a neurotic habit which the patient cannot shed, any more than he can alter the contours of his face or the colour of his hair, simply by wanting to; and such a habit should be treatable by conditioning, if the appropriate technique can be found. But my own feeling, and I have no evidence but hunch on which to back it, is that the Pavlovian theory will be found to be of value only in this type of case; and that the Freudian theory, though perhaps wrong in details, will be found to be nearer the truth in most serious neuroses, and in illness in general.

To begin with, the idea that, say, facial twitches are learned habits which can be unlearned without reference to what causes them does not accord with my observation of people who suffer from them. A business man of my acquaintance occasionally has a movement of his nose which is half sniff, half twitch. He was unaware of it until he began to notice that his secretary, of whom he had previously had a poor opinion, had suddenly grown much more tactful; she seemed to be able to sense when he was in difficulties, particularly over rows with his managing director (which were not infrequent), and to offer him the consolation he needed at those times. With some skill she kept from him the reason for her improved performance; it was simply that she had noticed that his twitch always came at these difficult times.

On the Pavlovian thesis, his twitch might be a hangover from some early experiences; in fact Pavlov and Freud might here have joined hands and traced it to a reaction begun out of fear of his father. But the important thing (as the secretary grasped, even if the business man didn't) was not the twitch, but the fact that he allowed himself to get into a state when dealing with his boss: a feeling of inferiority and repressed hostility which was bad for him as a person, and bad for his prospects as an employee; the boss traded on his inferiority. To remove the symptom without trying to find, and if possible banish, the reasons for the inferiority and hostility would obviously be foolish.

Conditioning, too, has an obvious danger. To cure a patient of something by conditioning is—as can be seen in much Pavlovian literature—only a short step from conditioning a person *to* something: perhaps to a person who is more acceptable to his masters, to his family, or his neighbours. Brainwashing is a form of conditioning of this kind. And the danger lies not simply in that psychiatrists, or the men they serve, sometimes have unpleasant ideas of the aims of conditioning: it lies also in the deprivation of a symptom which may represent the fulfilment of a need for the patient (if the Freudian theory turns out to be right, after all); or which may be a sign that something is wrong which ought to be put right—a sign of a rebellion within the personality which may need to be encouraged, if the patient is to be set on the path to health again.

The most startling evidence yet provided of the need to tread warily in dealing with neurosis is the extraordinary case history related by two doctors, Corbett Thigpen and Hervey Cleckley, and later adapted into a book (and a film) with the title *The Three Faces of Eve*.

The story seemed barely credible. A depressed, harassed-looking woman came to an Augusta, Ga., clinic for psychiatric treatment, complaining of headaches; and eventually the psychiatrists discovered that she was a dual personality—split not in the usual schizophrenic pattern, but more on the model of Jekyll and Hyde. Jekyll—Mrs. Eve White, a dutiful if resentful wife and mother—was wholly unaware of the goings-on in local nightclubs of her other self, Eve Black—a psychopath. Eve Black, on the other hand, was aware of her second self; she despised the meek, downtrodden White, and occasionally deliberately made mischief for her—though, with a psychopath's craft, Black avoided making White's life utterly impossible, or both of them would have been locked up.

Significantly, there were many physical indications of the difference between White and Black. The doctors were amazed at the change in appearance when Black emerged; her posture, her movements, her walk, her look, were all completely altered; and it was White who suffered from the headaches, the depressions. A curious detail was that Black, rather than White, was allergic to nylon; when wearing nylon stockings she suffered from itching. A more detailed physical study might have shown many more discrepancies of this kind.

The White/Black case was very far from being an isolated phenomenon. Instances of dual personality—apart from schizophrenia—have been reported many times, and in many parts of the world. Some are relatively uncomplicated, as when people suffer from fits of loss of memory, and lose touch, for a while, with their old identities; the episodes are usually regarded and treated as if they represented a momentary aberration. Others are more spectacular, like the case William James related of Ansel Bourne, who led a totally different life in a different place for a couple of months before waking up with a fright, unable to recall how he had come to be in his new surroundings. "Dissociation" is extremely common in some primitive societies, where the capacity of men and women to lose hold of their identities and go into various trance states is part of standard religious procedures. What was strange about Eve White was the improbability that anybody so ordinary as her should lead so extraordinary a double life; and the fact that her evil genie Black could not be pushed back into the bottle; Black kept on mischievously emerging.

Confronted by this phenomenon the psychiatrists, not unnaturally, had little idea what to do about it; and fortunately they did what in the circumstances was the best they could have done: nothing. That is, nothing drastic. They gave the patient(s) somewhere to discuss her problems without fear; they did not try out a battery of violent "cures"; they waited, in the hope that something would eventually emerge. It did: a third personality, separate from both Black and White, but watching over both of them with interest and sympathy. The third party did not represent the woman's final personality (she turned out to be, literally, too good to be true) but she provided a bridge across which the other two joined hands to form a fourth and, the doctors hoped, a final, stabilized personality.

As things transpired, they were wrong; Eve's troubles were not over, and according to newspaper reports she underwent yet another change of personality some years afterwards. But the failure to solve her personality problem is of less importance than the evidence accumulated in the attempts to solve it; and here, the doctor's own tentative explanation is interesting:

> "Let us compare the minor and isolated symptoms of neurosis to the various disturbances of the peace that occur continually throughout a nation, but are kept in check by the police. So, too, we might find an analogy between the schizophrenic psychosis and a violent rebellion by anarchists who without definite purpose destroy a civilization and leave it in chaos. Let us consider another sort of revolt, that of an organized conspiracy by a vast secret party with carefully devised aims and plans of its own. If such a party becomes strong enough before its existence is suspected, and suddenly rises and over-throws the existing government, we may here find a good analogy to the development of dual personality."

The analogy is admirable, in its indication how and why the personality may not necessarily be identical with the person. Most of us have come across casual examples, like the gentle, kindly fellow who becomes maniacal in drink; but it is also true in a deeper, and alarming sense. Our cards of identity may have been stacked against us by circumstance: the personality which has emerged may merely be the one which happened to secure control of our police and their weapons (conscience, habit) at an impressionable age—its police having sat firmly on revolutionary activity by the other, perhaps the real personality, ever since.

Yet a revolution may have been desirable—as it was in this case. It was an extremely fortunate chance for Eve that her doctors were not tied to any psychiatric party line. They make some entertaining comments on the way the case could have been twisted into making a textbook example of whatever theory the psychiatrist had happened to believe. Any of a number of different treatments could have been used—brain operations, drugs, spiritualism or multifarious forms of "healing"—and any of them might have worked, in the sense of enabling White to reorganize her police forces and stamp out the Black revolutionaries. Victory won, the case would have been noted up as "cured". That there was another, more worth-while personality trying to emerge would never have been suspected.

The Three Faces of Eve is not merely a remarkable case history in its own right. It is also a thumping denunciation of much current psychiatric practice, with its emphasis on symptoms, rather than on the emotional problems which give rise to them. Symptoms, both mental and physical, express a need: they may have to be encouraged, in certain circumstances, rather than "cured", if the patient is really to be helped. Lindner once described a case where he actually joined in a psychotic's fantasy life, in the belief (subsequently justified) that it would be easier to make contact with him there than in reality. Orthodox and Pavlovian psychiatry, with their concentration on symptom removing, and their habit of marking up cases where symptoms are successfully removed as cures, are dangerous in such circumstances; so, also, may be psychotherapy, if it seeks to equate cures with successful adaptation to environment. Either method might have succeeded in making Eve White remain Eve White; but it would have been a sad day for her if either had.

4

FREUD'S WAY

THERE are a number of different analytical schools; and even the Freudians, the largest and best known, are by no means united. That there should be differences of opinion is a healthy sign—there would be good grounds for suspicion if complete uniformity prevailed; but the animosity with which their quarrels are conducted is often disagreeable. Freud himself was partly to blame: the good humour with which he fought his detractors from other camps broke down when he had to deal with rebels in his own: Adler and Jung.

I do not propose to go into the differences here. Adler, as I have said, may have had a better notion of psychosomatic medicine than Freud; and Jung's more glamorous notions about the unconscious mind (in Freudian hands it tended almost to be regarded as a ragbag of repressions: Jung is more interested in it as a repository of the wisdom of the ages) may turn out not to have exaggerated the mind's potential. For simplicity, though, I am going to confine myself to the Freudian technique of analysis; and this, rather cursorily, for reasons I shall come to in a moment.

The assumption on which the technique of psychoanalysis rests is that man in his normal, adult state is an emotionally mature and healthy being; if he is not, it is either because he is suffering from external and often identifiable strains—the thousand and one trials that we have to contend with in life; or because he is suffering from some internal emotional disturbance of whose nature and origins he is ignorant, because it is repressed.

The more progress that is made in the elimination and modification of externally-induced illnesses, the greater becomes the need to devote attention to this internal enemy; conflict within the personality. Two methods can be used: either an attempt can be made to find out the reason for the disturbance—to discover what is being repressed, and why, in order to release the pent-up emotion; or, search for causes can be called off as unprofitable, and treatment concentrated on enabling the patient to "live with" his difficulties. This is not materially different from the principle on which treatment is based in most physical illnesses: doctors ask themselves, shall we operate, and remove the cause of the stomach trouble? Or, shall we put the patient on a diet so that even though the cause may remain, he will not suffer pain?

Obviously the first method—the discovery and removal of the causes—is, other things being equal, the more satisfactory. But before Freud, nobody had been able to suggest a way of treatment which might enable the causes of neurosis to be found. Many cures had been claimed for faith healing, and for other methods, but none of them had been explained on rational grounds. Freud offered an explanation not merely of how his new method—analysis—worked, but of why it worked. He owed this explanation, he said, to his friend Joseph Breuer, who had made the highly significant discovery that in the case of hysterical phobias and obsessions an understanding of how they had arisen was in itself treatment: as soon as the patient realized the origin of his symptoms, the symptoms began to disappear. The difficulty, however, remained: how to get patients to discover and understand the symptoms' origins. It was for this purpose that Freud evolved the technique which is known as psychoanalysis.

The technique is probably more easily explained by reading actual case histories, such as those given by Lindner in his *Fifty-Minute Hour*, than by attempts to describe the theory. Suffice to say here that Freud found that by getting neurotic or hysterical patients to eliminate the critical spirit in which they normally viewed the thoughts floating up to the surface of consciousness—by persuading them to prattle on, saying whatever came into their heads and suppressing nothing, no matter how irrelevant or nonsensical it might seem—he could get them to recall much of what they had forgotten; memories, perhaps, of intense desires felt as children, but banished altogether from consciousness, because they gave rise to painful feelings of guilt. And with the rediscovery of the repressed desires, which in the light of adult knowledge were revealed to be harmless, a great weight of guilt was lifted; phobias and obsessions vanished because the emotional pressure of which they had been the symptoms was no longer being kept stifled by repression, but could release itself, through feeling, in the way emotion normally releases itself.

People often find it hard to credit that the free association method, which sounds rather silly, should give results. It has been made the target of a great number of jokes, of which one of the commonest would surely have delighted Freud, so comical a piece of evidence is it in favour of his theories. The joke appears in a variety of forms, but usually in connection with some of the words used by psychologists in certain free association tests, where the patient has to say what each word brings to his mind. To the word "banana" most patients say "fruit" or "shop" or "tropical"; but one patient says "women". 'Ah,' says the psychologist, waking up; 'that is very interesting indeed. Now, why does a banana make you think of women?' 'Because,' says the patient, 'everything makes me think of women.'

"Precisely!" Freud might have said.

The value of the free association method—which can be used either through such formalized tests, or by getting the patient to ramble on on his own—is that it can break through the censorship barrier which stands between most of us and our unconscious minds. The barrier, Freud held, is actually broken through more frequently than we realize, not merely in dreams (if we can interpret them), but in everyday life—for example, in slips of the tongue. The frequency with which some people say the precise opposite of what they meant to say—something hurtful, instead of an intended compliment—suggests that repressed feeling is always on the look-out for a chance to escape by making us say, or do, what it would like us to say, or do, if it were not repressed—if the censor did not stop us from knowing what it wants. The free association method is designed to provide it with a chance to escape, by taking away the censor's power to intervene.

That the method is not more successful is due partly to the censor's vigilance, partly to our resistance to the whole project. It is difficult to compute the extent of our determination not to find out what is the matter with us, because it is rarely conscious —and, in so far as we are conscious of it, we put up rationalizations to justify it. That we should resist exploration of our minds is understandable; the whole point of repression in the first place was to spare ourselves from conflicts which threatened to overwhelm us, so it is not surprising that we should fight any attempt to revive the memory of the conflicts (as we do not know what they were about, we cannot realize how unnecessary they were, and how trivial they may seem on examination). So we cling to our repressions; part of ourselves remains cut off, and fails to develop.

The object of analysis might be said to be assisting people to grow up—to become their complete selves. Its object is not the assisting of people to become what somebody—their doctor; their society; Big Brother—thinks they ought to be. Whether the final fusion of "Eve" into a new unified personality would have occurred under analysis is impossible to tell, but at least it would have been her analyst's object to help her towards such a solution; not to iron out her symptoms by "conditioning", or to persuade her to "live with" her neurosis, and conform to the demands of her environment, as represented by husband, home and family life. Analysis aims to help people realize their full personalities; and it works on the assumption that people fail to realize them not because of any fundamental moral or emotional weakness, but because they have failed to grow up emotionally, in some way; part of their personality has been retarded by the existence of repressions which have prevented them from experiencing feeling in the way a normal human being should.

The success of analysis, in fact, does not depend on the individual's intellectual discovery of what he has repressed, but on his feeling the feelings which have been repressed; feelings whose existence he has not even suspected, and would hotly have denied had anybody accused him of having them. As Carl Rogers puts it in his essay on "Client-centred Therapy":

> "the client experiences, clearly and in awareness, some hitherto denied emotional facets of life. It seems as though for the moment he *is* his fear, or his anger, or his tenderness, or whatever. He is experiencing this particular feeling without any defensive barriers, exactly as it is occurring in his organism . . . The feelings are not all negative: a father comes to the point where he suddenly realizes that love for his children is not an obligatory attitude that he must possess, but is a spontaneous, surging, tender feeling in him which he has never dared to recognise, because it seemed unmanly. He sits quietly with tears in his eyes while this feeling flows through him".

The mystical experience which some people feel at the time when they are converted to acceptance of a new religious faith may be a way of spontaneously achieving some of the results of a successful analysis; before his God, possibly, the newcomer is able to hurl down all his defences—among them, though he is not aware of it, repressions—and out flows the feeling, transmuted into love. The cure is not always so lasting, though, as successful analysis, perhaps because of the failure to recognize what has happened, on an intellectual level; but it can on some occasions produce remarkable results, turning crabbed spinsters and crotchety business men into different beings; loving, and beloved by, their fellow workers and their families.

Religious conversion, however, cannot be laid on as a treatment. Analysis can; and the question arises how far it has proved of value. But first some misconceptions have to be removed.

There are three widespread illusions about psychoanalysis; the first being that its success is dependent on the discovery of some single traumatic event, the one which caused the repression, that it is the analyst's job to find. To begin with, it is not the analyst's job; it is the patient's; all the analyst can do is give informed guidance. But in any case there is no single emotional cause, any more than there is a single physical cause, of illness. There is, or can often be, a single traumatic event which precipitated or is linked with the illness—and which, when the patient recalls it, may help him to recapture his feelings at the time, and understand how his troubles have arisen; but too great a concentration on the search for the single traumatic event—it might be called "the woodshed complex"—is not helpful, and may easily be misleading.

The psychoanalytic technique, too, with the analyst listening while the patient unburdens his mind, is still often confused with the technique of confession, as employed by the Catholic Church. The two are quite distinct. A man in the Confessional retains his critical faculty about what he is revealing; he recounts only what he believes to be his sins. This, too, may have a therapeutic effect (it is wonderfully described in James Joyce's *Portrait of the Artist as a Young Man*); but it does not attempt to discover the reason for the lapses—that being already established, for Catholics, as original sin. Nor, as a rule, does it prevent Catholics from continuing to do things which they believe to be morally wrong, even when they know they will later feel guilt.

Nor is psychoanalysis something esoteric. It has acquired a cabalistic climate; to the public, the analyst is still often seen as a kind of devil's disciple, dabbling in the arcane to transform his patients' personalities. But, as Lindner has argued:

> "Nothing could be further from the truth. Neither the science of psychoanalysis nor the art of its practice depend upon extraordinary agencies. As a matter of fact, the only medium employed by the analyst is the commonest instrument of all—his own human self, utilized to the fullest, in an effort

to understand its fellows. . . . A psychoanalyst is nothing more than an artist at understanding, the product of an intensive course of study and training which has—if it has been successful—rendered him unusually sensitive to his fellow men. And it is this sensitivity—in short the analyst's own person—which is the single instrument, the only tool, with which he performs. Only on himself, and on nothing else, does he depend."

Lindner's defence is sound in theory; in practice, psychoanalysts have unwittingly encouraged the growth of the popular legend that they are necromancers. It is not entirely their fault, as it stems from the time when the Freudians had to contend with passionate, prejudiced and grossly unfair criticism. As Franz Alexander has recalled:

"Most, if not all, of these early polemics were motivated by emotional 'resistance' due to the fact that psychoanalysis aims at making conscious that psychological material which is excluded from consciousness because of the person's unwillingness to recognize and admit it. This led then to an inclination amongst us to reject criticisms from outsiders and to consider deviation from what was supposed to be the 'official' view as signs of 'resistance'. There was a readiness among analytical authors not to deal, in the first place, with the intrinsic merits of a criticism or a new formulation or technical deviation but instead to interpret the author's psychology, remarking, for example, that the author had not been fully analysed, or wanted to be original at any cost, or had an unresolved conflict with authority, or was a compromiser ready to sell out to the enemy."

Freud himself, though in some respects his humility was remarkable, could be vain and touchy; he could even suggest that people who had not been analysed were not in a position to criticize analysis—a most dangerous line of argument, as it can be used to justify every crackpot religion or treatment; but it has continued in use by some of his followers, who have thereby contrived to insulate themselves not only against hostile outsiders, but also against intelligent self-criticism. For example, Freud's lack of interest in the psychosomatic aspects of illness is shared by many analysts to such an extent that for many of them, the divorce of mind and body in treatment is almost as clear-cut as it is with most physicians; they are consequently often ignorant of the progress that has been made, which hampers them when they encounter patients whose neuroses are expressed in physical symptoms.

The trend towards the establishment of orthodoxies (and heresies) which Alexander mentions has led to excessively rigid objective patterns of analysis being laid down from which the analyst must not depart even when his hunch tells him that an individual patient needs a different approach. In fact it may lead the analyst to regard his hunches with suspicion. Where analysis breaks down—as well it may, under such circumstances—escape-hatches have been provided; such as that the patient is "unanalysable" (which is rather similar to the physician's excuse that a patient's illness is "functional"). Eysenck mentions another common analyst's device: to have things both ways. One idea, patented by Jung, is that persons who are outwardly introverted are unconsciously extroverted, while those who are outwardly extroverted are unconsciously introverted, thus making it possible to "explain" any type of conduct simply by referring it either to the conscious or to the unconscious portion of the patient's personality. "It is this feature of analytic thought," Eysenck justly complains, "more than any other, which serves the analyst as a defence mechanism, because all reactions whatever can thus be explained after a fashion, even if none can be predicted." This is not to argue that such contradictions do not exist; they obviously do; but their existence can be put to dangerous use in controversy.

The very impact of Freud's genius, too, was so striking that it has had an unfortunate effect on his followers; and Eysenck, as a Pavlovian, can hardly be blamed for pointing out the similarities between the development of Mesmerism and that of psychoanalysis.

> "In both cases there is a strong personality as a founder of the cult; there is a large congregation of pupils, fanatically devoted to the furtherance of the master's teaching; there are the splits and the formation of different schools; there is a formulation of unusual, unorthodox, and unlikely theories on the basis of highly questionable evidence. In both cases there are reports of cures achieved, and in both cases there is an absence of the controlled experiment which alone could verify the claims made. Only the future can tell whether the Freudian libido will join animal magnetism on the heap of discarded hypotheses for which science has no use."

Although the comparison is unjust to Freud, who was himself a scientist, and a man of uncompromising intellectual honesty, it is true that he set his followers on a number of paths which, though promising, are full of pitfalls—notably dream interpretation. Dreams have proved useful in analysis, and form a staple adjunct to psychotherapy; their value is not in doubt. But the method chosen by Freud to explore the dream world is dangerously similar to that which is used by Baconians to explore the works of Shakespeare. Just as it is possible, by the manipulation of codes and cyphers, to demonstrate surprisingly effectively that Bacon (or somebody else) wrote Shakespeare, so interpretation of dreams by symbols, and through word association or puns, can be extended to explain almost anything. Even if it is granted that there is a basis of good sense behind it, dream interpretation can easily develop into an elaborate game, a kind of psychoanalytic crossword puzzle. This may not matter much so long as the interpretations, however far-fetched, help the analysis along; but they are too often used to justify assumptions, and thereby to discredit the technique of analysis.

There is a possibility, too, that analysis has deeper effects on the personality of the analysed than is at present recognized or admitted. An analyst normally takes elaborate care to avoid making any use of the power that he attains over his patients, as his object is not to mould his patients' personalities in the way he thinks is right for them, but to enable them to build up their own personalities. But suggestion is not made by word of mouth alone: an analyst may, without knowing it, be "willing" his patients in certain directions. Little is known about the capacity of one unconscious mind to reach out and influence another; but there is plenty of evidence that such a power exists. It has been exploited, in certain circumstances, by mediums, witches, and medicine men. The rationalist reaction, which has led to stories of the power of witchcraft over the minds of men being sceptically received, has gone too far; there is at least a possibility that the particular relationship of analyst and patient can lead to the influencing—it might be described as the unconscious brainwashing—by the one of the other.

This is a risk that analysis needs to guard against: so, too, is the possibility that analysts will be corrupted by the importunities of patients. Where analysis can be bought, it can become fashionable, as it became in America; and rich people with nothing to do with their money may take up fashionable analysts just as they take up fashionable photographers or dress designers, a process which is bad both for the individual analyst and for the reputation of his profession.

Things are difficult enough without these complications, for analysis is a long, tedious, and costly journey, with no certainty of safe arrival. Indeed there have been some analysts who feel that its value so far has lain less in what it has done for patients than in what it has revealed about the workings of the mind. Where analysis brings results, patients are often so entranced with what they discover about themselves that they refuse to believe the journey is not at an end, and leave before they are in a proper condition to walk alone; or, where it could bring results in time, patients may despair, and abandon it, because progress is so slow.

Defending the analytic method, Lindner agreed that it is a commonplace at a certain stage of treatment for everything to appear to be the same with a patient as before it was begun—even for things to seem worse—

> "but in the mental underground, unseen by any observer and inaccessible to the most probing investigation, the substructure of the personality is being affected. Insensibly but deliberately the foundations of neurosis are being weakened while, at the same time, there are being erected new and more durable supports on which, eventually, the altered personality can rest. Were this understood by the critics of psychoanalysis (or, better still, by friends and relatives of analysands who understandably complain of the lack of evident progress), many current confusions about the process would disappear".

Lindner was probably right; but it is not fully established that analysis, on balance, has benefited those who have been treated by it. Admittedly the scales are weighted against success, because the majority of patients would not have consented to be analysed had they not been desperate; the kind of people whose difficulties might easily be disposed of by analysis are the kind of people who do not get bad enough to feel compelled to ask for it. The technique, too, is only half a century old: too young for its results to be fairly assessed. I feel reluctantly compelled to give it relatively little space—and to fill much of that with criticisms—because for practical purposes it is not so much, as yet, a method of treatment as a research technique. This is not to deny that many people have been helped—their reason, perhaps, saved—by analysis; but in relation to the sum total of illness, the amount analysis can hope to do in the form of direct treatment is insignificant.

Psychoanalysis nevertheless represents the most striking medical discovery of our time, and possibly of all time. Its importance extends far outside medicine; it is revolutionizing the whole study of mankind. It will in time provide the means whereby illness, all illness, can be examined in its relation to the individual personality, so that the powers of the mind can be used not, as they now so often are, to make us ill, but to prevent us from falling ill, and to speed our recovery if we are ill. But this is in the future; for the moment, its chief therapeutic value lies not in the small number of people it helps directly, but in the growing number it now helps, and the huge number it could help, indirectly—through psychotherapy.

5

PSYCHOTHERAPY

THE case of Eve White suggests that illness can be symptomatic of revolutionary forces at work within the personality; and stress disorders often arise in much the same way, though the clash is less dramatic. In these cases, the Pavlovian technique of reconditioning is not applicable; and full Freudian analysis, even if desired, is rarely available. The need has therefore grown for a form of everyday treatment that will apply some of the lessons learned from analysis and other research into the mind; and this method has come to be called psychotherapy.

It is difficult to make a definition of psychotherapy comprehensive enough to be of any value which is not also so wide as to be meaningless. "Treatment of mind and body through the mind" gives the general idea; but this might be held to include suggestion, or exhortation, or even "bedside manner". In an essay on the subject Wittkower has made a sensible distinction; "Bedside manner may be defined as an unsystematized understanding of a patient's emotional needs, whereas psychotherapy is their conscious, systematized counterpart." It is theoretically possible (in practice, a frequent occurrence) for a doctor to help his patients much more by his presence, his calm, his good humour, and his general air of competence, than by his treatment; but his method cannot properly be called psychotherapeutic, because it is not based on any system. The prefix "psycho" has led to some confusion with psychoanalysis. Analysis is a form of psychotherapy, and most psychotherapists' work is influenced by, sometimes based on, the lessons learned from analysis; but there is no necessary connection between the two. Other systems can be put forward which ignore or reject or modify Freud's teaching. But all systems of psychotherapy take as their starting point the need for the patient to heal himself. The therapist does not give treatment, in the usual medical sense. He provides the means for the patient to understand himself; the beginning of a process which in time may lead to the disappearance of his stress, and of his symptoms.

At present there are not so much different schools of psychotherapy as different attitudes of mind to it. On one side, there is the practice of what Franz Alexander has called—an uncomfortable title—"psychoanalytically oriented psychotherapy"; the Freudian theory is accepted, its rules being adapted and applied to everyday treatment. On another, there is what has come to be known as "client-centred therapy". Its foremost practitioner is Carl Rogers—who, like Alexander, works in Chicago. "We see therapy," Rogers has said, "as an experience, not in intellectual terms; we treat the client as a person."

Rogers's methods have been criticized by Freudians as unsystematic and undisciplined; he does not work from any theory of the mind's processes. But his method is not completely haphazard; he accepts the Breuer/Freud hypothesis that patients need to recognize and to express their inner feelings; where he differs from the Freudians is in his belief that there can be no rigid formula for therapeutic procedure. In Freudian analysis the analyst tries to efface himself; to keep his own feelings out of it. For Rogers:

> "it appears essential that the therapist be genuine, or whole, or congruent, in the relationship. What this means is that it is important for the therapist to be what he is, in his contact with the client. To the extent that he presents an outward façade of one attitude or feeling, while inwardly or at an unconscious level he experiences another feeling, the likelihood of successful therapy will be diminished. It is only as he is, in, this relationship—a unified person with his experienced feelings, his awareness of his feelings, and his expression of

> those feelings all congruent or similar—that he is most able to facilitate therapy. It is only as the therapist provides the genuine reality which is in him, that the other person can successfully seek the reality in himself. The therapist is non-defensive about the reality in himself, and this helps the client to become non-defensive".

Freud himself opposed the idea that analysts should be "non-defensive" with their patients; partly because he saw the destructive effect of involvement in individual cases, where analysis broke down as a result; mainly, I suspect, because he wished to make analysis as far as possible scientific, which it was easier to do if the analyst was kept as a theoretically constant factor. But my own belief is that Rogers is right; that the therapist ought to be what he is; that he ought to represent a congruous human being to the patient, not a disembodied voice at the end of the couch. Naturally the therapist will have to exercise his ordinary common sense on how far he can express his feelings; he may occasionally need to dissimulate for a specific purpose, just as he does in everyday life; but he should be a friend to his patients; he should meet them and greet them, man to man.

Client-centred therapy has also a distinct advantage over the psychoanalytically oriented variety—though it also involves certain risks—because it makes possible a greater degree of flexibility in training and in methods of treatment. Where the Freudians require of their pupils a long period of training, and the ability, proved in cases conducted under supervision, to carry out analytic technique according to the book, client-centred therapy makes more demands on the personality of the therapist than on his knowledge. A man with no formal training, provided he fulfilled the qualification that "he knows the genuine reality which is in him" and has the necessary interest in and sympathy with people, could very quickly become a useful therapist; whereas all the training and experience in the world could not convert some of today's psychoanalysts into therapists on the Rogers's model.

This may turn out to be important, because if the stress theory of disease becomes more widely acceptable to the public, the medical profession will not for some time be in any position to handle the changed type of treatment required; and psychoanalysts already have more work than they can cope with. The need, therefore, will be for more psychotherapists, and a conflict is bound to develop between the two views; one, that nobody should be allowed to practice as a psychotherapist without three years' training, including analysis; the other, that personality is much more important than training, and that any attempt to institutionalize psychotherapy will merely exclude people who, though eminently suitable, have not got the time or the money to follow the courses prescribed.

The Freudian argument is that short cuts are dangerous; to embark upon psychotherapy without intensive training means placing too much reliance on the therapists' intuition and common sense, neither of which, the lessons of analysis have shown, are always reliable guides. Yet knowledge, training and qualifications do not make the psychotherapist any more than the cowl makes the monk; and they may even make it more difficult to preserve the essential requirement (again to quote Rogers) "to sense the client's private world as if it were your own, but without ever losing the 'as if' quality . . . to sense the client's anger, fear or confusion as if it were your own, yet without your own anger, fear or confusion getting bound up in it".

The future of psychotherapy largely depends on the ability of all those concerned in it to come to terms on this point; and this will not be easy, because there is little unity, though there is more disposition to realize the need for it than there was ten years ago. At present there are four main categories of psychotherapist. First, psychiatrists, who may or may not be analysts. Second, psychotherapists proper, who have no medical qualifications but have been through a course of training (if Freudians, they will have been analysed and have conducted analysis under supervision; they then practise psychoanalytically oriented psychotherapy under a doctor's supervision—strict or non-existent, according to the doctor). Third, clinical psychologists, who commonly work with a psychiatrist, carrying out various routine investigations and examinations for him—IQs, Rorschach (inkblot) tests, and so on; clinical psychologists do not normally give psychotherapy themselves, but often they know much more about it than the psychiatrist they are working for: some of them practise under his supervision. Finally, there are psychiatric social workers, a heterogeneous collection ranging from avid but unqualified Freudians to Marriage Guidance Counsellors with no lecture-room knowledge of psychotherapeutic theory. These categories are not clear cut; in different countries the groups range themselves under different names or coalesce into different subdivisions; but they represent the basic pattern.

It would require another book to discuss the various techniques of psychotherapy; but they all have the same objective, which is to enable the patient to get something off his chest. At first the patient tends either to deny that he has got anything to worry about, or, more often, to attribute his worries to the failure of people—wives, parents, employers, workmates, neighbours—to understand him. The fact of being able to talk about his difficulties is usually in itself therapeutic, in much the same way as confession is usually good for the body, as well as the soul; and it is at this point that the technique of psychotherapy really begins. The therapist uses the rapport he has established with patients to help them realize that their worries arise not out of the machinations of others, but in themselves. He does not say, in so many words, "your wife is a good woman, now go back to her, kiss, and make up", because he knows that to persuade patients to act against the run of their feeling may be unwise. What he tries to do, instead, is help patients to want to resume easy relationships with wives or workmates; which they often do, after they have blown their tops freely in the consulting room—because in discussing the reasons for the outburst, they come to a better understanding of themselves.

The psychotherapist helps by judiciously prompting patients

when they get stuck in their self-examination, or by putting into words what they have begun to feel, but have not fully understood. In this second capacity, as a putter-into-words of previously disorganized sentiments, his influence can be enormous, as can be seen where psychotherapy has achieved its most striking success: in child guidance. Dr. Spock and others have made this impact not by the intellectual conviction of the reader, but because they have put vague feelings and ideas which the reader already had into a palatable form; they have translated Freud into language he can understand and adopt without doing violence to his beliefs. Where a reader of the *Ladies' Home Journal* might once have scoffed at the notion that a child's neuroses arise out of jealousy for a younger brother she can see the point immediately when Dr. Spock (quoting a woman psychiatrist) tells her:

> "Imagine what it would feel like if your husband came home from work one afternoon, leading by the hand a gorgeous hussy, and said to you: 'I've decided that since it has been good to have one wife, it will be even better to have two. I love this girl Marilyn and I know you'll love her too.' It's preposterous to think that a wife could be delighted with such a stranger, but that's just what we expect of the very young child."

It is interesting to observe that Dr. Spock has been becoming more of a "client-centred therapist"; he has joined in the reaction away from orderliness in child training, towards the encouragement of intuition. Twenty years ago the tendency was for psychotherapists to replace one set of rules (such as rigid feeding times) with another. Mothers were asked to believe that, say, punishment was bad for children; and they restrained themselves from spanking a child even when instinct told them that it was just what the child needed. Now, the feeling is that a child who is not spanked may be being deprived of something he needs; and that in any case, it is better for parents to indulge their feelings, within reason, than to bottle them up out of deference to any book of rules.

Knowledge of the workings of a child's mind—and by extension, of adult minds—has also been extended through techniques evolved by Melanie Klein. For obvious reasons, it is not possible to psychoanalyse young children in the way adults are analysed; for a time it was thought that the difficulties in the way of treating them were insuperable. Dr. Klein found, however, that if she provided children with toys, and watched them at their play, she could observe them acting out their feelings. Dolls representing parents or brothers and sisters would be treated by a child in ways the child would have liked to, but could not, or dared not, treat them in real life; they were hugged, or ignored, or smashed to pieces. By watching children in such circumstances, a therapist is provided with clues which help her to deal with their problems.

"Play therapy", as it has come to be known, is now widely used, though there are still many differences of opinion among the various schools, even among the Freudians themselves, over how far children should be allowed to act out their feelings. Child guidance clinics in which this and other methods of psychotherapy are used have become common; parents' resistance to sending their children to them has largely broken down. But as yet there are few signs that adult resistance to psychotherapy is also breaking down. Its use is still largely confined to the treatment of mental or emotional symptoms which have become bad enough to make the patient's (or his family's) life a misery, but not bad enough to necessitate his removal to a mental hospital. It is, of course, also used in mental hospitals; but I shall consider it here as a method of treatment at home.

★

There are two main categories of psychotherapy, "supportive" and "uncovering": the one designed to palliate; the other, to cure. Supportive is the more general method: its aims have been described by Alexander in his *Psychoanalysis and Psychotherapy*: as first, to gratify patients' dependent needs while they are in a state of stress, thereby reducing their anxiety; second, to give them the opportunity to release their pent-up feelings; third, to review objectively their stress situations, and offer help in the making of judgements and the taking of decisions; fourth, to try not to remove neurotic symptoms but even, on occasion, to support them, where the therapist suspects they are defences against pressures too strong for the individual to deal with; and finally, to assist in the readjustment of the patient's way of life, if there is no other solution to his difficulties.

These methods are "supportive" in that they are not directed at finding the causes of neurosis, but at making life with it bearable. "Uncovering" therapy—analysis—is indicated when "supportive" fails, or when for some other reason it is held to be essential; but unless some way can be found to shorten and simplify the analytic process it is on its supportive merits that psychotherapy is likely to be judged.

This does not mean that it ought to be judged on its capacity to make men good, or useful, or respectable members of society; the adjustment should be to themselves, by a fusing of discordant elements in their personalities; not by submission to society, though obviously in his own interest a neurotic needs to be helped to keep within the law. In cases where patients suffer from, say, compulsive swearing, a therapist may be reluctant to stop the flow of obscenity for fear of bringing on some worse symptom; but he should at least try to prevent the swearing from taking place in public, or the patient may find himself in jail.

The first step in psychotherapy is the establishment of a relationship between therapist and patient; and the first qualification for a therapist is the ability to enter into a bond of what may be called sympathy—though without that word's sentimental connotations. This bridge once constructed, it becomes easier for the patient to express, and thereby to some extent to relieve his feelings. It may be desirable for the therapist to advise, but that is incidental to treatment; the real aim is to restore the patient's morale so that he can begin to understand and cope with his own difficulties, and make his own decisions. As a friend of mine, a psychiatric social worker, has written:

> "we no longer moralize, *give* advice, take upon ourselves the initiative of solving practical problems—although we may have to give some help here. We do enter into a special relationship which is conveniently but unilluminatingly called a 'casework relationship'. Through this relationship a patient comes to understand more of the nature of his own difficulties and can, therefore, the better handle them, because he can talk at length to the case worker, and project on to her some of his need for love and understanding which he lacked long ago".

Most of us have become so conditioned to the idea that treatment is something which is imposed from the outside, in the form of a prescription, and that the object of treatment is cure, or remission, of symptoms, that we find it hard to grasp that the purpose of psychotherapy is neither to receive advice, nor to be cured of our symptoms. In his *Being Lived by my Life* Charles Berg describes an occasion when a prominent psychiatrist, "Dr. Top-Notch", boasted at great length about the large number of psychoneurotic patients cured in his enormous mental out-patients' department.

> "Thereupon a true psychologist amongst us arose and asked naïvely whether the great doctor really thought it necessary to deprive all those poor sufferers of their only means of relieving their tensions. Maybe it was more natural for them and more comfortable, more consistent with health, to have their symptoms than to learn to suppress them. Symptoms only disappear healthily when a readjustment or new distribution of energy is made within the mind which enables the tensions which give rise to them to find an alternative outlet more satisfactory to every level of the mind. Without such a redistribution of psychic energy, it may be more natural for some people to have symptoms than not."

Berg goes on to express his conviction that "so far from the ordinary cures 'doing people any good' I am convinced by dint of long experience both in organic medicine and in psychiatry, that all our illnesses, including organic disease of every description, are essentially the fruit of these 'cures'". A psychotherapist, therefore, should be approached in a very different way from that in which a doctor is approached; we should not go with the intention of showing him our symptoms, and asking him to remove them. We do not even know whether the symptoms should be removed—unless they are so painful or unpleasant that it is impossible even to begin psychotherapy while they are there.

Going to a psychotherapist, patients also need to realize that to talk over their troubles is a routine way of dealing with physical, as well as mental, illness. At present it is still quite widely believed that when a doctor suggests psychotherapy, he is implying that it is mental illness which is suspected. Take the case I related earlier of my friend B., who had fits. If the specialist had said that, as no physical reason could be found for B.'s fit, a psychotherapist should be called in, B.'s family would have been horrified. They would have assumed that B. must be suffering from schizophrenia, a form of mental illness which some films had made rather fashionable; and which would have suggested itself because B. had a split mind, of a sort—he could exclude from it anything he did not want to remember. The family would not have thanked the specialist for implying that the trouble was "mental", in this sense; yet he got great kudos out of a negative diagnosis: the family were so delighted to hear B. did not have epilepsy that they did not worry over the fact that his fit remained unexplained.

There was another reason why it might have been wise not to employ a psychotherapist, even if the specialist had thought it desirable, and the family had agreed. B. was the kind of person to whom psychotherapy would have been a release from his responsibilities; he would have used the fact he was being treated, as long as he could, to excuse his failure to face the problems of his ordinary life. As things turned out, the fits themselves—he had three or four more of them—were a form of treatment. They provided him with an escape hatch when things got too difficult for him, enabling him to face reality at normal times, because the escape hatch was there, for use in emergencies. In this way the fits eased the transition into marriage, and the responsibilities of a family. The desire to run away and hide, or to bluff his way out of difficulties did not wholly disappear; but it ceased to be dominant. In time the fits, too, ceased.

In retrospect, though I did not realize it then, this seems to me to be worth remembering. B.'s family regarded themselves as intelligent people; although it would have alarmed them, they would have accepted the suggestion, had it been made, that a psychotherapist should be called in. But they would have expected him to "cure" the fits; and they would have been dissatisfied had he not done so. They would not have realized that the fits might be in themselves a cure, any more than the reporters I had worked with had realized their colds and headaches were cures—providing a release from difficult situations.

This is not an argument against psychotherapy; it is only another reason for not calling in psychotherapists to act as symptom removers. As it happens, though, they may not be called in to act in any capacity. Even today, some doctors tend to by-pass psychotherapy; to ignore neurotic symptoms, or treat them with tranquillizers or placeboes—unless they get really menacing, and then to call in a psychiatrist, who, conceivably, is a believer in drugs or shocks or operations (or whatever physical treatment happens to be fashionable). Even where psychotherapy is agreed upon, there may be difficulty in finding a qualified psychotherapist, so thin are they on the ground. Still, the number of social workers with an interest in, and sometimes a fair knowledge of, psychotherapy, is growing; and consultations with them—particularly if they have interest and sympathy, far more important than diplomas—may provide what is needed.

There have also recently been encouraging developments

in group psychotherapy, originally tried as a desperate expedient where there were more patients than could be dealt with individually. The personal patient-therapist touch is lost, but there are some compensating advantages; individuals in a group learn that other people have the same, or worse problems; and in trying to help others, a patient may learn to help himself. Although the difficulties created by the absence of privacy, leading to reticence, and by the possibility of clashes between members of the group, make group therapy difficult, the recent success of bodies such as Alcoholics Anonymous shows that much can be achieved, along these lines.

Normally, though, psychotherapy is based on a relationship between psychotherapist and patient, with the aim of helping the patient to understand himself so that he can cope with his problems. The decision who is best fitted to act as therapist depends to some extent on the nature of the symptoms; obviously when the neurotic symptoms take serious or dangerous forms, it will be necessary to call in a specialist. But in ordinary cases, the best qualified therapist, other things being equal, is somebody who knows the patient. And there is one person who is pre-eminently suited to the task: the family doctor.

At first sight this may seem surprising. Why not a specialist psychotherapist? But this would bring disagreements and wrangles over the boundary between ordinary medical practice and psychotherapy; probably leading in the end to an arbitrary division into physical and psychological illness which would bear no relation to the facts of neurosis. If neurosis manifested itself only in emotional symptoms, or in obvious neurotic afflictions like twitches, the two might be kept distinct; but if, as seems to be the case, most of the physical symptoms brought to doctors arise out of stress, this line cannot be drawn. And, the family doctor, as the man in possession, is in the best position to take on the work.

The choice of the family doctor as psychotherapist has other advantages. To begin with, he already holds the confidence of his patients (presumably; or he wouldn't have patients). And if he retains charge, there is less risk that treatment will ignore or underrate the importance of physical causes of illness—something which is apt to happen in psychotherapy.

> "One of the most persistent errors in this field," Alexander says, "is the belief that if emotional etiology in a case has been established, somatic medical management becomes unnecessary and the patient can be turned over to a psychiatrist. This error is the reverse of the earlier misconception: namely, that if a patient has somatic symptoms, his case belongs exclusively to the domain of the physician or specialist outside of psychiatry—no matter whether its etiology is of emotional nature, once there is an active ulcer in the duodenum, therapy must attempt to remedy this local lesion. Such a patient requires general medical care, dietary management, and pharmacological treatment, or even surgery. . . . Psychotherapy aimed at the specific emotional factors of etiological significance is a long range product and must be co-ordinated with the rest of the medical management. Above all, it must be correctly timed."

The family doctor is also likely to be the only person knowing the patient's background who can discuss intimate matters without embarrassment. This is very desirable if stress symptoms are related to the patient's constitution and circumstances—to his life at home and to his work. Recognition of physical symptoms is becoming of less importance than personal acquaintance with the strains that brought them on—job difficulties, family difficulties, sex difficulties, or any other of the sources of worry with which people have to contend. The family doctor is in a unique position: the position once held by the priest. It is to their doctor that most patients would now turn, if he let them, as their father confessor.

I do not wish, though, to minimize the difficulties that confront the family doctor as psychotherapist. To begin with, he needs to take a very much wider range of things into consideration, in treatment. Take the case I mentioned of the girl from my home village who suffered from asthma attributable to family trouble. At any given time she could be temporarily "cured" by simple separation from her family. But treatment is never so simple. Her family doctor, had he considered her asthma to arise out of emotional stress, would have had to take many other things into account before deciding that separation from her family was what she needed. He would have had to consider her family's circumstances (they might not have been able to afford to send her away for long); and their attitude (they would certainly be horrified at any hint that her asthma was due to some incompatibility with them). To find out the truth about the incompatibility, the doctor might want the parents to go away for a while; both together, and separately, to see how the child reacted. Supposing that such an experiment could be arranged, might it not have other adverse effects? There are worse things than asthma; what the child might be craving was not less attention, but more—greater affection, perhaps, from her parents. And if, in the end, the attacks of asthma could be shown to arise from the child's emotional demands, this knowledge would not necessarily end them permanently. A doctor, therefore, even if he is convinced that the symptoms have an emotional basis, may be forced to decide that the safest thing to do is to palliate them as best he can with drugs and injections—to do just what he would be doing if he had never heard of the stress theory.

Not that the doctor as psychotherapist is always so helpless. When he realizes that children's emotional disturbances are reflected in stress symptoms, he may be able to show parents that, instead of fussing over their child's illness, they should ask themselves whether their own lives, and the life of the family as a whole, is the reason why the family difficulties arise. In such cases, everything depends upon the way in which the father and mother are approached. If they are lectured, let alone hectored, they are certain to react in the wrong direction. If, on the other hand, they can be induced to take an interest in the stress theory, even if only out of curiosity, the prospects are very much brighter. Delicately though such advice needs to be given, at least the family doctor is in a much better position to know how to handle parents than a psychotherapist who is meeting them for the first time.

But this postulates the existence of family doctors; and I have already mentioned that the family doctor is now a rarity. He is becoming extinct, a process accelerated by bureaucracy but really caused by the trend towards specialization. Whereas the family doctor was once *the* doctor, sending on patients to specialists only when he had satisfied himself that there was something wrong with them which required hospital treatment or the special skill of a physician or a surgeon, he now tends to have a mean view of his own capabilities either as diagnostician or therapist; he sends on patients at the slightest excuse for a specialist opinion, or for tests, X-rays and examinations. In doing so, he has to a great extent lost the personal touch he used to have with them and their families. And the family doctor may not merely have little knowledge of the theory of psychotherapy; he may have a bias against it. He knows that patients who most require it, too, are often those who are apt to be the greatest nuisances, the hypochondriacs and the hysterics, whom his chief desire is to avoid. As few doctors learn more than a smattering of psychotherapy in their student days, and as afterwards they are too busy to take it up, their training and cast of mind alike conspire to make them treat almost all their patients as if they are ill from physical causes—even though when they examine patients dispassionately they realize that most of them are not.

Yet is the difficulty in reversing the trend, in restoring the pre-eminence of family doctors who know the symptoms of stress, and who understand the individual needs of their patients as great as it appears? Balint argues that the need is not so much for the doctor to do different work, as to do the work he is now doing with a difference. If family doctors would begin to think about what they are doing, and why, they would soon realize that their tendency to think of themselves as second best to the specialist is justified only in relation to a disease; in relation to a patient their knowledge is, or should be, vastly superior and more reliable than the specialists. If, therefore, the family doctor can get himself back into his old habit of mind, when his patients were what mattered—when he knew all about them, their circumstances, their families, their work, their love affairs, and their hobbies—he will be in a position, even if he does not know much about psychotherapy in theory, to begin again to learn about it in practice.

Little theoretical knowledge is needed for a doctor to start on this road. All he requires is to persuade himself to regard his patients as individuals, not as diseases; and to listen to them—useful treatment not only for the patient, but for the doctor himself. In the case Balint cites of Mrs. D. (the woman who kept returning with different varieties of stomach trouble), the doctor who first treated her as a person and not as a walking mass of symptoms, immediately noticed a marked improvement. Balint suggests that this might mean not that she was better, but that the doctor was. He had approached her case with a difference; the improvement might simply reflect the change in their relationship. The first need in psychotherapy, he concludes, is for the doctor to get better—which he can do by beginning to understand his patients' complaints as symptoms not so much of diseases as of their life histories. But to achieve this, the doctor must become less dependent on—that is, more critical of—hospital medicine and specialists; and more confident about his own observations.

Again, it will be objected that a little learning is a dangerous thing: that for untrained men, even if they are qualified doctors, to engage in psychotherapy is putting their patients to the hazard. But doctors every day are putting their patients to much more serious hazard, by filling them up with drugs about whose long-term effects little is known, and whose short-term benefit is doubtful. And as it happens, psychotherapy on the everyday level where it can be practiced by general practitioners has few risks. Analysis may be dangerous, as readers of Lindner's *Fifty-Minute Hour* or Nigel Balchin's *Mine Own Executioner* (which incidentally, also gives an entertaining picture of the warring "psycho" factions) will remember; but casual listening to patients is, at worst, only a waste of time. True, the doctor who starts using his common sense may make mistakes, some of which will delay patients' progress; but they should, if he recognizes them, help the doctor not to make the same mistakes again.

In any case, there is no need for a doctor to embark unaided upon psychotherapy. He can attend courses and seminars provided, though there are all too few; and he can enlist the help of trained psychotherapists. These, admittedly, are also too few; but as relatively little use is made of their services by doctors, any doctor who needs one should not have difficulty in getting one. And with a trained psychotherapist's assistance the doctor's opportunities expand enormously—a view shared alike by two such otherwise dissimilar men, Balint and Jack Ferguson. Ferguson even claims that the family doctor is the father of psychiatry, "it is this man that sees mental illness start. He practices soft-shoe psychiatry with over half his patients every day. And I believe the public wants its competent modern general practitioners to handle its family and mental and emotional problems . . . they want the family doctor because the word 'psychiatrist' brings to their minds thoughts of couches, of years of interviews, of big doctor's bills—and of ridicule."

There is no reason why patients, too, should not be encouraged to learn the elements of psychotherapy. No doctor would argue that the public should be prevented from learning the elements of first aid—how to deal with minor cuts, or burns, or to give artificial respiration—on the grounds that a little learning is dangerous. Nor can there be any objection to the public getting sufficiently knowledgeable about neurotic symptoms to be prepared for them, rather than to try to ignore them. Everybody should know enough about himself to be aware of his own limitations; enough to realize that certain physical symptoms point to the existence of emotional disturbance; some of them positive, like headaches, or skin trouble, or indigestion; some negative, like lassitude or ill humour or depression or worry; all of them a reflection of the individual's reaction to his environment. His environment may be uncongenial; his home life, his job or his friends ill-attuned to him. Or, the failure may be his own in not making the necessary adjustments to them. But at some stage—if the individual's environment grates on him too much—there is going to be trouble. He is unlikely to be able to diagnose what is wrong himself. But there is no reason at all why he should not have enough knowledge of the subject to perform the equivalent of "first aid"; to recognize the symptoms, and to realize when they get serious enough to require a visit to his doctor.

Simple curiosity about the stress theory may itself be a help. I have mentioned earlier a newspaper column I wrote about a surgeon's heretical views on stomach ulcers; and in passing I commented that this came at a time when the ordinary layman was only just beginning to accommodate himself to the fact that asthma had an emotional basis. A few days later a letter arrived in the office which I might have answered perfunctorily, had it not been for the fact that the address was in my home village. The writer had been interested, he said, in my reference to asthma, as he had ideas on the subject himself; but he had found himself up against local medical prejudice. He had a son aged nine suffering from asthma, for whom the doctors could do virtually nothing; could I give him any more information?

I did not keep a copy of my reply, nor can I remember what I said; but I have a letter he wrote some time afterwards, saying that I had started him "on a new line of approach to our own particular problem, and whether by luck, coincidence, or Providence, it has shown distinct results". The admission that luck, coincidence or Providence might have a hand in it suggests that here, at least, was a parent who had the right idea; that he was prepared to regard his son's asthma not as a symptom to be removed by short-term medical remedies, but as a challenge to himself and to his whole family. Such efforts of parents over children, even if amateurish, are never wholly wasted—provided that they are the product of a desire to understand and help, and not simply of a wish to make the children less of a nuisance around the house.

*

Up to this point I have been discussing psychotherapy on the assumption that it is, or can be, a useful form of treatment; but it has been argued, particularly by the Pavlovians, that it does not work.

The case against psychotherapy has been often and vigorously made by Eysenck, notably in his *Sense and Nonsense in Psychology*. In an earlier book he had complained that of the fifty or more papers describing the effectiveness of psychotherapy, not one had made use of a control group; and as people suffering from neuroses may and often do get better without treatment, there was consequently no evidence that treatment, rather than natural causes, had caused the improvement noted in the experiments. Since that time, Eysenck writes,

> "a proper experiment has been recorded from California in which matched groups of neurotic subjects were respectively treated by psychotherapy and not treated at all. The outcome of the experiment was very much in line with my previous conclusions. The treated group improved to a considerable extent, but the untreated group improved equally. Without the existence of such a control group, the erroneous impression would have been given that psychotherapy was responsible for the improvement".

This is true; most accounts of experiments in psychotherapy have been coloured by the enthusiasm of the experimenters. But the California test was palpably absurd; nobody who knows even a little about psychotherapy would fall into the trap of imagining you can dispense it on a large scale, like a drug—let alone base statistics on its use in that way. It is possible by taking certain precautions to ensure that neither the doctor who gives a pill nor the patient who takes it knows whether it is a drug or a placebo; consequently it is relatively easy to make an objective study of what effects a drug has. But there is no way of disguising who is getting psychotherapy, and who is not. As we have seen, too, psychotherapy is not a one-way traffic; it depends on the therapist doing his job properly, as well as the patient; whether or not the necessary rapport has been established between the two of them, and how satisfactory it is, cannot be measured by scientific means, any more than whether or not two people have fallen in love, and how deep their love is, can be measured by scientific means. Consequently the evidence in favour of psychotherapy (and of love) is, and must remain, "anecdotal".

The overwhelming anecdotal evidence of psychotherapists is that psychotherapy gives results. Granted some of them are prejudiced in its favour, but not all of them—not such men as Jack Ferguson, Pavlovian by training and inclination, but forced by the evidence to recognize that scientific research techniques are not applicable here. As de Kruif says, relating a conversation with him:

> "'You understand,' says Jack, 'it would be a half-baked experiment to test the new drugs as many are now doing—I mean, throwing the chemicals into half the patients and leaving the rest for controls. Controls are only real controls if the sickness of the treated and the untreated is identical.' Jack went on to din it into me that the disease of every one of his 1,000 patients is *different*, 'That's why you've got to watch every one of them constantly, closely.' "

The only people who can prove or disprove the claims made for psychotherapy, Balint believes, are individual family doctors. Research "can be conducted only by general practitioners; no one else, certainly no specialist, has access to the patient's material. The answers can be obtained only in a close and constant relationship with the patient which is the essence of general practice."

Other arguments are sometimes heard against psychotherapy; one being that it is designed to change or mould the character of the patient. This can be true of some other forms of psychiatry, notably of Pavlovian conditioning; but it is certainly not true of psychotherapy, except when a therapist is unscrupulous or wrong-headed enough to use powers which he may obtain over his patient in the course of treatment for his own purposes. The fact that it can be abused is in any case not a conclusive argument against psychotherapy, any more than it is against hypnotism, so long as the real purpose of psychotherapy continues to be the encouragement of the patient to find his own personality—not an effort to give him a new one.

Next, there is the common argument that psychotherapy encourages the patient to become irresponsible; to attribute his personality defects to the misfortune of having a cruel father or a feckless mother, and to adopt the attitude that he cannot be expected to behave himself, because of his unhappy childhood. Psychiatric evidence in the courts has tended to give this impression by suggesting that people with emotional troubles traceable to childhood suffering deserve what in the German army used to be called a "shooting license"—a right to make nuisances of themselves. But this is directly contrary to the real aim of psychotherapy; the aim is to make the patient more responsible—to give him back the sense of responsibility which he is trying to shed by falling back on his symptoms. The truth is that the present physical bias of medicine is much more of an encouragement to irresponsibility, of an unconscious kind, by which the patient claims the right to be recognized as ill; whereas psychotherapy, by making him realize why he is getting ill, aims to enable him to do without his symptoms; and to become a fully-developed healthy, adult personality.

Psychotherapists do not tell a patient to "grow up", or "be his age", because to do so is pointless. But there may well be occasions when a rebuke is needed, if the patient starts to be a nuisance. Just as electric shock treatment can shake a man out of a terrible fit of depression, so in ordinary human relations a shock may be what somebody needs to wake them up; from which point the psychotherapy can proceed. When the shock should be applied, and what form it should take, depends on the individual and his circumstances; but psychotherapy does not prescribe endless indulgence, in which everything the patient does, no matter how silly or dangerous or obnoxious, is explained away and justified. Even when he obviously is not entirely responsible for his actions, it may be a necessary part of rescue operations to make him think he is—just as it is a necessary part of childhood training to give the child the feeling that he has certain responsibilities, even when in fact he has not.

Finally, it is often argued that psychotherapy, by relying so much on introspection, is liable to lead patients to too great a concentration on themselves. This is certainly a risk. For many people, the need is less to inquire into what has upset them emotionally, than to enable them to release themselves from bondage by that form of spontaneous emotional combustion seen in lovers, artists, and converts. The therapeutic effect of falling in love, whether with a fellow creature or with an ideal, can be immense—as Tolstoy found, and described in *Anna Karenina;* in the episode when Levin spends his ecstatic night before securing the Scherbatsky's consent to his marriage with their daughter. Levin

> "had passed the whole night and the morning in a complete state of indifference to the material conditions of existence. He had neither eaten nor slept; had been exposed, with almost no clothing, to the cold for several hours; and he not only was fresh and hearty, but he felt freed from all the slavery of body, master of his powers. . . . What he saw that day he never saw again".

Were a method available of inducing love artificially, there would be far less need for psychotherapy. But at least psychotherapy can gradually free people, and in time make them capable of love, where before they were too caught up in their worry and guilt to be able to love—except to love without hope.

6

HEALING

At the beginning of his short story, *Lord Mountdrago*, Somerset Maugham describes a psychoanalyst who had adopted the profession by accident; he had discovered in the course of the First World War that he could allay certain pains by the touch of his hands, and induce sleep by talking in a low monotonous voice, resolving conflicts and phobias and effecting miraculous cures. After the war he went to Vienna to study analysis, in the hope of finding a theory to account for his skill. But though he got to know all that Freud and Jung and the rest had written, "he was not satisfied; he had an intimate conviction that all their theory was hocus-pocus, and yet there the results were, incomprehensible but manifest".

Maugham's story poses a question to which too little attention has been paid: how far is "healing", in the old biblical sense of the word, a force in medicine: not merely in analysis, but in all branches of treatment? Most doctors concede the possibility of faith healing in theory; but even those who are firm believers in the Christian faith are inclined to scoff at cases of successful faith healing should they occur in their own home town, or attribute them to hysteria. The method Jesus used, summed up in the words "thy faith has made thee whole", are in disrepute; anybody who possesses similar powers and seeks to use them for the relief of suffering is apt to be persecuted as a quack, even when his character and motives are above reproach.

In any consideration of healing today a complication arises: that for the most part healers are not aware of the real nature of their powers. They try to explain them away on pseudoscientific grounds. This is particularly true of the fringe groups of medicine, which range from comparative respectability (like the osteopaths and homoeopaths in Britain) to the quacks who peddle coloured water at fairs. Some of these techniques have a sound scientific basis; with homoeopathy, indeed, a much sounder basis than most of current present-day medical practice. Others, however difficult it may be to explain the reason, give consistently better results in practice than orthodox medical treatment. In Britain osteopathy once almost broke through into complete respectability as a result of the genius of Herbert Barker, whose work during and after the First World War brought such general respect that he was awarded a knighthood (though this did not prevent the profession from hounding a qualified anaesthetist, who worked for him, off the medical register). To this day, there are many general practitioners in Britain who advise patients with backache to go not to a hospital (where "slipped disc" will probably be diagnosed, and the patient immobilized in a variety of uncomfortable plaster jackets and steel corsets) but to visit the nearest osteopath, who may set him right in a few sessions of manipulation.

Still, it seems probable that many of the osteopaths'—and certainly of the American chiropractors'—successes resemble the psychiatrist's in *Lord Mountdrago*. Partly because they have been infected by the mechanistic trend, partly out of an understandable desire to attain respectability, the tendency recently has been towards codifying their methods of treatment, and trying to justify them on scientific grounds. But as the successes of chiropractice are often due to the healing power of suggestion the attempt to explain them scientifically merely leads to absurdities—such as the advertisements, common enough in American newspapers, in which chiropractors try to explain why their treatment gives good results for, say, asthma:

"The cause of asthma is excessive contraction of the bronchial muscles due to an improper supply of vital energy through the nerves. Tiny telegraphic messages carried by nerve fibres cause these muscles to contract. The Chiropractor regulates and brings back to normal the nerve supply to the bronchial tubes by adjusting the spine where the nerves supplying this area is impaired. . . ."

No doubt such manipulation of the spine, the common denominator of chiropractice, benefits some patients directly; but most of the beneficial results (where the results are beneficial) can reasonably be attributed not to the manipulation but to the patient's faith in its results—just as the great majority of benefits from pills and medicines are simply a reflection of the patient's faith in them.

It is, therefore, less sensible than it might seem to send an *agent provocateur* around chiropractors and naturopaths, who claims to be suffering from certain diseases; and then to arrest them for unlawful practice of medicine if they prescribe or give treatment—round-ups which are not infrequently carried out in America today. People would not go to a chiropractor if they were satisfied with their doctor; chiropractice flourishes only because orthodox medicine is not giving results. Many of the manipulations and medicines prescribed by chiropractitioners are valueless; but the same is true of most of the manipulations and medicines prescribed by doctors.

But apart from the members of these fringe groups, there are healers, proper; and generally speaking they fall into three categories. The first consists of men and (more rarely) women attached to religious sects. Sometimes there is a healing centre, like Lourdes, where the waters (or in other places, the relics of saints) are believed to have miraculous properties; sometimes it is an individual who possesses the healing powers, like "Padre Pio", or the late William J. MacMillan—an American, who, after failing for priesthood, came over to England, found himself able to heal people, and established himself as a healer, with the approbation of some Church of England dignitaries who had been impressed by his results. Second, there are the believers in psychic powers, some of them spiritualists. In Europe, for example, Jesse Thomas has for years been demonstrating before sceptical audiences, sometimes drawn from the medical profession, that he can put himself in a trance and perform a "psychic operation" on the patient's "astral body"; curing diseases which have defied the doctors. Third, there are people who have no spiritual or psychic pretensions of any kind, but are simply possessed of powers of healing; they are still very often to be found in country districts. Some of them pick up a certain amount of psychic mumbo-jumbo, or in time come to think of themselves as divinely accredited; but most regard their powers as natural, if inexplicable, and use them without trying to explain them.

Scepticism prevails on the extent to which claims for healing are justified, even when they are well attested. In his *Eleven Lourdes Miracles*, Dr. D. J. West has analysed, as far as it is possible to do so, the cases which have most recently been officially accepted by the Catholic Church, after prolonged scrutiny, as inexplicable except in miraculous terms. West's verdict is that "in no case was the evidence really satisfactory, and in certain cases the evidence suggested a perfectly natural alternative explanation". He points out that of all the cures claimed as miracles, an unduly high proportion are of T.B., a disease where sudden dramatic changes frequently occur; and of these the majority were of women, in whom hysterical disorders are common, so that there may have been a "functional" element in many of them. No self-evident miracles—no instance where lost eyes or amputated fingers have been regenerated—are recorded and in the cases where the appearance of miraculousness seems strongest, the evidence is often untrustworthy, containing incomplete data and insufficient consideration of alternative diagnoses.

If West's verdict is accepted, many of the Lourdes' cures (and in all probability many similar cures elsewhere) are genuine, but not miraculous; they merely illuminate the extent to which the patient's emotional state is capable of changing his physical condition. An acute sense of guilt may bring on paralysis; an acute sense of spiritual well-being may remove it. Nor need it be assumed (as West tends to assume) that the process only works with functional symptoms, where the people who are cured have not had real, organic illnesses. In view of "Tom", and all the other instances of how rapidly emotional and physical states interact, there is no reason to doubt that many organic symptoms can be made to disappear so suddenly as to give the appearance of a miraculous cure—particularly in the case of T.B.

The same thing is probably true about all forms of healing. Jesse Thomas has, in fact, recorded a number of cases where his patients were cured of organic diseases which had been formally diagnosed, in order to test his powers, and pronounced incurable.

It remains to consider how healing works; but this is something about which next to nothing is known. The simplest analogy is to liken it to the passage of an electric current, from healer to patient—the emotional, psychic or spiritual energy travels from the healer, with his charged battery, to the patient, whose battery has gone flat. This would help to account for the feeling Jesus referred to—"goodness has gone out of me"—when the woman touched his garment; a feeling shared by many healers, who find themselves in a state of exhaustion after effecting a cure. It is not inherently improbable that certain people have the capacity to release, in a way not yet understood, their emotional energy, and transfer it to others. This would also help to explain why it is that, while some chiropractors and osteopaths insist on the importance of a knowledge of anatomy, others are indifferent, and a few even argue that such knowledge is a handicap. Intellectual awareness may inhibit the use of healing powers; or it may distract the practitioner from his real task, which is to get the patients' own recuperative powers working again.

The potential value of healing has been ignored for a number of reasons; chiefly because of the reluctance of profession and public to admit the extent to which unconscious motives can determine the course of health and illness. What is generally known as "the will to live", most doctors would admit, can play a very important part in a patient's recovery; but psychoanalysis has revealed that what people believe is their will to live may in fact mask deeper contrary desires; and this has been confirmed by investigation into combat exhaustion among soldiers. Sargant, after studying the evidence, asserts that the virtues normally recognized and praised as "will-power" and "courage", where they are the product of conditioning, may actually exhaust the brain—so that it cannot stand stresses. This theory has received experimental confirmation in tests on animals; "when dogs co-operate in experiments testing their tolerance to stress, they are all the easier to break down; the loyal efforts they make prove their own undoing". It is not improbable that the existence of an intense conscious desire to live because, say, of family responsibilities may impede a patient's chances of recovery by denying access to, or by preventing the fuller understanding of, those deeper unconscious motives which are pulling him in the opposite direction.

Healing is disconcerting to the medical profession because it does not deal with patients' consciousness; it is not even dependent upon patients' awareness that the process is at work. There have been many reports of cases where healing has been successfully conducted from afar, unbeknownst to the patient—just as there have been many reports of cases where a curse has been laid from afar, with destructive results. Once a common practice in witchcraft, it is still found among primitive tribes: a spell is laid upon an enemy, who gradually wastes away and dies. If the emotional current can flow one way, there is no reason why it should not be made to flow the other; the existence of the power to make people ill is not to be scoffed at as a traveller's tale.

A further reason why healing is viewed askance by the profession is that it is so difficult to study. A few half-hearted efforts have been made to investigate it; in 1954 the Church of England actually persuaded the British Medical Association to set up a committee of investigation. But the committee consisted almost exclusively of doctors, who approached the subject along orthodox professional lines; they made little attempt to explore the subject dispassionately, concentrating instead on reviewing their stock prejudices, and arguing that what has been claimed as spiritual healing has in fact usually been the result of mistakes in diagnosis or prognosis; of alleviation, or remission; of spontaneous cure; or of cure due to a combination of spiritual and other treatment. "We can find no evidence," their report concluded, "that there is any type of illness cured by 'spiritual healing' alone which could not have been cured by medical treatment, which necessarily includes consideration of environmental factors."

At least the importance of environment was conceded: the report even admitted that all the functions of a personality react on one another, so that "we cannot afford, especially in critical illnesses, to disregard any means at our disposal which may lead to the restoration of a man's health". Yet this is precisely what the profession is doing; disregarding any evidence that what it thinks of as organic disease can be cured by spiritual or psychological means. And this reflects the general attitude of doctors everywhere to healing: a mixture of indifference and hostility.

Some of the hostility is understandable. Healers are often difficult people to handle, truculent and arrogant; and their work may reek of abracadabra; it looks bogus, even when it is not. The mystical passes used by divine healers, the operations on "the astral body" by "psychic surgeons", often seem to be on a plane with witchcraft—as indeed they are. But this is not necessarily a condemnation. The report of the Committee on Divine Healing mentioned a couple of cases of successful witch doctoring, which led to a brief correspondence on the subject, some correspondents having the temerity to argue that orthodox medicine has still a good deal to learn from a study of the techniques that witch doctors employ. One writer pointed out that some of these bear a remarkable resemblance to those which are currently being used by psychiatrists—drug abreaction, for one: and "surely it is a cause for wonder and study when we find similar techniques in Africa, which have been developed by rule of thumb, to those developed here since Freud". The work of the witch doctor, he suggested, ought to be looked into "in spite of his omission from the medical register".

The writer might have added that orthodox medicine has also a good deal to learn from all the various fringe medical groups—as things are, qualified doctors may be utterly unfitted for the profession of healing; while, next door to them, may live a man with healing as his gift, who cannot use it as it should be used because the profession dare not admit that his powers are real.

It will, of course, be argued that not to have the present strict limitation on entry to the profession would leave the public at the mercy of quacks. But the public is already, in a sense, at the mercy of quacks in the profession. How else can the initial success of so many wonder-drugs be accounted for, when later scientific tests, with controls, have shown that the drugs had nothing like the powers claimed for them? That they had remarkable results in the early stages of their use is equally undeniable; presumably these results must have been the product of suggestion—not necessarily direct suggestion, but operating through that contagion of enthusiasm which can spread among groups of any kind—crowds; audiences in cinemas; doctors, nurses and patients in hospitals. And this is, by the strictest professional standards, quackery. Doctors may have thought they were curing or alleviating patients with the drugs; in fact, they were using a form of healing.

Many problems arise, though, if healing is to be brought within the orbit of the profession. Wherever there is a healer today, he has his denigrators; rumour credits him with every malpractice, from extorting money from his patients under false pretences to using his trade as a cover for sexual orgies. And often there is some fire under the smoke; the tag "power corrupts" is true of healers as of anybody else; they can become arrogant in the use of power, just as doctors do, but without the safeguards against exploitation of patients that exist in the case of members of the profession. Still, simply to ignore healers because some are rogues, and to persecute them for practising their skill, is unjust and unwise; the need is now to find ways to make better use of their abilities, and to enable them to give the service they undoubtedly can give to the public.

7

HYPNOTISM

If a lesson is to be learnt from healing, it is that more attention must be paid to unconscious processes. The chief obstacle to the development of psychotherapy, it can be argued, is that doctor and patient are in the main compelled to deal with each other on the conscious level. Play-therapy may reveal the unconscious desires of children; and analysis of dreams, or of the chatter of patients indulging in free association, may expose the inner feelings of adults; but normally the therapist is faced with a protracted and wearisome task whenever he seeks to get behind patients' consciousness—and the worse their trouble, the more defences they may have erected, and the longer it takes to break them down. Naturally, anything which might provide a short cut to the understanding of patients' unconscious minds, provided it has no ill-effects, would be an incalculable advantage; and the most promising method, which has been fairly extensively tried out, is hypnotism: the means whereby patients can be put into a state of trance in which the therapist can talk direct, as it were, to their unconscious minds.

Basically, hypnotism is a way of increasing suggestibility by concentrating the patient's mind, to an extent it rarely, if ever, is in normal life, on whatever it is he wants to do, or know. To hypnotize him it may be necessary that he should drift into what appears to be sleep, but in fact it is only the body which is relaxed; the mind is highly charged, so that instead of letting impressions go, as the saying is, in at one ear and out at the other—as we do with most impressions we receive—we seize on them and make them a part of ourselves; so much so that if we are told under hypnosis that we will perform a certain action, such as getting up and opening a certain door ten minutes after we have come out of our trance, we will get up and open that door at the time stated, even if we cannot account for our action. Through suggestion under hypnosis, too, our physical faculties improve; the same amount of exercise will take less out of us; or we can be made to play a game above our usual form.

Hypnotism is not in itself a treatment; it is a means to facilitate treatment. It is used in either of two ways; to enable the doctor to penetrate the barriers put up by our censorship, and thus to collect clues on what we are repressing; or to provide him with a way of removing symptoms by suggesting that they will disappear—as in the case of the "rhino boy". Autohypnosis can also be taught, so that patients in effect can hypnotize themselves for therapeutic purposes.

There is clearly a vast field for treatment under hypnosis of minor but irritating, painful or unsightly symptoms. Why hypnotism has not been used more extensively for this purpose is hard to understand. Admittedly, prejudice against it still exists; it is associated to some extent in the public mind with the esoteric and sometimes disreputable practices of men like Mesmer; and also with undignified antics of hypnotized people on the stage. But doctors who practise it have found that the prejudice is easy to break down; nor is it hard, as a rule, to put people into hypnotic trances. And although the medical profession has never been enthusiastic about hypnotism, it has not actively discouraged its use. As more doctors find how easy it is, and more patients reap its benefits, the chances are that we shall see a great extension of the practice.

Yet hypnotism has certain dangers. It presents a standing temptation to the physical and Pavlovian schools of psychiatry, whose test of success is the removal of unpleasant symptoms and the reconditioning of patients. Nor is it in principle a very happy arrangement where one man, in full possession of his conscious faculties, is in charge of another man who is to all intents his slave; for the traditional safeguard of hypnotized people—that their moral sense is retained so that they do not commit what in normal life they would consider sins, or crimes—is by no means absolute. In his *Sense and Nonsense in Psychology*, Eysenck describes an experiment in which hypnotized subjects were ordered to throw nitric acid over a laboratory assistant; a number of them did so (the substance was not, in fact, nitric acid, but they thought it was—and on one occasion, owing to an oversight, the laboratory assistant actually did get nitric acid thrown over him; fortunately he was able to wash it off before it did him any damage).

If the thesis is accepted that symptoms are often necessary to the patient, to protect him from or against worse things, it is obviously risky to allow doctors who know nothing about psychotherapy to experiment with so potent an instrument. Freud began to practise psychotherapy through hypnotism, using it to break through to the patient's unconscious mind far more easily and more swiftly than he could hope to do by ordinary analysis. But he found that the removal of patients' resistance to analysis had two bad effects; it prevented him from observing where their resistances lay (from which much can be learned); and it meant that though a certain field of the unconscious was freed for the analyst to study, the patients' resistances appeared to be pushed back and dammed up at the boundaries of the field; at that point, they became insurmountable.

A further limitation is that in psychotherapy patients need to be ready for the revelations of their unconscious desires. An analyst has to prepare their conscious minds for the shock of realizing what these unconscious desires are, much as we prepare somebody for the shock of hearing of a bereavement. In providing a way out for the flood of unconscious memories pent up in a patient's mind hypnotic suggestion may be too sharp an instrument: as Lindner wrote, "sometimes it penetrates into the unconscious too far for safety. At such times, particularly with the near psychotic, it dredges the hidden recesses of the mind before the patient is prepared to receive and digest what is brought up. Confronting an unprepared ego with these unconscious contests may, in these cases, unhinge the precarious balance of the mind".

But, as I have said, the fact that powers can be abused is not a reason for rejecting their assistance, where safeguards are provided. The medical profession might reasonably make it a rule that no doctor should practise hypnosis on patients who has not first attended a course on the subject; at least this would give him some warning of the snags, which he could then study at his leisure. And much more research needs to be done—for example, on the possibility of both doctor and patient being hypnotized, so that their unconscious minds can meet, as it were, face to face. For the present it may be wise to play down the possibilities of hypnotherapy, to prevent it from becoming fashionable before its uses and limitations are better understood; but its promise is very great.

CONCLUSIONS

To arrive at methods of medical treatment more attuned to patients' needs will be difficult; the present emphasis is so strongly mechanistic, the bias so firmly against acceptance of the stress theory (particularly in connexion with the influence of the unconscious mind on the body), that any change must be slow. But this is not wholly a disadvantage. To provide what might appear to be a ready-made system of treatment would be extremely undesirable; for we have got to begin to realize first the extent that we are responsible for our own illnesses, before we can see why "treatment", in the sense we ordinarily use the word, is no longer relevant. Henceforth the aim of treatment is not to be cured by somebody of something, but to release in ourselves —if necessary with somebody's help—feelings which have been bottled up and which, like wind in the stomach, will continue to cause us discomfort until we find how to release them.

The analogy is useful in another way. I have mentioned some of the forms which resistance to the stress theory takes; but there are two questions so commonly asked about it that I have kept them to consider here. One is "I am quite willing to concede that there may be sides of my personality I do not know about—that are, as you call it, 'repressed'. But, wretched creature though I am, how do I know that I will not be even worse if the new 'me' you are so anxious about were to be revealed? Thank you: better the demons I know than the demons I don't know!" The answer is that the uncovering of repressed conflicts does not change the personality; it merely releases the personality from its chains. We are no more altered when we let loose a repressed emotion than we are when we let loose a belch —except that, with every such release we give ourselves greater freedom; and our personalities may benefit from it. We would become different only in cases like that of Eve White, where the real personality had long been subordinated to a false one, and where a palace revolution in her own mind was needed to reveal it.

The second objection consists of the query "If we are responsible for our own illnesses, why can we not keep well simply by telling ourselves we can keep well?" For a few people this autosuggestion method is effective, as M. Coué found; the formula "every day and in every way I feel better and better and better", repeated morning and evening before washing the teeth (more often, if desired), had some successes in curing afflictions like stammering, and even in a few more serious diseases. Many of us are readily suggestible; and autosuggestion is only a form of self-hypnosis. It may be strong enough to remove symptoms. But it does not do anything to help them find out why the symptoms arose, and its benefits are likely to be transitory. Much the same applies to the practice of Christian Science; like Coué, Mary Baker Eddy was right in grasping that the individual has within himself the power of well-being; and she also sensed the need for something outside the individual to which his desire for well-being can be dedicated. To the extent that health is related to the capacity to release feeling, enabling emotions and intellect to grow up together, it is helpful to have somebody on whom the feeling can be lavished; the analyst; the beloved; or, in the Christian Scientist's case, God.

And this is the reason why the Coué and Christian Science methods, though they may be helpful to individuals, cannot be the whole answer. Health lies in an intimate relationship with our capacity to release our real feelings; and this in turn is related to our capacity to love. To be able to love is to have health within our reach. But, as Anna Karenina lamented, "you talk of energy; but the foundation of energy is love, and love does not come at will". Neither does health. If in considering the stress theory—

in relating what has been done in research—I have tended to regard human beings as clinical entities, only a grade superior to the rats strapped to boards in Selye's laboratory, it is because that is how we in fact think of ourselves, in relation to disease. We look on ourselves as the victims of forces beyond our control. What we now have to realize is that the power to control our health lies within us—but only in the sense that the power to love lies within us. We can no more will ourselves to be healthy than we can will ourselves to love; or, if we can, it is a shallow form of health—just as it is a shallow form of love.

In love, lies the key to health; not only to the immediate physical relationship (of the kind noted in T.B.), but in a wider sense. For Jesus, it might be said, love and health became inseparable. In due course the nature of this relationship will be more closely examined, and apparently unromantic clinical conclusions may emerge; that love is connected with a state of enhanced suggestibility, giving the patient the opportunity of successful autosuggestion; or that it provides a way of releasing repressions; or that it helps us, by concentrating our attention on somebody else, to acquire something of the non-attachment which Eastern philosophies consider the basis of health. For the present, it need only be said that love and health coexist; that in the capacity to love lies the capacity to banish, or to overcome, stress.

★

There would be less resistance to acceptance of this idea if people realized that it represents not a break from, but a return to, tradition. "It is simply the correction of a mistake," Flanders Dunbar has said, "to which leaders like Socrates, Hippocrates, and Plato called attention, centuries before our present system of counting centuries began. They said, in effect, the greatest error in the treatment of sickness is that there are physicians for the body, and physicians for the soul . . . Body and soul are indivisible." The profession, therefore, is not facing a leap in the dark, but a return towards the Hippocratic light.

So firmly has the physical, mechanistic theory established itself, though, that the stress theory appears to be an entirely new idea; and there are three stages, Almroth Wright once complained, before a new idea is accepted: first, when it is repudiated as absurd; second, where it is allowed to be reasonable; third, where it is belittled as obvious. But the really disconcerting thing is that doctors frequently hold all three views together at different levels of their imagination. Although, as I have said, doctors often assert that the discoveries of Freud or the stress theory are little more than clinical common sense translated in high falutin' language, they rarely think of using the "common sense" in treating their own patients; if it is suggested they should do so, they find some excuse not to. And how many doctors, even those who know that neurosis is a real, distressing, and often disabling disease, treat it with the same sympathy that they treat, say, pneumonia?

It is not enough to "know" about the stress theory in the sense of having read some books or articles on the subject—which is all most doctors have done. The need is for them to know at a deeper level: the level at which knowledge becomes part of us, in that we use it automatically, unconsciously, in our lives. For only in this way can the doctor begin to regard his patients as people—as friends. Chesterton once defined a priest as a man who must touch with a benediction those whom most people would not touch with a barge-pole; and the doctor, whether he likes it or not, now finds himself in the same situation. As the "sins" which used to be confessed to a priest are often in reality compulsive neurotic actions, the doctor will actually need to take on some of the priest's functions. In general, once it is realized that neurotic symptoms, mental or physical, can be satisfactorily treated only through the therapist's knowledge of, sympathy with, and interest in, the neurotic, an entirely new concept of treatment arises.

A formidable obstacle exists in the habits of mind of doctors, reinforced by their training; they are unlikely, except in a few individual cases, to be attracted to the stress theory on its own merits. But it has one attraction which in the long run may be decisive: it will help to re-establish the family doctor as the most influential force in medicine—and in society.

The family doctor will be the master instead of, as he is now, the servant of the specialist. At present, he tends to throw off responsibility for his patients once they are dispatched to specialists' hands. His attitude is "I have done all I can for you: you are now in more expert care." But if he accepts the stress theory he cannot do this, because the surgeon or physician, however expert, are only his advisers. He will send patients to a surgeon in much the same way as he now sends specimens of their blood to a pathologist, for an expert opinion: but he will not necessarily have to accept the surgeon's recommendations as law, any more than he now accepts the pathologist's; always he will have to evaluate it, and decide from his knowledge of the patient's personality, constitution, and circumstances whether he would benefit most from the operation recommended by the surgeon, the drugs recommended by the physician, the shock treatment recommended by the psychiatrist, the manipulation recommended by the physiotherapist (or chiropractor), or the group therapy recommended by the psychotherapist. And in the end he may decide that all the man needs is a holiday at the sea.

No doubt the realization of the extent of their responsibilities will alarm many doctors; nor will they relish the prospect of sitting and listening to a neurotic patient's catalogue of worries. Still, there are compensations; chief among them being that they need no longer despair when they diagnose neurosis, or fail to find any cause at all. They will not need to fall back on the diagnosis "functional"; psychotherapy gives them a weapon with which to meet the challenge; and, knowing that something can be done, they will be less likely to run away from, or lose their tempers with, the neurotic nuisances who once irritated them beyond endurance.

For a real change in the profession's attitude, though, there will have to be a change in its training. The training of a good family doctor ought in certain respects to resemble the training of a parish priest—with two reservations: that he is less concerned to bring his patients' souls healthy to Paradise than to keep their minds and bodies healthy on earth: and that for a doctor the palace of wisdom is often reached by the road of excess. A doctor who has never been drunk is not well fitted to deal with what will certainly be a recurring problem of some of his patients: still less, a doctor who has never had sexual intercourse. Naturally there are common-sense limits: a family doctor does not have to become a drug addict to cope with drug addicts, any more than he has to chop his leg off to cope with amputations. But the more, within reason, that a doctor has experienced the joys and the woes, the ecstasies and the hang-overs of his patients, the more likely he is to handle his patients successfully. Medical training should seek to produce a rounded personality: not a clinical digest.

I have already mentioned a few welcome signs that this is beginning to be realized, particularly in America. Perhaps the most striking advance has been in the medical school at Western Reserve University in Ohio, where the traditional separation between pre-clinical and clinical teaching has been broken down into an integrated three-phase course. The first phase is designed to introduce the student to medicine in the widest sense of the word, with teaching by anthropologists and social workers as well as by scientists; the student is also assigned to follow a pregnancy for a month before the child is born, and thereafter to follow the progress of the child during the first year. In the second phase he deals with disease; in the third, with patients. Each student has his own work-room, which he can arrange to his own design; instructors come to help him in his own laboratory, rather than vice versa. And several other medical schools in America have adopted integrative schemes of one kind or another, on a smaller scale.

Any change in the method of teaching will need to be accompanied by a change in the nature of research. An obvious outlet for any funds that become available is in extending out-patient facilities for psychotherapy; for in this way it is possible to combine research with treatment.

The early results of one pilot experiment in England, at Worthing, where out-patient treatment has been provided so that only the most serious cases have to enter a mental hospital, have gone far beyond the expectations of its sponsors; the number of entrants to the mental hospital in the area dropped by almost two-thirds in a year—at a time when admissions to mental hospitals outside the area were rising. And as people are less reluctant to visit out-patient clinics than go to hospitals, they are prepared to take their troubles for treatment sooner, which increases the chances of dealing satisfactorily with them. More money, too, should be provided for the training and employment of psychotherapists and psychiatric social workers, to work alongside family doctors. Even if they have no better qualifications than the capacity to be good listeners, and to relieve the doctor of some of the listening time which he will otherwise have to put in, they would be valuable; but some of them will be of more positive assistance, providing the doctor with the specialist knowledge in which he himself, owing to his defective training, is lacking.

★

These changes within the profession cannot come about unless there is also a revolution in public opinion: and again, it is necessary to emphasize that this cannot be obtained simply by a change in what the community "knows" about medicine. "There is knowing and knowing," Freud once said; "they are not always the same thing. There are various kinds of knowing, which psychologically are not by any means of equal value." Freud was speaking of the relationship between doctor and patient: it is one thing for the patient to know what is the matter with him, because the doctor has told him so; quite another for the patient to know, because the significance of what the doctor has said has become clear to him. All of us are aware in our own lives of these different levels of knowledge—of how a play, or a piece of music, or a poem which we think we know, can be transformed into something immeasurably more important to us by a fresh interpretation, by a new production or recording, or by listening to it in a state of heightened sensitivity. "He that sings a lasting song," Yeats wrote, "thinks in a marrow-bone"; and it is in the community's marrow-bone, rather than its mind, that the rethinking must be done.

There is no point in minimizing the difficulties. I have already discussed the inevitable resistance to any change in habits of thought and feeling; it will be intense, and angry; and it will be fostered by those numerous members of society who regard everything that is strange to them with disfavour. But in addition, we will have to realize that it is not merely a question of accepting the stress theory of disease; if it is to be accepted, a great many conventional gods will have to topple, as well as the deities now worshipped by the medical profession.

For example: the aphorism "the child is father to the man" which once could have been considered merely a glimpse of the obvious, is now shown to have deeper implications; Pavlovians and Freudians, not to mention research workers with no particular theories, are agreed on the significance of a child's early upbringing and training in moulding his adult personality. But this is being recognized at the very time that the basis of family life in the West—the Christian ideal of strict monogamy—is breaking down; particularly in America, where divorce can be bought for little more than the price of a train fare to States where marriages are set aside without reference to the needs of the children.

Whatever its deficiencies, the old Christian ideal of strict monogamy provided children with security; they grew up in the certainty that however great the tension between mother and father, or between parents and children, there was no question of the family unit being voluntarily broken. As research is showing that it is more important that children should be secure than that they should be happy, it is necessary, if the Christian family sanctions break down, to find new ones. In theory (it could be argued) no two people ought to have children unless they can demonstrate to the community's satisfaction that they are getting married not just to indulge in compulsive concupiscence for a while, before changing partners; but with the intention of establishing a stable family unit. In practice the idea sounds comical; yet is it any more ridiculous than the present conception of marriage as a romantic social game for two players, in which the needs of the children can be ignored? It is not easy, admittedly, to see how new sanctions could be applied to restore the conception of the family as a stable unit, if belief in its religious significance disappears. Still, it will hardly be contested that the community must find some way of ensuring that, marriage or no marriage, the needs of the children must be safeguarded.

In education, too, fundamental changes will be required. Formal education, it is now coming to be realized, plays a much smaller part in developing intelligence than has been thought; so far from education being (out of respect to its Latin derivation) a "drawing out" process, it has tended to become a device for holding back the growth of the mind. Oscar Wilde's assertion, "nothing that is worth knowing can be taught", is now being shown by psychological research to be literally true; what is imposed on the mind by formal teaching is of little worth unless the mind is capable of assimilating it not merely on the shallow level at which we learn by rote, but at the deeper level when what we know fuses with what we are. Yet teaching is still very largely based on learning by rote, or by efforts of memory unrelated to what we are really thinking and feeling: what we learn in this way is of little benefit to us except in getting us through examinations. And not merely is it useless; it may be harmful, by causing us to build up unconscious barriers against learning. Many a child dismissed by his teachers as stupid, dull or dense (Winston Churchill was one) is in fact merely displaying innate character: refusing to learn because the subjects, or the way in which they are presented, hold no interest for him.

From Freud's researches, too, it is possible to see why intellect divorced from personality so often gives depressing results. In the arid academicism of universities and seminaries lie the skeletons of potentially brilliant minds starved of their proper nourishment: feeling. The barrier of the walls of the institutions in which they live are reinforced by the still more powerful barriers put up by their own skilful rationalizing; so that too many potential saints strangle themselves with the entrails of their casuistry; and too many "double firsts" sink into what Harold Laski once ridiculed as "that state of resentful coma which the universities call research".

*

A third aspect of society which will need drastic alteration is its attitude to the anti-social; to the breakers of the law. The extent to which, say, juvenile delinquency can be attributed to faults in early upbringing and other deficiencies in family life is now known to be very great. Scepticism is sometimes expressed on this point—particularly by judges, who resent the constant reiteration of defence counsel in trials, that the accused "never had a proper home"; that he was thrashed by his father, or neglected by his mother. But works such as John Bowlby's *Child care and the growth of love* have shown beyond all reasonable doubt the extent to which early misfortunes, though they are not the cause of delinquency, are linked with it. A good home is no guarantee of a good citizen, but it enormously increases his chances of becoming a good citizen; and the converse is also true.

It follows, then, that we should stop thinking of criminal tendencies as something which are in all citizens' conscious power to control; and that we should consider the extent to which they may, like a neurotic twitch, be something which can be controlled only when the citizen is capable of understanding them. In this context Samuel Butler's *Erewhon*, published close on a century ago, has a particular interest.

The Erewhonians believed that illness of any sort was immoral and criminal:

> "in that country if a man falls into ill-health, or catches any disorder, or fails bodily in any way before he is seventy

years old, he is tried before a jury of his countrymen, and if convicted is held up to public scorn and sentenced more or less severely as the case may be. There are subdivisions of illnesses into crimes and misdemeanors as with offences against ourselves—a man being punished very heavily for serious illness, while failure of eyes or hearing in one over sixty-five, who has had good health hitherto, is dealt with by fine only, or imprisonment in default of payment. But if a man forges a cheque, or sets his house on fire, or robs with violence from the person, or does any other such things as are criminal in our own country, he is either taken to a hospital and most carefully tended at the public expense; or if he is in good circumstances, he lets it be known to all his friends that he is suffering from a severe fit of immorality, just as we do when we are ill, and they come and visit him with great solicitude".

True, the Erewhonian who embezzled funds would be flogged by a doctor, and put on a diet. But because the flogging was given as a cure, and not as a punishment, the Erewhonian accepted it with the same calm, and even pride, as an Englishman accepts the news that he must have a serious operation.

Research into the relationship of disease and crime suggests that Samuel Butler was close to the truth. They are often different effects of the same causes: what makes one man insane may make another man a criminal; and it is absurd to treat the two as if they were completely separate: to send the lunatic to hospital, while sending the criminal to jail. It may be necessary to restrain the criminal, to insulate him from society, just as it may be necessary to isolate patients with psychoses, or with infectious diseases; but to isolate him as a punishment is unsound.

Not merely is it unsound; as I mentioned earlier, there is reason to believe that it is positively dangerous. Punishment is often not a deterrent; it actually creates crime. This is partly because "a community is infinitely more brutalized" (Oscar Wilde again) "by the habitual employment of punishment than it is by the occasional occurrence of crime", so that to some extent, the more punishment is inflicted, the more crime is produced. It is also because a craving for punishment, arising out of repressed feelings of guilt, is widespread. The reason why most of us do not give way more openly to our masochistic urges is that conscience makes cowards of us all; it tends to be the people with imperfectly developed consciences, the psychopaths, who commit crimes because they crave punishment—and to indulge their craving merely encourages them to commit more crimes.

This is not to argue that henceforth the jail doors should be thrown open, and that anybody who commits a crime should be patted on the head, told that his parents were to blame for not training him properly when he was young, and sent back into society. With a few criminals, this system would succeed—just as A. S. Neill found it did in his school: where a boy did something really infuriating Neill would reward him with extra pocket-money, and the trick often worked. It only worked, though, because Neill stood in a personal relationship to the boy, something that cannot be achieved where society, rather than an individual, is guardian. In fact society has great difficulty in persuading otherwise strictly moral, honourable men to obey its laws and by-laws—a man who would not dream of stealing a penny from his worst enemy will cheerfully wangle thousands from the taxpayer in spurious expense accounts. Sanctions there have to be, even if their design should be mainly prevention and reparation. Such sanctions, though, are irrelevant to the real problem: the criminal who acts from compulsive motives—the psychopath. Properly to deal with psychopaths, it will be necessary to convert the local jail into a hospital.

★

The implications of such changes in the public attitude to marriage, education and the law are more serious even than I have here outlined; but my aim is only to show the problem of health and illness can no longer be regarded as something to be solved by doctors and scientists. It can only be solved by a new conception of society; and on the recognition of this fact, society may depend for its survival; because stress is becoming a far more formidable problem than it has ever been before.

This is sometimes disputed. Our ancestors, it is pointed out, often bore far greater stress loads than we do. Consider pain, alone: without analgesics or anaesthetics, imagine the torments that they must have suffered during illness, and the horror even of falling ill! But, as I have tried to show, stress of this kind is relatively of little importance in disease, however horrifying it may be in terms of human suffering. The human mind has an astonishing capacity for overcoming stresses to which it is resigned, pain among them; "what can't be cured, must be endured", and endured it is. The stress that is the main danger to health is that which arises out of repressed feelings where we cannot see our adversary, or where we fight him with wrong weapons.

In *A theory of Disease* Arthur Guirdham gives one reason why stress, in this sense, should have increased. Proneness to disease, he believes, is related to the degree of development of the personality and to the individual's awareness of it; the pattern of disease reflects the religious and philosophic outlook of the community and the individual; and the value the individual sets on his own personality "stands in direct relation to his proneness to psychosomatic and neurotic disorders . . . the contagious and terminal diseases are to be regarded as the more natural forms of disease, and as part of the lot of man, whereas the psychosomatic and neurotic forms of illness are the result of *the excessive development of the cult of personality*".

In other words: where man believes himself to be in a state of utter dependence on his gods, whose will is interpreted by priest or witch doctor, he is more likely to avoid the type of stress that induces neurotic or psychosomatic symptoms. His illnesses, pains, and tribulations are endured because they have to be; it does not occur to him that there is any alternative to them.

But where he becomes a Protestant, in the loose sense of that term—where he disputes the right of priest or witch doctor to infallibility—to his other stresses, is added that of uncertainty; he has to begin to make his own interpretations of the Divine Will. Even then, he may firmly believe (as Joan of Arc did) that the voices he hears come from God: he may act on them with complete conviction of their divine origin. It is when he cannot accept the existence of a divinity, that uncertainty is increased to the point where he has to rely on himself; the cult of personality is on the way to becoming complete.

It is not necessary to accept Guirdham's reliance upon the findings of religious experience, rather than of psychiatric research, to realize that he has hit upon one convincing reason why civilized communities tend to suffer from stress disorders. And there is another: that the higher the degree of civilization, the more difficult the journey that a child has to travel to convert the atavism of infancy into the respectability of adulthood; the greater the risk of collecting repressions on the way. As if the journey were not hazardous enough, too, we have added to its dangers by allowing the disintegration of the marriage tie, thereby depriving many children of the very stability and security they need if the journey is to be successfully begun.

And the disruption of the marriage tie is not caused, as is sometimes argued, by the decline in religious feeling or in moral standards. The main reason for it, probably, is that wives in many countries are now in a position to leave their husbands when they want to, and earn their own living. There seems every likelihood that casual marriages—some entered into with no disposition towards permanence, others embarked upon with romantic zeal but liable to break up in time of crisis owing to the absence of sanctions to sustain them—are on the increase; and that the strain imposed on children in infancy and early childhood will increase also, leading to more neuroses and illness of other kinds. Perhaps the greatest single problem confronting communities today, and certainly the first objective of the revolution in medicine, is to learn how to prevent the child's teeth being set on edge by the sour grapes of his parents' broken, unstable, or unhappy marriages; for it is in children's lack of security, and lack of love, rather than from the pace of life today, or from any other of the outward strains imposed by modern civilization, that the stresses and stress disorders characteristic of modern times have their origin.

ACKNOWLEDGEMENTS

In a work of this kind, where so much depends on frequent chance conversations which bring up fresh ideas, it is hopeless to attempt to thank everybody to whom my thanks are due; but I am particularly grateful to Sidney Phillips, of Criterion Books, who suggested that I should write it; to Dr. Alfred Byrne, Dr. Kathryn Cohen and Mrs. Penelope Balogh, for their encouragement and advice in its early stages; to Drs. R. R. Bomford, Rory Childers, A. J. Hawes, and Desmond O'Neill, for their comments and criticisms; and to the many members of the profession whom I have bored with questions and contentions in the past.

BIBLIOGRAPHY

I have included only general works on and around the subject, except where it has appeared to me that the book is so illuminating on some particular aspect that it should not be kept out. Some of the authors, notably Flanders Dunbar and Harold G. Wolff, have written a number of books on stress and psychosomatic disorders: I have given the most representative volumes only. Most of the works included have been published both in England and in the United States: the place and date are of first publication. Specialist works dealing with psychiatry, psychoanalysis and related subjects are not included (a useful list of sources on psychoanalysis can be found in *Psychosomatic Medicine* for March/April, 1958).

Alexander, Franz. *Psychosomatic Medicine* (New York, 1950).
Association for research in nervous and mental diseases. *Life Stress and Bodily Disease* (Baltimore, 1950).
Balchin, Nigel. *Mine Own Executioner* (London, 1945).
Balint, Michael. *The Doctor, his Patient, and the Illness* (London, 1957).
Beers, Clifford. *A Mind that Found Itself* (New York, 1908).
Bowlby, John. *Child Care and the Growth of Love* (London, 1950).
Clark-Kennedy, A. E. *Human Disease* (London, 1957).
Dunbar, Flanders. *Mind and Body: Psychosomatic Medicine* (New York, 1955).
Eysenck, H. J. *Uses and Abuses of Psychology* (London, 1953).
Sense and Nonsense in Psychology (London, 1957).
Gorman, Mike. *Every Other Bed* (New York, 1956).

Groddeck, Georg. *The Unknown Self* (tr. London 1929).
The Book of the It (tr. London 1935).
Guirdham, Arthur. *A Theory of Disease* (London, 1957).
Halliday, J. L. *Psychosocial Medicine* (New York, 1948).
Hamilton, Max. *Psychosomatics* (London, 1955).
Lindner, Robert. *The Fifty-Minute Hour* (New York, 1955).
Must You Conform? (New York, 1956).
Munroe, Ruth L. *Schools of Psychoanalytic Thought* (Ohio, 1945).
O'Neill, Desmond. *A Psychosomatic Approach to Medicine.* (London, 1955).
Sargant, William. *Battle for the Mind* (London, 1957).
Selye, Hans. *The Stress of Life* (New York, 1956).
Shaw, Bernard. *The Doctor's Dilemma* (London, 1911).
Stafford-Clark, David. *Psychiatry Today* (London, 1952).
Thigpen, Corbett H., and Cleckley, Hervey M. *The Three Faces of Eve* (New York, 1957).
Walker, Nigel M. *A Short History of Psychotherapy* (London, 1957).
Weiss, Edward, and English, Spurgeon. *Psychosomatic Medicine.* (Philadelphia, 1943).
Wittkower, Eric, and Cleghorn, R. A. *Recent Developments in Psychosomatic Medicine* (Toronto, 1954).
Wittkower, Eric, and Russell, Brian. *Emotional Factors in Skin* Disease (London, 1953).
Wolf, Stewart, and Wolff, Harold G. *Human Gastric Function* (New York, 1943).
Wolff, Harold G. *Stress and Disease* (New York, 1953).

As will be obvious from the text, as well as from this bibliography, I have consulted only works published in Britain and the United States. Research in the psychosomatic field is, of course, in progress in other countries; but few reports of it are available in English, and the prospect of trying to translate them was too alarming.

GLOSSARY AND INDEX

I have used the index as a glossary to define terms, either where they are not in colloquial use or when their colloquial use can be confusing or misleading. I have not bothered to define them if they are mentioned only in passing; or if they are defined in the text (normally, on the first page they are mentioned: where they are not, I have put "definition on p. —"). In a few cases, where terms appear frequently in the text, I have given brief definitions in the index as well.

D

E

F

G

H

I

J

K

L

M

N

R

S

T

U

V

W

Y

Z